WHERE SHOULD WE CAMP NEXT?

A 50-State Guide to Amazing Campgrounds and Other Unique Outdoor Accommodations

Stephanie & Jeremy Puglisi

Published by Sourcebooks
P.O. Box 4410, Naperville, Illinois 60567-4410
(630) 961-3900
sourcebooks.com

Printed and bound in the United States of America.
SB 10

Once again, to Theo, Max, and Wes.

»» ———————————————————→

This book was completed during a very difficult
time for our family, and for all families. But
you constantly reminded us to take joy in the
moment, and to dream of better roads ahead...

For that we can never thank you enough.

CONTENTS

The Campgrounds

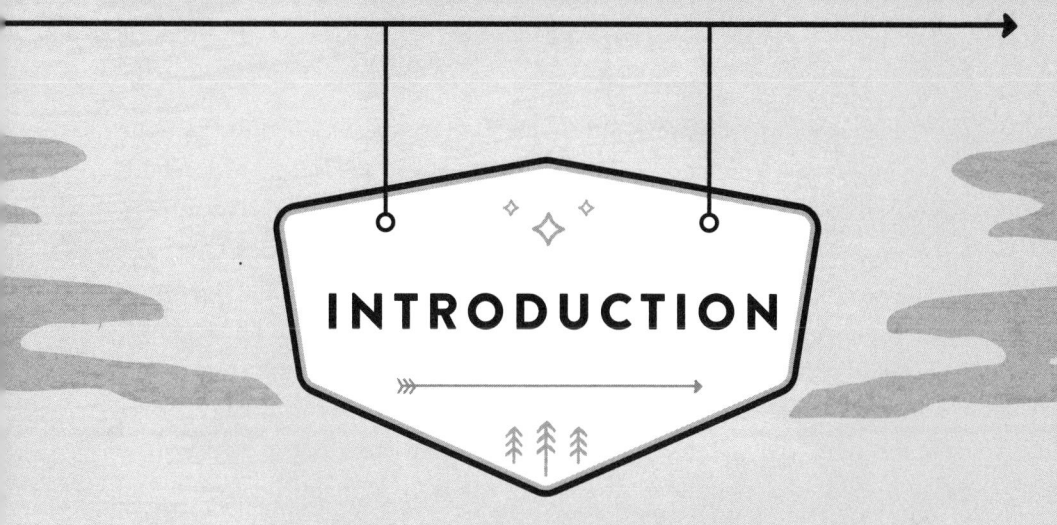

INTRODUCTION

Over a decade ago, we found ourselves with twin baby boys and a serious case of cabin fever. So we bought a pop-up camper hoping it would provide a more comfortable way to road-trip with our kids. It provided that in spades, but it also introduced us to a pastime that has changed our family forever—camping. We loved our time at the campground so much that we began blogging and podcasting about it, then we started writing magazine articles and books. Camping has inspired us to spend more time with our children, family, and friends in the great outdoors, and we love to encourage other people to experience the magic of the campground.

We've been camping as a family for more than ten years and sharing campground recommendations for almost as long. We decided early on that instead of reviewing every campground we visited—giving thumbs up or thumbs down—we would only share the ones we absolutely loved on our website TheRVAtlas.com and our podcasts *The RV Atlas* and *Campground of the Week*. We've spoken and written about hundreds of our favorite campgrounds across the country and invited other passionate campers to do the same. Those campground recommendations are the inspiration and backbone of this book.

Although many of the campgrounds in this book are personal favorites from a decade of family travel, this collection is so much bigger than our own camping experiences. We love talking to adventurers from around the country who camp in unique ways. Some prefer dry camping at remote state parks in Utah. Others choose RV resorts with full hookups and pull-throughs whenever they have the choice. We are truly in awe at the range of amazing camping opportunities throughout this beautiful country and have worked hard to demonstrate that there is no one way to camp and no one type of perfect campground. We've built a community of campers over the years that offer different points of view for what makes a great campground, and we hope this book represents those inspiring voices. Our podcast listeners message us regularly with campground suggestions and often help us plan our future camping adventures. The members of our private Facebook group have introduced us to the wonders of places that were never even on our radar.

With the help of this diverse and expansive community of campers, we've gathered up a dreamy collection of state park campgrounds, national park campgrounds, RV resorts, and unique glamping destinations. We love them all—the rustic Cedar Pass Campground in the Badlands, the Jellystone Park Camp-Resort near Shenandoah National Park with waterslides and hand-dipped ice cream, and the canvas glamping tents on the Oregon coast. We have tried to select a wide variety of amazing campgrounds. No matter where you are in this country or what type of camping sparks your wanderlust, we hope you find some inspiration in the pages of this book.

See you at the campground,

Stephanie + Jeremy

GETTING STARTED

HOW TO USE THIS BOOK

There are great campgrounds in every single state. That was a guiding principle for us as we wrote this book. *Where Should We Camp Next?* is our handpicked selection of the best campgrounds in the country, arranged by region and state. But it's also much more than that. We hope this book serves as that garrulous friend who sits around the campfire all night recommending the best campgrounds, hikes, food, books, movies, fishing holes, and off-the-beaten-track activities that no one else knows about. We all deserve a friend like that, don't we?

We separated the campground reviews in each state into two categories: "Best in State" and "Also Great." Best in State campgrounds are featured on the maps that start each chapter. In many cases the slimmest of margins separated campgrounds in each category. Sometimes a campground earned Best in State honors because of some subjective quality that was very personal to us. In other cases, we simply felt that these campgrounds had the broadest appeal to most campers. However, we also wanted to start a conversation and spark a debate with our readers. Our Best in State might be different than yours. That would be a fun conversation to have around the campfire one night, wouldn't it? If you are just starting out as a camper, maybe you have no basis to agree or disagree. In that case, we hope this book inspires you to get out there and start forming your own opinions.

We also created a system of badges to highlight campgrounds that have very distinct personalities. These badges do not mean that these are the best campgrounds in the book. Instead, we hope that they help you seek out certain types of experiences in a quick, easy, and fun fashion. We have also arranged the campgrounds by badge in an appendix in the back of the book for easy browsing by campground personality.

 If you want to experience comfort and luxury in the great outdoors, we suggest you take a look at the campgrounds that earned our *Glamping Badge*. Think high linen counts, organic soaps, and craft roasted coffee in the morning.

 If you are feeling desperate and need a weekend away from the kids (or work, or whatever!) we hope that the *Romantic Weekend Badge* inspires you to head out there with someone you love. Most of these campgrounds have options for fine dining and/or nightlife nearby.

 Do you just want a simple camping experience far from the maddening crowd? Then check out the campgrounds with a *Rustic Camping Badge* to find your inner Thoreau.

 If you want to park your RV or tent (or rent a cabin or glamping tent) somewhere with spectacular views, then look for campgrounds with our *Waterfront Views Badge*.

 Camping with kiddos and want lots of options to keep them entertained? Then seek out our *Family-Friendly Badge* for high-energy campgrounds where boredom is not an option.

Of course, you could have a romantic weekend anywhere. And, in a certain sense, most campgrounds are kid-friendly. But some places are better designed than others for particular types of experiences—and we want you to be able to find these types of experiences quickly and easily.

We hope that you dip in and out of this book whenever you get that familiar feeling of wanderlust during the long, boring winter months. We also hope that you keep a dog-eared copy of it with you and read it while you are sitting around the campfire planning the next day's adventures. Just don't forget to look up at the stars, okay?

WHAT'S YOUR CAMPING PERSONALITY?

There is a campground out there for every camping personality. The tricky part is finding your perfect match. Campgrounds are not one-size-fits-all, and you need to understand what you want out of a camping experience so you can look for a campground that will fall in line with your expectations. If you long for large, private, quiet, wooded campsites, you will be miserable at a resort. If you want paved campsites for your big-rig RV with access to a pool and activities for the kids, most state parks will not fit the bill. We can't count how many times we've heard people complain about things like golf cart traffic at a campground or a lack of good Wi-Fi.

Honestly, that type of issue should not be a surprise if you've done the proper research before making a reservation. As long as you know your own personal camping style, you should be able to use review sites and a campground website to determine in advance if a campground will be a good match. We've stayed at hundreds of campgrounds all over the country. Some of them are amazing and some are just okay, but rarely are we surprised by small site size or road noise. We know what we are looking for, and we do our due diligence to make sure a campground measures up.

What type of location do you want?

There are campgrounds in the middle of the action and campgrounds far off the grid. Each one comes with a unique set of pros and cons, depending on your perspective. There is an RV resort one block away from the French

Quarter in New Orleans. If you are looking for proximity to nightlife in the Big Easy, there is no better spot. If you want scenic views, it may be your worst nightmare. It's also important to remember that connectivity is often negatively correlated to natural beauty. Don't expect to be in the middle of nowhere with cracking Wi-Fi. If you opt for a national park campground, you'll probably be offline during your stay.

What type of campsite do you prefer?

Most campgrounds will offer two basic campsite styles for RVers—back-in or pull-through. A back-in site will usually give you more privacy and more space. A pull-through is typically less private and spacious, but easier to access for big rigs and new RVers. Campsites also come with a variety of hook-up configurations. Rustic tent and RV sites will have no hookups at all. Many state and national parks will offer some sites with just electric hook-ups. These are not just desirable for RVers—tent campers love to have access to electricity for charging devices and using small appliances in their camp kitchen. Another common campsite hookup combo is water and electricity. You'll be able to plug in a camper and run potable water to your RV sinks. Full hookup is water, electric, and sewer. Sometimes cable is also included in a full hookup configuration. If you are.looking to camp in state and national parks, you should be comfortable with dry camping—camping without any water, electric, or sewer hookups—or camping with just electric or water. Full hookups are more common in private campgrounds, and if you want to use all the RV bells and whistles, that's what you'll need.

What amenities will you use?

There is no standard amenities package for campgrounds. Each comes with its own unique blend of offerings from pools to playgrounds to dining options and golf cart rentals. Generally, the more amenities a campground offers, the more expensive it is. There's no reason to pay for a bunch of stuff you won't use, so avoid campgrounds with water parks if you won't go near them. A campground with more amenities tends to be busier as well. If you want peace and quiet, don't go to the campground with themed karaoke nights, okay? Instead, you might want to look for a state park campground with on-site hiking, fishing, and kayaking.

Create your own personal punch list of campground preferences, and make sure to find campgrounds that are a good match. It might take you some time to figure out, but that's okay—those campground mistakes often create some of the funniest family memories of all.

UNIQUE GLAMPING, RVING, AND TENT CAMPING EXPERIENCES

Even though there are plenty of traditional campgrounds out there, a new type of camping experience has emerged over the last decade, and the popularity of unique glamping and boondocking locations has exploded. Perhaps you have absolutely no camping equipment at all but still want to escape to the woods and sleep under the stars. Or maybe you own an RV and are tired of parking it just a few feet from another rig in a rack-em-and-stack-em campground. Or you could be like us and own a tent and RV but still crave new and adventurous camping experiences. There are more fun places popping up all the time that will give you a chance to step outside of the box and make memories with your family and friends. Here are some of our favorites right now.

Tentrr

Tentrr has almost 1,000 camping sites around the country, and they are growing quickly. Private landowners with beautiful, natural locations can purchase a kit that includes a platform, canvas tent, and furniture for a turn-key glamping setup. There are also backcountry sites for those who wish to pitch their own tent.

>> tentrr.com

Under Canvas

Under Canvas is one of the most well-known glamping outfits, and it offers a luxury camping experience that comes along with king-sized beds and daily housekeeping. The locations are limited (less than ten at the time of this writing), but they are located near some of the most popular national parks and memorials in the country, including Grand Canyon, Zion, and Mount Rushmore. Enjoy s'mores around the nightly campfire and organized camp activities. There's also an on-site concierge to help you book your national park adventures.

》 undercanvas.com

AutoCamp

What started with two luxurious California locations near Yosemite and the Redwoods has now expanded to the East Coast with the recent addition of a Cape Cod AutoCamp. The idea is to provide guests a combination of camping and resort-level hospitality. The accommodations include custom Airstreams and canvas tents situated around mid-century-styled, clubhouses.

》 autocamp.com

Collective Retreats

Collective Retreats includes five luxury camping resorts in iconic locations like Vail, Colorado, and Hill Country, Texas. Like many of the glamping retreats, it offers canvas tent accommodations outfitted with chandeliers and opulent linens. It adds in gourmet dining experiences with on-site chefs who create meals inspired by local ingredients and cuisine.

》 collectiveretreats.com

Hipcamp

Hipcamp is a campground search engine that focuses on connecting people with campsites on traditional public lands but also on ranches, vineyards, farms, and nature preserves. You can filter for the type of site or preferred location, and the listings include campsite description and amenities. It also tells you about on-site and nearby activities. The website also features user-generated reviews, which, while somewhat limited in number, are very helpful.

>>>> hipcamp.com

Harvest Hosts

Harvest Hosts is an affordable membership program for RV owners looking for something other than the traditional campground experience. There are more than 1,000 wineries, farms, and breweries that offer overnight camping for self-contained RVs. There are no hookups, and folks traveling with pets should be aware that many farm locations don't allow furry family members on their properties. Members are allowed to park at these locations for no more than twenty-four hours, free of charge, and are encouraged to purchase something from the business as a gesture of gratitude.

>>>> harvesthosts.com

Boondockers Welcome

Boondockers Welcome is a subscription service offering RV owners free overnight parking at more than 1,000 private property listings around the country. It costs $50 to become a member, then you have access to the contact information for individuals who allow you to park your self-contained RV overnight in their driveways. By signing up as a host, people earn subscription credit for themselves.

>>>> boondockerswelcome.com

CAMPGROUND PRICING

How much does it cost to camp? People ask us this question over and over, and there's no easy answer. The truth is...it depends. It depends on the location, the type of campground, and the amenities the campground offers. However, it can also vary greatly within a campground itself. A single campground might offer tent sites for $20; electric and water RV sites for $35;

and paved, pull-through, full hook-up sites for $55. Nevertheless, after more than a decade of camping all over the country—in both private and public campgrounds, with rustic and resort-style amenities—we can offer some general price ranges that will help you weigh the affordability of camping and budget for your own adventures.

Remember: Campgrounds are real estate, and prices will often coincide with how expensive the real estate is in a particular region. Expect to pay significantly more in coastal and urban areas on the East Coast and West Coast, or in popular vacation destinations like the Smokies and Rockies.

Public Campgrounds

Public campgrounds are located in state parks, national parks, county parks, U.S. Army Corps of Engineers (COE) parks, national forests, or on any other government-managed land. These are hands down your most affordable campgrounds. Many of the campgrounds are rustic, with limited hookups or on-site amenities, although this is not the case across the board. In this book, we highlight many state and COE campgrounds that have water and electric, or full hook-up facilities. Some public campgrounds, especially in the West, have camping fees as low as $10. However, most fall into the range of $20–$40 for tent and RV sites. Cabins range from $50–$100. Rooms in lodges are often $100–$150.

Standard Private Campgrounds

Private campgrounds are owned by individuals or corporations, and there is a huge range of campsite quality and amenities in this category. For the purposes of giving a general price range here, we are talking about private campgrounds that offer full hookups and a standard level of amenities, which may include a camp store, laundry facilities, playground, and pool. They may also provide some organized activities on the weekends or during peak season. In other words, they have the basics, but nothing particularly fancy. This category would include the KOA (Kampgrounds of America) Journey and Holiday campgrounds. These are perfect for a clean, safe place to stop on the way to a destination or for a long, relaxing weekend getaway. The price range for this type of campground is from $40–$70 per night, depending on the type of amenities offered and the location. Cabins cost anywhere from $75–$175 per night. The biggest differentiator in the cabin pricing is the number of beds and bathroom or kitchen facilities.

Private Campground Resorts

Campground resorts are becoming more popular every year. What's the difference between a typical private campground and a resort? It's all about the on-site level of amenities and service. Campground resorts don't just have pools; they have multiple pools, probably heated ones, and additional water features like spray grounds or waterslides. Perhaps they have hot tubs and lazy rivers. One of our favorite campground resorts has an adults-only pool with a swim-up bar. True resorts also offer dining options and full activity schedules for kids and adults alike. The price tag for this type of campground ranges from $70–$125 in general. Cabins cost anywhere from $150–$300 per night. A notable exception is Fort Wilderness, the resort campground at Walt Disney World in Orlando, Florida, which has prices as high as $200 per night for campsites and $500 per night for cabins.

Dynamic Pricing

A decade ago, campgrounds offered pretty transparent pricing that was stable throughout an entire camping season. While most public campgrounds still have a standard price for each type of site (tent, electric, electric/water, electric/water/sewer), times have changed for many private campgrounds. It is becoming more and more common for private campgrounds, especially resorts, to use the dynamic pricing model that hotels have used for decades. Prices for the same site at the same campground can vary greatly depending on the day of the week and month of the year. A full hook-up campsite at a resort might be $70 per night on a Wednesday in early June and $125 per night on a Saturday in July. If you are looking for the amenities without the high price point, try to camp during the week or in the shoulder seasons.

CAMPGROUND RESERVATIONS

Folks who have been camping for decades loudly complain about how difficult it has become to make campground reservations. Camping has indeed exploded in popularity over the last decade as RV sales have increased dramatically. Three types of campgrounds have experienced the most pressure in terms of demand outpacing the supply—state parks, national parks, and resort campgrounds.

If you are looking to reserve a popular state or national park campground, find out when the reservation window opens. This is different for every single state and national park in the country, and that fact alone makes it difficult for new campers to snag a coveted site. Some state park reservation systems open twelve months in advance, while others open eleven months or six months in advance. Some of the systems open at midnight; some open at 9:00 a.m. Find out the details for the public campground you are looking to book, and set a reminder in your phone calendar.

The most popular resort campgrounds are often open for reservations a year or more in advance, especially for summers and holiday weekends. Fort Wilderness is actually open for reservations up to 499 days in advance. Some resorts have started offering guests first dibs on booking a campsite for the following year while they are staying at the campground in order to ensure that their loyal campers get to return. In general, experienced campers and RVers are making reservations in the late summer and early fall for the next year. This booking window often comes as a bit of a shock for newbies.

If you already missed the boat on early reservations for the upcoming camping season, we have an insider tip for you. With more and more people reserving so far in advance, cancellations have increased as well. We've nabbed some premium campsites at popular state parks, national parks, and resorts at the last minute by stalking cancellations on a daily basis.

USING ONLINE REVIEWS

We never book a campground without doing our homework, and that includes researching campground reviews from a variety of our favorite sources. Don't just look at a star rating to make your decision. You'll also want to do a good amount of reading to make sure you are getting a holistic idea of the campground vibe. Here are our tips for successfully navigating online campground reviews.

Take reviews seriously.

Sometimes we hear people complaining about a campground, and when we do a little research, it turns out that the place has years' worth of bad reviews with no response from management. If more than one review mentions late-night partying, bad customer service, or dirty bathhouses, you should believe them. Also note when a review was left. Sometimes campgrounds change ownership and you'll notice the reviews shift dramatically over the course of time. Don't believe everything that every reviewer writes, but do look for patterns.

Look for reviews from people who are camping like you are.

If you are tent camping, look for reviews from tent campers. The same is true for RVers or cabin renters. The different types of accommodations and campsites can often be run very differently, even at the same campground. For example, some popular resorts with beautiful RV sites have tent sites that are small and exposed to the elements. Likewise, cabin guests will very often have complaints that are irrelevant to an RV camper, like lukewarm bath water or uncomfortable beds. Make sure you look for the reviews that focus on the type of camping that you will be enjoying at that particular campground.

Pay attention to the specific amenities that are critiqued.

Some perfectly acceptable campgrounds in beautiful places have specific features and amenities that you might not care about at all. For example, we prefer to use our RV bathroom and rarely walk into the bathhouses at campgrounds. It really doesn't matter to us if a bathhouse isn't perfectly maintained, since we probably won't use it. However, if you are tent camping or you don't use the RV bathroom, this may be the single most important campground amenity. The same could be true of playgrounds, pools, or fitness centers. Pay attention to feedback on things that are important to you personally.

Follow up with additional crowdsourcing.

There are so many camping Facebook groups that make it easy to double-check your campground choices. In The RV Atlas Facebook group, people get feedback on campgrounds across the country in minutes, often confirming that they are picking a fantastic location. They also receive helpful tips from the crowd, perhaps being warned that the mosquitoes are bad in July or the river sites tend to flood in the spring. Crowdsourcing campground info is easier than ever, so take advantage whenever possible.

CAMPGROUND REVIEW RESOURCES

TripAdvisor

The TripAdvisor website is fairly ubiquitous for hotel reviews, but it has only recently come into its own as a place to find campground reviews. The website now features a healthy number of current ratings and photos from travelers. Also, the campground owners/managers have the option to respond, which lets you get both sides of the story in the case of a negative review. Be aware that many of the reviews come from cabin rentals, so you need to look carefully at whether the feedback applies to your specific situation.

Campendium

Campendium offers a great website and app focused primarily on campground reviews, including established campgrounds, popular boondocking spots, and even dump station locations. Know that these are user-generated reviews, so the actual quality of the review varies wildly. We find that there are more reviews of the western half of the United States than the eastern half.

The Dyrt

The Dyrt has a website and app, and it is pretty much the hip new kid on the block in the campground review space. The website is definitely aimed at the state park, national park, and tenting crowd in both branding and content. However, their review base is expanding constantly, so look for more private campgrounds to appear in the future. We particularly like that they have a description of each campground followed by reviews, providing a little more information and insight than a simple review site.

Campground Reviews

The Campground Reviews website has been around a long time. The great thing is that the reviews are written by experienced RV owners. You'll find a healthy amount of reviews for almost every campground out there, since this website was one of the first in this space. However, it is important to note that many campground reviews are written by older RV owners, so they may not be looking for the same things you are in a campground. Also, without an app, they aren't exactly attracting a younger crowd of RVers. Finally, you have to pay attention to the date of the reviews. You'll find some that are pretty old and may not reflect the current status of the park.

KOA

KOA offers a website and an app with an extensive number of reviews for its 500 U.S. campgrounds. Most of the KOA campgrounds actually allow reviews to be left right there on KOA's landing page, and they don't seem to be censored. KOA actually sends a review request by email after a campground stay, so these are verified guests offering a broad range of responses. It's admirable when a campground is willing to post the good, the bad, and the ugly reviews. It's also helpful when campground owners respond, giving you more insight into the situation. The downside to this resource is that you'll only find KOA campgrounds.

Campground of the Week

Of course we're biased, but we happen to think our *Campground of the Week* podcast is a great resource for finding amazing campgrounds in many of the most popular destinations across the United States. Over the years, we have offered hundreds of campground recommendations, interviewing folks who had visited and could offer specific details like best sites and local attractions. Even though we stopped producing new episodes, you can still listen to all the previous ones in your favorite podcast app, or you can read the reviews on our website at TheRVAtlas.com.

The RV Atlas

Even though we no longer produce new episodes of *Campground of the Week*, we do continue to pump out campground reviews on *The RV Atlas* podcast. We offer specific, detailed campground reviews for popular destinations like Glacier National Park and Zion National Park. We also provide roundups, bringing on locals to share their favorite Georgia State Parks or RV resorts. You can listen to these episodes in your favorite podcast app or at TheRVAtlas.com.

SEASONAL CAMPING

Seasonal camping is when you reserve one campsite for an extended period of time, and you are free to come and go at your own convenience. Most seasonal campers own an RV and leave their rig on the site and set it up to enjoy whenever they can escape for a few days or more. Seasonal camping has become an increasingly popular way to enjoy the camping experience, especially for busy families juggling work, school, and extracurricular activities. Seasonal camping rates and schedules vary greatly from one campground to another, so you will have to do a bit of research to find one that suits your family.

Why do people become seasonal campers?

They can't store their RV at home.

Some homeowners' associations do not allow recreational vehicles or boats to be stored in the driveway or yard. If you have to pay RV storage fees either way, you should crunch the numbers on a seasonal spot. It may not cost that much more to find storage *and* a permanent campsite for your travel trailer or motor home.

They want to camp more.

Many people love their time at the campground, but they find it difficult to make plans and reserve spots in advance. With a seasonal site, the RV is parked and waiting. All you have to do is show up with some clean clothes and a bag of groceries.

Work and activity schedules get in the way of extended vacations.

The two-week family vacation has vanished from many workplaces in America. Many of us struggle even to squeeze in a long weekend away. If a job makes it difficult to schedule time off in advance, a seasonal campsite offers a quick break from the daily grind.

They want to maximize time at the campground and minimize packing, setup, and breakdown.

Short weekend getaways become even shorter when you factor in all the preparation and cleanup. Seasonal camping eases the packing and unpacking workload. There are also no check-out times when you are a seasonal camper, so many people enjoy that additional flexibility.

They love the region or area close to their home.

Seasonal camping is particularly popular in places that have vacation destinations nearby, whether it's a lake, state park, or beach. This can be a way to have an affordable, camping version of a lake house.

How to find a seasonal campground

If seasonal camping sounds like a good fit for your family, make sure to do the research and find a campground that will truly be your happy place for an entire camping season.

Find a place that you love going back to again and again.

Lots of campgrounds are just fine for a night or two, but how enjoyable is the campground for repeat visits? Think about the location, the amenities, the campsites, and the overall atmosphere as you consider how often you'd like to camp in a particular park.

Do your research and ask the right questions.

There are a lot of elements to consider when you are looking at a long-term spot. Are other seasonal campers happy with their experiences at this park? Will you be surrounded by other seasonal campers or overnighters? Can you get Amazon deliveries? Can you store stuff outside of your RV? Try to think about all the items that contribute to a great experience, and think of things that make the long-term experience different from a short-term stay.

Check out the surrounding area.

If you are returning to the same campground again and again, chances are you will also be exploring the local area. Does it offer the kinds of activities, restaurants, shops, and amenities you will need and enjoy? As with buying a home, think *location, location, location.*

Do a trial run of weekends.

Try out the seasonal camping experience by renting a spot for a couple of weeks. Leave your RV, and see how you like the experience of coming and going. You'll soon figure out how far of a drive works for your situation. Be sure to include a holiday camping weekend to see how much the atmosphere at the campground changes.

Calculate your costs.

Does the cost of a seasonal spot make sense for your budget? A seasonal site may cost anywhere between $2,000 and $10,000 per year, depending on location and amenities. Make sure you understand what is and what is not included. (For example, some campgrounds charge extra based on usage for electricity or water on seasonal sites.) Find out the exact dates that are included. Some seasonal sites can be rented for the whole year, while other parks offer shorter seasons. Ask whether you have to pay the fee up front, or if there is a pay-by-month option. Also, you may want to check into any cancellation fees if you decide the park isn't for you.

HAPPY TRAVELS!

Our last book, *See You at the Campground: A Guide to Discovering Community, Connection, and a Happier Family in the Great Outdoors* is also a terrific resource for learning more about camping culture, whether you are interested in buying or renting an RV, tent camping, cabin camping, or glamping. We hope you check out that book too. But the most important thing we can tell you is this—there really is no wrong way to go camping. The only mistake you can make is staying home.

The CAMPGROUNDS

NEW ENGLAND

Connecticut

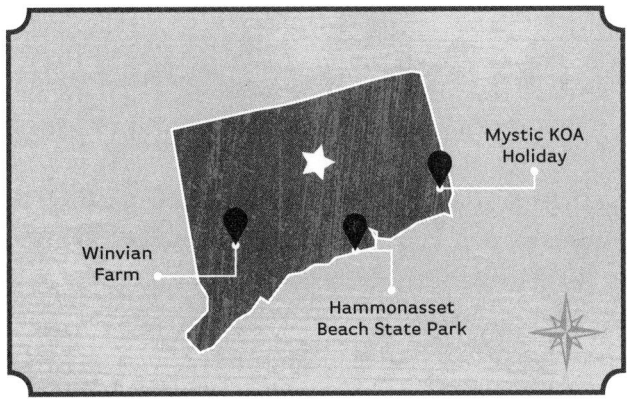

Connecticut is not a top camping destination for most folks in the United States, mostly because there just aren't that many campgrounds there. However, many people do find it to be a convenient stop when traveling north or south along the I–95 corridor to more popular camping destinations like Maine or South Carolina. The good news is there are some great campgrounds to break up the drive and explore this southernmost New England state. It's also a popular escape destination for millions of New Yorkers. So be prepared for traffic and crowds if visiting the beach areas on summer weekends.

BEST IN STATE

Winvian Farm

▷ Litchfield Hills, Connecticut

▷ winvian.com

▷ Luxury Cottages, Tree House, Log Cabin, Indoor Campsite

Set on over 100 acres of pristine woodlands and rolling meadows, the eighteen luxurious resort cottages at Winvian Farm were designed by fifteen different architects and each provides a unique environment for its guests. All of them are exceedingly posh. Some of them, like the Connecticut Yankee and the Hadley Suite, have very little to do with glamping no matter how much we stretch the definition. But other cottages, like the Treehouse (which is suspended 35 feet above the ground) and the Camping (which is designed to be like an indoor campsite) fit very nicely into the burgeoning glamping scene. Winvian takes both of these charming accommodations straight over the top—the Treehouse has a full bar and a jacuzzi, and the Camping has two wood burning fireplaces and a jacuzzi. Prices are sky high for this kind of pampering, but the experience will be unforgettable. Book a session at Winvian's delightful spa and a table dinner at its five star Seed to Table restaurant. A full breakfast is included at no additional cost, and each cottage includes complimentary bicycles for guests to use.

Mystic KOA Holiday

- ▷ North Stonington, Connecticut
- ▷ koa.com
- ▷ RV and Tent Sites, Deluxe Cabins, Camping Cabins

Mystic Seaport is an absolutely delightful slice of New England history and culture. Where else can you step aboard and explore historic whaleships and coal-fired steamboats? If you want to camp nearby, then the Mystic KOA is an obvious choice. The campground is huge and can get quite crowded in the summer, so we recommend visiting during the week if at all possible. Our boys loved the great facilities when we visited. The pool is large and clean, and the playgrounds and bounce pillows are modern and well kept. The quality of the RV sites varies depending on your location within the campground, and many of them are not shaded or private. We recommend calling and asking for a larger, more private site if at all possible. Cabins are cute and cozy, and the campground offers basic models without bathrooms and deluxe models with bathrooms and kitchens. Many of the cabins are nested back along the tree line and have privacy and shade. The highway is nearby, so if you are sensitive to noise at night please take that into consideration when booking any site, particularly if you are tent camping.

Mystic Seaport

Worth a day trip, this famous seaport is home to the *Charles W. Morgan*, the last remaining wooden whaleship. In addition to touring the ship, we enjoy the live performances and ship-building demonstrations. There are plenty of kid-friendly activities, including a children's museum and play area of model ships.

Hammonasset Beach State Park

▷ Madison, Connecticut

▷ ct.gov

▷ Tent and RV Sites, Rustic Cabins

Hammonasset Beach State Park is beloved by locals and receives over one million guests a year. The 2 miles of coastline here are the best in Connecticut, and the park also boasts excellent hiking and biking trails and a nature center that offers educational programs all year long. The campground has grassy sites, which is unusual for East Coast beach camping, and most of the sites are out in the open. There are a good number of trees in the campground, and some sites do offer shade and privacy. Good luck getting one of those sites on a busy summer weekend—or getting any site at all, for that matter. This place gets packed on the weekends. Some campers complain that things can get a bit rowdy, and that the campground is not well monitored, but we have found that the campground is generally very family-friendly. Connecticut added one hundred new cabins to its state park campgrounds in 2013 to celebrate the one hundredth anniversary of the park system, so the cabins at Hammonasset are relatively new and some of them are in cozy, shaded spots nestled along the tree line.

ALSO GREAT

Black Rock State Park

▷   Watertown, Connecticut

▷   ct.gov

▷   Tent and RV Sites, Rustic Cabins

Black Rock State Park campground is rustic and charming. The sites are wooded and offer privacy but are best for tent campers or those with smaller RVs, like pop-up campers. Four basic, two-room cabins are also available. Bring your hiking boots and fishing gear to enjoy a back-to-basics camping experience nestled among the pine, hemlock, and oak trees that form a ring around Black Rock Pond.

Seaport RV Resort and Campground

▷   Old Mystic, Connecticut

▷   sunrvresorts.com

▷   RV Sites, RV Rentals, Tent Sites

This clean and family-friendly resort campground makes a great base camp for exploring coastal Connecticut and Rhode Island. The basketball, volley-ball, tennis, and bocce ball courts are all excellent. Rainy days are also made tolerable by the comfy rec room that features a pool table and shuffleboard. Grab a burger and a beer at the nearby Captain Daniel Packer Inne, which has the look and feel of a classic whaling tavern from New England's storied past.

Dinosaur State Park

Dinosaur State Park has one of the largest dinosaur track sites in America and has easy trails for stretching your legs after time spent in the car. The Exhibit Center contains 500 tracks made by the Dilophosaurus, a carnivorous dinosaur from the early Jurassic period. Pack your own lunch to enjoy at the park's picnic area.

Tips for Eating at Abbott's Lobster in the Rough

Connecticut is the southernmost New England state, as such we consider it our starting point for all seafood shack dining adventures. If you have never been to a New England seafood shack, you might need a brief tutorial to fully enjoy the experience. They are all unique and have their own idiosyncrasies, but suffice it to say visitors should not expect a traditional eat-in dining experience. Here are a few tips for first timers:

▷ Don't try to make reservations. They are not accepted at Abbott's (or at most other famous seafood shacks).

▷ Go early. Most seafood shacks involve waiting in line to order at a window, and lines at the most popular places get shockingly long. Get there at the beginning of service.

▷ Bring a blanket. Abbott's has a large lawn that looks out over the water. There is a smattering of picnic tables, but many folks bring blankets for a picnic experience.

▷ Bring your own wine or beer. We learned this the hard way. Most seafood shacks serve alcohol, but Abbott's does not. Folks bring bottles of wine to enjoy with their feast.

▷ Order the hot lobster roll. You can get a hot lobster roll in northern New England, but Connecticut is the true home of this warm, buttery lobster roll delicacy.

P.S. The chowder at Abbott's is Stephanie's very favorite, and she's eaten her fair share of chowders on the East Coast.

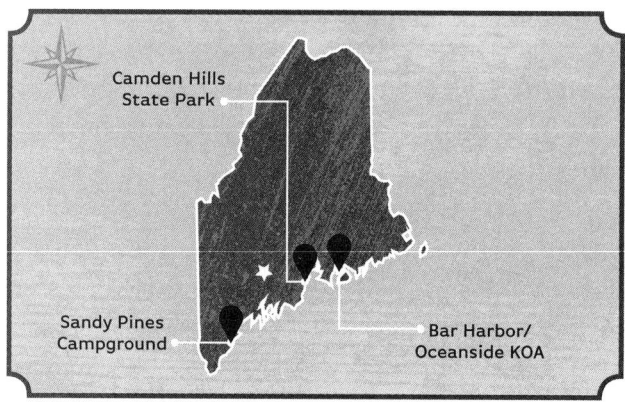

Maine

Camden Hills
State Park

Sandy Pines
Campground

Bar Harbor/
Oceanside KOA

Maine calls itself Vacationland, and anyone who has played tourist in this state will surely concur. It is truly heaven on earth, as long as you visit during the months of June through October, when the days are warm and sunny, and the nights are crisp and cool. Make sure to plan your camping trip after Father's Day to avoid experiencing the wrath of the legendary black flies. And while the foliage is stunning in early October, be prepared for winter temperatures to arrive at any time.

There are quite a few distinct regions in Maine, each one holding its own vacation magic. Old Orchard Beach along the southern coast is a favorite beach town getaway for many folks in New England, so expect all the touristy boardwalk attractions and lots of crowds. Head north to mid-coast Maine for a quieter, more picturesque experience. There you'll find quaint villages like Bath, Camden, and Rockland with downtown boutiques, bookstores, and coffee shops. You'll also find a lobster roll on every corner.

Head a bit north to find the wild wonder of the great outdoors. Acadia National Park is one of the top ten most visited NPS sites in the country, with accessible hiking and breathtaking views around every bend in the road. Trek far into the northern wilderness and visit Mount Katahdin, the highest mountain in Maine, and the northern terminus of the Appalachian Trail located in Baxter State Park. If you want the experience of a truly off-the-grid camping trip, this region will check all the boxes. Former Governor Percival Baxter gifted the land to Maine and wanted it to be "forever wild." To this day, there is no electricity or potable water in the entire park.

Before you go...

▷ **Read:** *The Lobster Coast* by Colin Woodard

BEST IN STATE

Sandy Pines Campground

▷ Kennebunkport, Maine

▷ sandypinescamping.com

▷ Tent Sites, RV Sites, Glamping Tents, Cottages, A-frame Huts, Airstreams, Covered Wagons

If a state park and a resort campground fell in love and had a baby, its name would be Sandy Pines Campground. This magical retreat feels miles away from the hustle and bustle of Kennebunkport, and the rustic tent sites are tucked back along the water's edge. The RV sites are spacious, shaded, and perfectly manicured. The glamping accommodations look like they leapt off the pages of a magazine. While the campground offers the natural beauty of a state park, the amenities are resort quality. There's a beautiful pool; activity field with corn hole, ladder ball, and badminton; and a delightful kids' craft tent. Guests can rent paddleboards, kayaks, and bikes from a local vendor. They can also enjoy coffee and fresh pastries at the camp store each morning and burgers grilled by the pool for lunch.

Camden Hills State Park

▷ Camden, Maine

▷ maine.gov

▷ Tent Sites, RV Sites

The campground at Camden Hills State Park, which is nestled along the base of Mount Battie, is a gem in Maine's sparkling state park system. Here, tent campers and RV owners can take their pick between deeply wooded or sunny sites. When we visited in our pop-up, we were delighted to pull into a gigantic site next to an open field. Kids have to make their own fun at most state park campgrounds, and Camden Hills is no exception. Amenities are sparse. Activities are non-existent. But beautiful, natural space and the smell of pine trees and salty ocean breezes are abundant. Let the kids run wild and free on the huge field, or take them for a hike to the top of Mount Battie for spectacular views of Camden Harbor and Penobscot Bay. Campground bathhouses and showers are clean and inviting for those camping in tents or pop-ups.

If you get tired of smelling pine trees and chasing fireflies, you can head into town for posh boutiques, coastal galleries, and well-curated bookshops, both new and antiquarian. Don't forget a scoop (or two) of Gifford's ice cream before you head back to the campground. We prefer Moose Tracks.

How to Spot a Moose in Maine

Even though moose appear on almost every sweatshirt and mug in souvenir shops across the state, it's trickier to spot one in the wild. First of all, don't expect to catch sight of a moose in Acadia National Park. Wildlife experts claim there is no permanent, breeding population on Mount Desert Island. You'll have more luck in the northern wilderness, specifically in Baxter State Park and the aptly named Moosehead Lake. Keep your eyes open at dawn and dusk from May through July when they are most active.

Bar Harbor/Oceanside KOA Holiday

▷ Bar Harbor, Maine

▷ koa.com

▷ Tent Sites, RV Sites, Cabin Rentals, Airstream Rentals

The sunsets at this KOA are incredible, and so are its waterfront RV sites with views of Acadia National Park in the distance. If you can't book a waterfront site, we suggest that you wait to schedule your trip until one opens up. Your kids will spend hours playing in the tide pools each day, and each evening will end with a lobster dinner served up fresh right at the campground. Prices are better here than in town. Save a little room for the pie guy who drives around the campground each night selling his wares out of an old station wagon. The cookies are good, but the blueberry pie is to die for, especially when it's heated up in foil over the campfire and served with a scoop of vanilla ice cream. Not Moose Tracks. Vanilla. Trust us.

Don't worry. You'll burn up all of those calories hiking in Acadia National Park and taking in the breathtaking views atop Gorham and Cadillac Mountains. More adventurous souls will hike to the top of the Beehive or Precipice Trails and behold the majesty of the Atlantic Ocean sparkling beneath their feet.

ALSO GREAT

Terramor Outdoor Resort

▷ Bar Harbor, Maine

▷ terramoroutdoorresort.com

▷ Glamping Tents

When KOA announced that it was reopening one of its corporate-owned campgrounds in Bar Harbor, Maine, as a glamping resort, it made a lot of heads turn. Industry insiders looked at this as yet another sign that glamping was no longer a fad, but a legitimate niche in the outdoor space. We camped on this property when it was a KOA. The property is deeply wooded and filled with fragrant pine trees, and the location near Acadia National Park is excellent. Terramor's centerpiece is a lodge with a restaurant and bar and concierge-level services. The glamping tents are also gorgeous and can accommodate couples or families of up to five people.

---------- **Favorite Spots for a Family Swim** ----------

The water may be pretty brisk even in the warm summer months, but that doesn't mean you shouldn't enjoy a refreshing swim while in Maine. Here are a few personal favorites:

✧ Goose Rocks Beach near Sandy Pines Campground

✧ Laite Memorial Beach near Camden Hills State Park Campground

✧ Echo Lake in Acadia National Park near the Bar Harbor/Oceanside KOA

Huttopia Southern Maine

▷ Sanford, Maine

▷ canada-usa.huttopia.com

▷ Glamping Tents, Cabins

Nestled in the woods just a few miles from Wells and Kennebunkport, Huttopia's glamping tents and fully equipped cabins serve as a perfect model for the brave new world of glamping experiences that are popping up from coast to coast. Everything about Huttopia is hip, comfortable, and aesthetically pleasing.

Bayley's Camping Resort

▷ Scarborough, Maine

▷ bayleysresort.com

▷ Tent Sites, RV Sites, Cabin Rentals, On-Site RV Rentals

Bayley's offers resort-style camping less than a mile from the beach. After a day spent enjoying the sun and sand, come back to the resort and listen to live music while soaking in one of its four hot tubs.

Schoodic Woods Campground

▷ Acadia National Park, Maine

▷ nps.gov

▷ Tent Sites, RV Sites

An anonymous donor developed the campground, bike paths, and facilities on the Schoodic Peninsula before turning over the property to the National Park Service. Located about an hour's drive from the main part of the park on Mount Desert Island, the Schoodic area has a rugged beauty and amazing views but none of the crowds that you will find on the Park Loop Road. The campsites are huge and paved, with electric hookups. B-loop sites have electric and water.

------------------ **Lobster Roll: Hot or Cold** ------------------

The traditional Maine Lobster Roll is served cold, tossed with a bit of mayo, on a warm, buttered bun. But don't worry, if you prefer a hot lobster roll, you'll be able to find that also at many of the famous Maine lobster pounds. We recommend trying them both, perhaps during the same meal. There's always room for more lobster.

Hiking in Acadia National Park

With over 120 miles of hiking trails on Mount Desert Island, you could visit Acadia National Park many times over and never walk the same path twice. These five hikes encompass the best that Acadia has to offer, with sweeping ocean views, dramatic granite cliffs, and landscapes filled with cedar, birch, and spruce.

Ocean Trail

This easy 4-mile-round-trip hike (also known as Ocean Path or Ocean Drive Trail) is the classic introductory hike to Acadia. Starting off at Sand Beach, the path brings you to Thunder Hole and Otter Cliffs, passing by one beautiful vista after another. There are many small turnoffs that can lead to dramatic views and also dramatic drop-offs. If you wander off the main trail, keep a close eye on your kids. There are also stretches where the path is right next to the road. Traffic can be fast and close, so hand-holding might be in order.

Reward yourselves after the hike with a swim at Sand Beach, just be prepared to squeal as you dive into the cold water.

Gorham Mountain Trail

One of the more famous family-friendly hikes within the Park Loop, this trail also rewards its hikers with stunning views of Sand Beach, Otter Cliffs, and Cadillac Mountain. We enjoyed this trail with another family, and all of the kids had a blast navigating the rocky terrain. The summit offered incredible ocean panoramas as well as a safe space for snacking and enjoying the view. If you are feeling more adventurous, take the Cadillac Cliffs trail spur—a short but fun 0.3-mile with rock scrambles, stone stairs, and iron rungs.

Wonderland/Ship Harbor Trails

If you want to get away from the crowds clustered around the Park Loop, drive past Southwest Harbor to the Wonderland and Ship Harbor Trails. Both of these trails can be done independently, or you can do what we did—hike out to the water on the Wonderland Trail, then head west along the rocky beach to the Ship Harbor Trail and complete a loop back to the parking lot.

Have time for just one of these two trails? We think Ship Harbor is your best bet, offering lots of paths down to the tide pools and, of course, great water views. We hiked these trails on a weekend during peak season and saw only a handful of people. This is truly the quieter side of Acadia.

Flying Mountain Trail

We get much of our travel intel from the recommendations of other campers. A friendly hiking dad named Chris told us that the Flying Mountain Trail would be perfect for our family. He was right. This 1.5-mile loop was great fun for the boys, giving them a good challenge at the beginning with a steep ascent and ending with beautiful views of the Somes Sound. The tricky descent kept them entertained, and there is a rock beach where the kids can play at the bottom. The hike ends with an easy walk via a fire road right back to the parking lot. Awesome hike. Thanks, Chris.

Great Head Trail

Great Head Trail is another classic family hike that has all of the best elements of Maine. You cross a sandy beach to get to the trailhead, pick your way up and around a rocky peninsula that overlooks the ocean with stunning views, and head inland to an incredible pine forest that smells like heaven itself—then you loop your way back to the beach for a cold water swim!

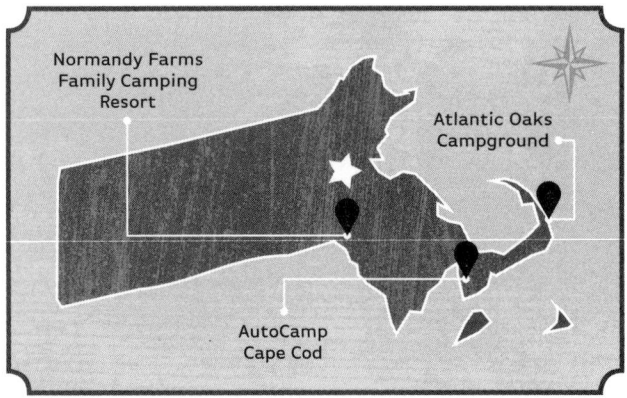

Massachusetts

For a small state, the regional diversity in Massachusetts is almost shocking. The eastern side boasts 192 miles of coastline that includes beautiful Cape Cod, and the famous and storied islands of Martha's Vineyard and Nantucket. Look to the west, and you will find the lush Berkshire Valley nestled between the Berkshire Hills and the Taconic Mountains.

A whole lot of history happened in this state as well. Visitors can walk the Freedom Trail in Boston, visit the Salem Witch Museum in Salem, and gaze at America's most famous rock located in Pilgrim Memorial State Park. From whale watching at the Stellwagen Bank National Marine Sanctuary to checking out the Green Monster at Fenway Park, there are plenty of adventures to be had in Massachusetts.

And there are plenty of places to camp. Cape Cod has something for every camping personality, offering rustic state parks and amenity-rich RV resorts. One of the oldest RV resorts in the country places you within spitting distance of Boston. The Berkshires has surprisingly few private campgrounds, but state forest campgrounds abound for folks who are willing to rough it.

--------- **Our Favorite Cape Cod Seafood Shacks** ---------

✧ Arnold's Lobster & Clam Bar. This popular spot is hardly a hidden treasure, but it is most definitely worth waiting in line for the creamy chowder, lobster rolls, and homemade ice cream.

✧ Mac's Market & Kitchen Eastham. This is the perfect place to pick up fresh seafood for a campground feast. We traditionally grab a couple pounds of shrimp and clams for a festive seafood boil with friends.

✧ Cap't Cass Rock Harbor Seafood. The clam plate and scallop po'boys are on point at this quaint and casual restaurant. Time your visit to Rock Harbor at low tide so your kids can play in the seemingly endless tide pools.

BEST IN STATE

AutoCamp Cape Cod

▷ Falmouth, Massachusetts

▷ autocamp.com

▷ Airstream Suites, Luxury Tents, Studio Suites

Cape Cod is one of our favorite camping destinations on the East Coast. It has great state park options, a handful of great mom-and-pop campgrounds, and a couple of good RV resorts. But up until now, there has not been a luxurious glamping destination. The birth of a new AutoCamp location in a high-end destination like Cape Cod makes all of the sense in the world. We love the custom designed Airstream rentals, and the luxury tents have fresh and modern design appeal. Food and drinks are available on-site, so you can have a tastefully curated meal and a cocktail (or two) and not have to worry about driving home. Leave the kids at home for this one, and check in for a romantic weekend that you will never forget.

Normandy Farms Family Camping Resort

▷ Foxboro, Massachusetts

▷ normandyfarms.com

▷ Cabins, Yurts, Pop-ups, Safari Tents

Normandy Farms is an early example of a fashionable luxury RV resort on the East Coast—and it still might be the best. This place has everything, and it may succeed at being all things to all people. It offers seemingly nonstop organized activities for kids and teenagers—like ga-ga ball and softball tournaments. And it also offers one-of-a-kind facilities, like a challenging bike park and a creative arts center for movie nights. Adults will love working out in the fitness center, getting a massage in the wellness center, and relaxing in the jacuzzi or reading a book in the adults-only loft. Four-legged camping companions will also love the gigantic dog park, which is the largest dedicated outdoor pet recreation area we have seen in a decade of camping. Everyone will love the four huge pools (one of which is indoors) and the well-trained staff who are present throughout the park. Some RV sites are out in the open, but many are shaded and private. Pop-up camper rentals can be delivered to your site if you don't have your own RV, and the safari tents are stylish and comfortable.

Atlantic Oaks Campground

▷ Eastham, Massachusetts

▷ atlanticoaks.com

▷ Tent and RV Sites, RV Rentals

Atlantic Oaks is a simple campground—and it is simply delightful. The location in Eastham—near the Cape Cod National Seashore and sandwiched between two classic seafood shacks—is near perfect. Most guidebooks choose Arnold's Lobster & Clam Bar as their top pick in Eastham, but we like the Friendly Fisherman even more. Either way, we love to take a bike ride up to the beach after dinner. The Cape Cod Rail Trail runs behind the campground and connects directly to the Nauset Bike Trail, which rolls up and down and eventually drops right off on the windswept beaches of the Cape Cod National Seashore. Things are pretty chill back at the campground. Groups of campers will be grilling up that day's catch, and they might even invite you over for a cup of hot chowder—even if you are wearing a Yankees cap. Ask us how we know... The sites are private and some are semi-shaded; the community lounge is comfortable, and the camp store is well stocked.

A Day in Boston

If you are staying at the legendary Normandy Farms, take advantage of public transportation and plan a day trip to Boston, just 30 miles away. The campground offers detailed trip guides and a concierge is on-site to help organize your city adventure.

- Walk the Freedom Trail
- Visit Faneuil Hall
- Eat at Quincy Market
- Picnic at Boston Common
- Catch a game at Fenway Park

ALSO GREAT

Beartown State Forest

- Monterey, Massachusetts
- mass.gov
- Tent Sites

There are only twelve campsites available at Beartown State Forest. A small handful of them are located on the shoreline of Benedict Pond. This is no-frills, back-to-nature camping at its best. Whether you are looking to disconnect completely or take that perfect photo for your Instagram gallery, this is the place.

> -------------------- **Before you go…** --------------------
> ▷ **Read:** *The Outermost House: A Year of Life on the Great Beach of Cape Cod* by Henry Beston
> ▷ **Watch:** *The Crucible* (1996)

Salisbury Beach State Reservation

▷ Salisbury, Massachusetts

▷ mass.gov

▷ RV and Tent Sites

Located directly on the Atlantic coast and at the mouth of the Merrimack River, this gigantic campground has almost 500 sites, and none of them have shade or privacy. But there is water everywhere you look. Those who love to fish, kayak, or swim will be in heaven.

Nickerson State Park

▷ Brewster, Massachusetts

▷ mass.gov

▷ Yurts, RV and Tent Sites

As far as we are concerned, camping in Massachusetts begins and ends in Cape Cod. And Nickerson State Park is one of the prettiest places on the Cape. Windswept beaches and a classic wooden bat baseball league are nearby—but Nickerson is all about thick pine and oak forests that surround the park's eight crystal-clear kettle ponds. There are no hookups on the sites, so be prepared to dry camp.

Get Outside on the Cape!

✧ **Bike the Cape Cod Rail Trail.** Twenty-two miles of beautiful, paved paths meander through state and national parks. We love to park at the Salt Pond Visitor Center and bike to the Coast Guard Beach.

✧ **Kayak at Nickerson State Park.** Flax Pond has a lovely roped off swimming area and plenty of room to paddle around the 48-acre freshwater kettle pond.

✧ **Hike at Wellfleet Bay Wildlife Sanctuary.** Arrive during low tide so you can hike the Boardwalk Trail all the way out to the edge of the salt marsh. Bring your bug spray!

✧ **Whale Watch in the Cape Cod Bay.** There are countless places to go whale watching in New England, but we think Hyannis Whale Watcher Cruises offers the very best experience. The tours are focused on conservation and education. Plus, the humpbacks almost always put on a show.

✧ **Drive It.** There's only one way to drive on the protected dunes of the Cape Cod National Seashore, and that's by getting in an SUV with the knowledgeable guides at Art's Dune Tours. You can pick from a variety of tour options, from a one-hour drive to a sunset experience that includes dinner and a bonfire on the beach.

· New Hampshire ·

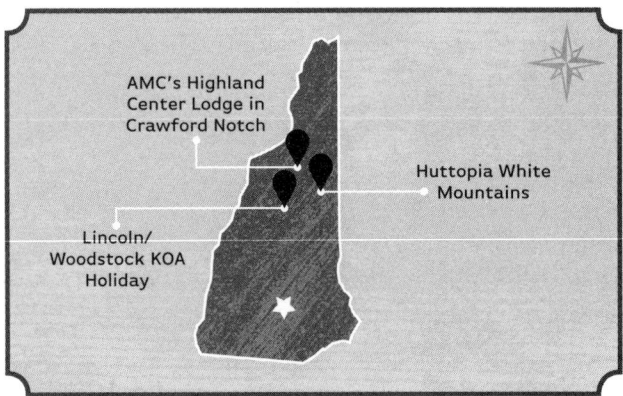

New Hampshire is rugged and wild, and camping here feels like an entirely different experience from anywhere else in New England. You won't find many quaint seafood shacks like in neighboring Maine, or endless charming downtowns like in Vermont. In fact, the last time we camped there, we drove over thirty minutes just to restock our grocery supplies.

The two most popular areas for camping in New Hampshire are the southern coast—where you'll find a small spit of sandy beaches packed between Massachusetts and Maine—and the White Mountains, where you'll find amazing hikes and, of course, a harrowing drive up Mount Washington. The state park system has stricter pet policies than most we have visited, so check those out in advance if traveling with four-legged family members. The entry fees for public attractions are also a bit higher here than in many other states, since the parks are self-funded and not subsidized by state taxes. Live free or die.

BEST IN STATE

Huttopia White Mountains

▷ Albany, New Hampshire

▷ canada-usa.huttopia.com

▷ Glamping Tents, Chalets

Whether you choose the Trapper, Bonaventure, or Canadienne tents, or upgrade to the bright and spacious chalet, you are in for a glamping adventure of a lifetime at Huttopia White Mountains. The tents are well equipped with cooking essentials, and the chalet has a woodstove, stocked kitchen, two bedrooms, and a wooden bathroom. Relax by the pool after a long day of hiking in the "whites" or rent a canoe or SUP and paddle into the sunset. Huttopia's lake has its own private beach, but during high season evening entertainment takes center stage. Outdoor movies and concerts are fun for the whole family, and cookery classes help couples reconnect. Bring your fishing poles—the lake is filled with trout, perch, and black bass. Basketball and volleyball don't sound very glampy to us, but it has those too, along with a popular Finnish throwing game called Mölkky that is good for glampers of all ages.

Lincoln/Woodstock KOA Holiday

▷ Woodstock, New Hampshire

▷ koa.com

▷ Camping Cabins, Deluxe Cabins, Safari Tents, RV and Tent Sites

This is one of the best KOA campgrounds in America. The White Mountains are filled with every kind of outdoor adventure imaginable, and this delightful campground is a perfect base camp for your adventures. Our boys loved the huge open field and the fun planned activities, like hayrides, that run most nights during the summer. Owners Rob and Darlene take pride in their park, and they can also guide you to the best local hikes and launch points for your kayak or canoe. The Lincoln/Woodstock KOA is also incredibly pet-friendly. Every KOA has a dog park, but this one is huge and really fun for your favorite furry friend. They also offer kenneling services for those who want to take day trips and leave their pups at the campground. We visited during the World Cup a few years back and enjoyed watching a game or two in the comfortable common area—and were always made to feel right at home.

··········· **Drive It: Kancamagus Scenic Byway** ···········

The Kanc for short, this highway runs 34.5 miles through the White Mountains, connecting the towns of Lincoln and Conway. Carve out plenty of time for this drive, since there are countless places to stop along the way and enjoy over-looks, photo opportunities, and hikes. The Lower Falls and the Rocky Gorge Scenic Area are a couple of our favorite places to explore. There's also a beau-tiful 3.1-mile round-trip hike to Sawyer Pond.

AMC's Highland Center Lodge at Crawford Notch

▷   Bretton Woods, New Hampshire

▷   outdoors.org

▷   Lodge Rooms, Family Lodge Rooms, Family Bunkrooms, Hostel-Style Bunkrooms

The Highland Center Lodge is not a campground by any definition. But we still want you to know about this magnificent lodge, which is centered around the outdoor experience in the otherworldly Crawford Notch section of the White Mountains. AMC's crown jewel lodge is surrounded by soaring waterfalls and hiking trails for every level of adventure. After a buffet-style breakfast, head into the great outdoors with one of the lodge's trained natu-ralists for a group hike, or venture out with your traveling companions for a self-guided adventure. Either way, make sure to plan on grabbing lunch and a cold beer back at the lodge. The food is delicious and the craft beer is local.

Our kids *loved* the "natural, outdoor, *Big Mountain* Playscape," and so will yours. They will spend hours crawling through the rock caves and testing their balance on the rope bridge while you relax nearby—unless you decide to play with them, like we did.

ALSO GREAT

Yogi Bear's Jellystone Park Camp-Resort Lakes Region

▷ Milton, New Hampshire

▷ lakesregionjellystone.com

▷ Cottages, Cabins, Bungalows, RV and Tent Sites

This shady, waterfront Jellystone is located on the shores of Northeast Pond and has two private, sandy beaches for swimming and kayaking. Basketball, volleyball, tennis, and soccer are available for the sports nuts in your family— and so is giant chess, if you are feeling silly and cerebral. RV sites near the water are nice—but we also love the wooded and shady sites a little further back. Cabin offerings are excellent for glampers and those getting their first taste of camping culture.

Riding the Coasters

The White Mountains has a surprising number of water parks and amusement parks for a famed outdoors mecca. We highly recommend two of these tourist attractions: Santa's Village and Story Land. Santa's Village is where the big guy spends his summers, and little kids have chance to tell him what they want for Christmas long before he arrives at the malls back home. It's also the cleanest amusement park we have ever visited in the entire country. Story Land is also a fun, charming experience for young kids, but includes larger roller coasters for teens and adults as well.

Hampton Beach State Park Campground

▷ Hampton, New Hampshire

▷ nhstateparks.org

▷ RV Sites

The campground at Hampton Beach State Park has an almost mythological status among East Coast RV owners. There is nothing incredible about the campground, but the location right on the beach is astonishing. So of course it is incredibly difficult to book a site here—we jumped up and down when we did so a few years back.

Ellacoya State Park

▷ Gilford, New Hampshire

▷ nhstateparks.org

▷ RV Sites

Sadly, pets are not allowed at this delightful campground, and neither are tents. But RV owners will be thrilled to find full hook-up sites on a spacious, grassy field with lovely views of Lake Winnipesaukee, New Hampshire's largest lake. The sandy beach makes for a great swimming spot just steps away from your RV site. Make sure you book this campground far in advance, as there are only thirty-seven sites and they are all highly desirable.

-- **Drive It (or maybe don't): Mount Washington Auto Road** --

Driving up to the Mount Washington Observatory was one of the more petrifying travel experiences of our lives. If you are squeamish about driving just inches away from steep mountain drop-offs, take the train or guided van tour to the top instead. Of course, you could also hike. The Appalachian Mountain Club (AMC) has the most reliable and thorough trail information for this legendary summit climb.

Favorite Family-Friendly Hikes in the White Mountains

Flume Gorge Trail

This is a busy tourist attraction, but if you arrive early enough in the morning, you'll be able to enjoy a quiet, serene 2-mile hike through a natural chasm.

Artist Bluff Trail

This relatively easy 1.5-mile hike does include some steep elevation gain, but the views of Cannon Mountain are worth the climb. Bring your bathing suits to swim in Echo Lake after the hike.

Basin-Cascades Trail

An easy 2.5-mile hike that includes lots of opportunities for waterfall photos and also plenty of chances to dip your toes in chilly mountain water.

Elephant Head Trail

A short, uphill climb with amazing views. Less than a mile round trip, and you can see Mount Washington on a clear day. Make sure you look up from the parking lot to get a good look at the "elephant head" above.

Arethusa Falls Trail

This one might be a bit more challenging for little ones, but it's worth the effort. Hike about 3 miles and arrive at some of the most beautiful falls in the White Mountains. Bring a picnic lunch and a change of clothes.

Rhode Island

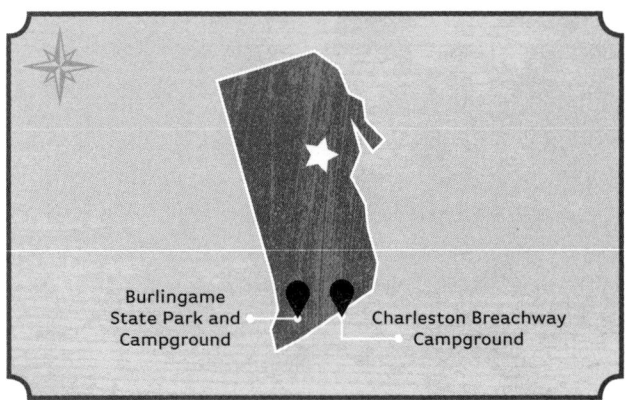

Burlingame State Park and Campground

Charleston Breachway Campground

Rhode Island may be small, but it punches above its weight in the camping category. Residents rave about the state park campgrounds, but you'll have to be prepared for a rustic camping experience—Fishermen's Memorial is the only one with hookups. You'll also have to be ready for a competitive booking experience. This is a densely populated part of the country with limited open spaces, so the best campsites are snapped up fast. And when you do reserve your spot, take a moment to celebrate the budget victory: accommodations start at just $18 for tent sites for residents and top out at $75 for cabins booked by out-of-staters.

Before you go...

▷ **Read:** *A Guide to Newport's Cliff Walk: Tales of Seaside Mansions & the Gilded Age Elite* by Ed Morris

▷ **Watch:** *The Great Gatsby* (1974) with scenes filmed at Marble House, Rosecliff Mansion, and Ocean Drive

BEST IN STATE

Burlingame State Park and Campground

▷ Charlestown, Rhode Island

▷ riparks.com

▷ RV and Tent Sites, Cabin Rentals

Burlingame Campground may be the most popular campground in all of Rhode Island—thankfully it has seven hundred campsites and twenty cabin rentals. The campground is nestled next to Watchaug Pond, and canoe rentals and a boat launch ramp make this a great spot for spending time on the water. The 29-acre Kimball Wildlife Refuge is located on the southern shore of the pond, and trails connect it directly to the campground. There are also beaches nearby for those who want to play in the waves. The rustic cabins are cute and cozy, but they book up early, so plan ahead. The RV and tent sites are also rustic and have no hookups, and most are well shaded and semi-private. Check the schedule for nature programs when you check in— kids will love them. The park can get crowded during peak summer weekends, so consider a trip during the week or in the shoulder months.

---------------- **Fancy a Game of Tennis?** ----------------

The International Tennis Hall of Fame just happens to be located in Newport, Rhode Island. Even if you are not a huge fan of the sport, who can resist experiencing a Roger Federer holographic theatre where visitors feel as if they are in the same room as one of the greatest tennis stars of all time? The museum prides itself on interactive and educational displays, including tennis trivia and a broadcasting simulator.

Charlestown Breachway Campground

▷ Charlestown, Rhode Island

▷ riparks.com

▷ RV Sites Only

Most folks fall in love with the Charlestown Breachway Campground almost immediately after parking their rigs. The seventy-five sites are only for self-contained RVs (those with bathrooms and holding tanks), and the beach is just steps away. The swimming and fishing are legendary, and you will probably end up meeting many families that have been coming here for decades. The sites are small and in no way private—and because there are no hookups, many campers run their generators all day long and into the night. There is little supervision here, and you need to cross your fingers and hope your neighbors are nice. But if you can get past the small sites and loud sounds of generators, then you will probably fall in love with the wide open and often uncrowded beach. There is only a small parking lot for day visitors, so campers have plenty of space to themselves. Bring lots of water if you go, and make sure you are prepared for a true dry camping experience.

ALSO GREAT

Melville Ponds Campground

▷ Portsmouth, Rhode Island

▷ melvillepondscampground.com

▷ RV and Tent Sites, Airbnb Airstream Rentals

Melville Ponds Campground started offering comfortable and stylish Airstream rentals a few years back, and they have been a smash hit. Rentals (which are listed separately on Airbnb) include a rehabbed 1972 Airstream Ambassador and a 1977 Airstream Land Yacht. Both have classic curb appeal and bright and fresh "Instaworthy" interiors. Downtown Newport's dramatic coastline is only 5 miles away.

George Washington State Campground

▷   Glocester, Rhode Island

▷   riparks.com

▷   Tent and RV Sites

Located directly on the Bowdish Reservoir, the George Washington State Campground offers an excellent rustic camping experience at an afford- able price. There are only forty-five sites, but they are spacious and private. Regulars are thrilled with the brand-new bathhouse and shower facility. Previously there were no shower facilities, and campers had to take care of their business in pit toilets.

------------------ **Drive It: Ocean Drive** ------------------

Also known as 10 Mile Drive or just The Drive, this road meanders along the coastline of Newport, Rhode Island. The drive might take an hour or an entire day, depending on how often you stop along the way. Here are some of the more popular points of interest along the drive:

✦ Fort Adams State Park

✦ Castle Hill Inn

✦ U.S. Coast Guard Station Castle Hill

✦ Brenton Point State Park

✦ Gooseberry Beach

The Charm of Rhode Island

Rhode Island is known for its collection of quaint seaside towns, each with its own unique character.

Newport

It's all about the Gilded Age mansions in Newport. Stroll the 3.5-mile Cliff Walk, then tour a selection of the summer cottages. The Breakers, a Vanderbilt mansion, is the grandest of the bunch. Other favorites include Marble House, The Elms, and Rosecliff.

Block Island

Twelve miles from mainland Rhode Island, Block Island is only accessible by boat or plane, so many visitors arrive using one of the ferry services. There are 17 miles of free public beaches in addition to miles of hiking trails and self-guided bike tours.

Narragansett

This classic New England beach town features the photogenic Point Judith Lighthouse, which is still an active Coast Guard station. Splash in the tidal pools at Black Point and go clamming at Point Judith Salt Pond, then enjoy a clambake back at the campground.

Jamestown

Packed with historic charm, this town also lays claim to two state parks: Fort Wetherill and Beavertail. Visit the Beavertail Lighthouse Museum and hike along the coastal granite cliffs.

Providence

Visit the Rhode Island School of Design Museum and tour College Hill Historic District, home of Brown University. Make sure to check listings for current art exhibits, live music, and theater while visiting this culturally vibrant town.

• *Vermont* •

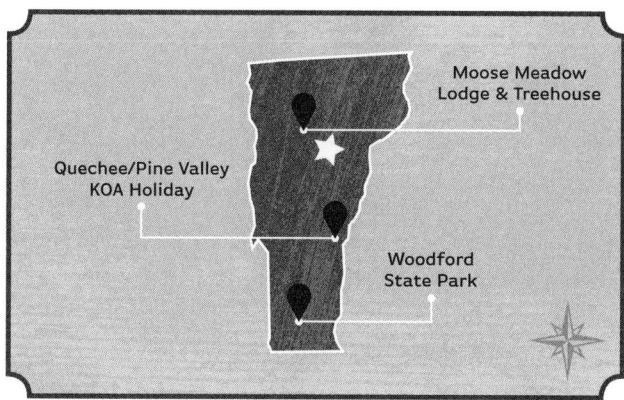

Vermont is the type of place that makes us wonder why we don't just move there whenever we visit. Our camping trips to Vermont are filled with hiking, biking, berry picking, and maple syrup tasting (yes, that's actually a thing). There are charming downtowns and farm stands overflowing with fresh produce. While better known for its skiing, we have had many magical camping adventures in the Green Mountain State.

BEST IN STATE

Moose Meadow Lodge & Treehouse

▷ Waterbury, Vermont

▷ moosemeadowlodge.net

▷ Treehouse

The Moose Meadow Lodge & Treehouse is like something out of a children's fairy tale. Is this camping? Glamping? Something else entirely? Call it what you want. A getaway in this magical treehouse is a great outdoors experience like no other. This handcrafted accommodation is actually supported by two mature pine trees and is built with cedar, pine, maple, and hemlock. Its thirty-one windows and wraparound deck make you feel like you are outside. Be forewarned—the bathroom, sink, and shower are on the first floor deck *so they are actually outside*, making this a true back-to-nature experience. But don't worry about your privacy, because there won't be anyone else around. Spend the morning rambling through the woods, then return to your cozy lodge-like rooms for lunch, afternoon tea, a book, a nap, or all of the above. There is room to bring the kids—but this place has "romantic weekend" written all over it.

Quechee/Pine Valley KOA Holiday

▷ White River Junction, Vermont

▷ koa.com

▷ Wide Range of Cabins, RV and Tent Sites

Owners Mike and Cindy make everybody feel welcome at this charming KOA, which is one of the very best private campgrounds in New England. The lovely pine trees that fill this KOA make it smell better than a Yankee Candle, and every inch of the property is kept Disney World clean. Everything flows naturally into the landscape here, including the lovely cabin and RV sites and the playground and camp store. Whether intentional or not, the landscaping feels inspired by classic English landscape architecture—and Mike and Cindy just keep making this place better and better. Families return to their favorite RV sites or cabin sites every year for peak fall foliage and the local balloon festival, which recently celebrated its fortieth anniversary. The location is also perfect. Quechee Gorge is nearby, as is the magnificent Vermont Institute of Natural Science (VINS). Opportunities for world-class hiking and terrific craft beer and local foods are also abundant. This is a quintessential Vermont camping experience.

Woodford State Park

▷ Woodford, Vermont

▷ vtstateparks.com

▷ Tent and RV Sites, Cabins and Lean-Tos

The Vermont State Park system is one of the best in the Northeast, and Woodford State Park is just one of many gems. Bring a kayak or canoe to take advantage of the lovely Adams Reservoir, which is surrounded by a thick forest of spruce, fir, and birch. Also be prepared for a rustic dry camping experience. The tent and RV sites do not have hookups, and the cabins do not have bathrooms. This park borders the George Aiken Wilderness Area, which is part of the Green Mountain National Forest—so abundant hiking, fishing, and boating options are nearby. But we recommend you hike the 2.7-mile trail around the lake at the campground to get started. If you don't have your own kayak or SUP, rentals are available at the park. While amenities are somewhat limited, they include a horseshoe pit and a regular series of nature programs that should not be missed by any budding young naturalists.

ALSO GREAT

Brattleboro North KOA

▷ East Dummerston, Vermont

▷ koa.com

▷ Glamping Retro RV, Cabins, Cottages, RV and Tent Sites

This delightful little KOA is known for its Fall Vintage Camper Rally that takes place at the end of September. Beautifully restored trailers from around the country are set up for an "open house" tour that is a blast from the past. There is much to do nearby, including hiking on Mount Putney and tasting organic foods from the farm market right next door.

> ---------- **Drive It: Green Mountain Byway** -----------
>
> This byway stretches 11 miles along Route 100 from Waterbury to Stowe, passing iconic points of interest like Smugglers Notch, Ben & Jerry's Ice Cream factory, and Cold Hollow Cider Mill.

Apple Island Resort

▷ South Hero, Vermont

▷ appleislandresort.com

▷ Cottages, Cabins, RV and Tent Sites

Apple Island Resort is packed with upscale amenities like a nine-hole golf course and a fitness room. It also has spectacular views of Lake Champlain just about everywhere you look. A wide variety of boat rentals are available, and the RV sites are spacious and manicured. Functional (but not exactly Instagram-worthy) cottages are available, as are primitive cabins.

> --------------- **Bike It: Vermont Rail Trails** ---------------
>
> When people in Vermont can't ski, they bike. Over the last few decades, Vermont has led the way in the rails to trails movement, which sought to turn unused and abandoned railroad corridors into public bike paths. Here are some of most developed and popular rail trails in Vermont. These trails have multiple points of entry, and traillink.com is a great place to go for more information about rail trails around the country.
>
> ▷ Lamoille Valley Rail Trail (33 miles)
>
> ▷ Missisquoi Valley Rail Trail (23.6 miles)
>
> ▷ Delaware and Hudson Rail Trail (20.5 miles)
>
> ▷ Island Line Rail Trail (14.5 miles)
>
> ▷ Montpelier & Wells River Trail (22.9 miles)

Our Favorite Small Towns in Vermont

Brattleboro

We love the quirky, hipster vibe of this downtown as well as the beautiful farmland surrounding it. Catch a flick at the 1938 art deco Latchis Theater, hike the trails at Retreat Farm, taste the samples at Grafton Village Cheese Company, and take pictures of the historic Creamery Covered Bridge.

Queechee

Some people say the Queechee Gorge is overrated, but those are probably the folks who don't hike down and stay awhile. Bring swimsuits and towels, and have a blast dipping into the cool water, and maybe riding the current down the river a bit. Once you dry off, visit the Simon Pearce Mill where you can watch the glassmakers create their works of art. Finish your visit with a fancy meal overlooking the falls.

Woodstock

The Marsh-Billings-Rockefeller National Historical Park is a mouthful, but also a treasure, with hiking and historic grounds just minutes from the charming downtown of Woodstock. Hike the short but challenging Precipice Trail to the top of Mount Tom. Then descend and head to White Cottage Snack Bar for some of the best burgers in America.

Dorcet

Nearby Stratton is more well known, but we love the Dorcet Quarry where you can jump from towering slabs of marble into the chilly 50-degree water, then warm up and do it all over again.

The
MID-ATLANTIC

· *Delaware* ·

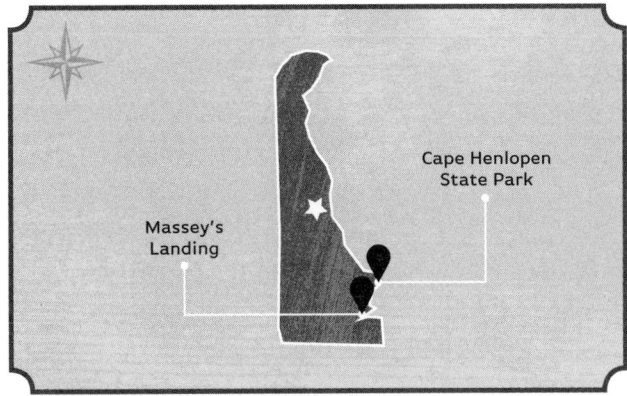

Cape Henlopen
State Park

Massey's
Landing

If you are familiar with the famous *Wayne's World* "Hi, I'm in...Delaware"
scene, you may be tempted to overlook the camping opportunities in this
state. Don't do it! It took us years to book our first campground here, and
we were definitely missing out. Insiders know that Delaware maintains
an impressive system of state park campgrounds, many providing direct
access to sandy beaches and boat launches along with surprising amenities
like the water park at Killens Pond State Park. Another thing that people in
the know love about these state parks? Some of the campgrounds are open
year-round, offering a great opportunity to shake off the winter blues over
a mild February weekend. The bottom line is that Delaware has a shocking
number of great campgrounds for such a small state.

BEST IN STATE

Massey's Landing

▷   Millsboro, Delaware

▷   masseyslanding.com

▷   RV and Tent Sites, Cottages

East Coast RV owners love resort-style campgrounds with luxurious amenities—and they are willing to pay $100 a night or more for sites. Massey's has been the talk of the town among this crowd for several years. We think the RV sites could be a bit bigger, but we love everything else here. The pool and bay beach are great for swimming, and the on-site Paradise Landing Tiki Bar and Jackspot Pool Bar means you can have a cocktail or two and walk back (carefully! Watch out for golf carts!) to your site. Massey's somehow manages to be a good-time campground for the adults while still maintaining a family-friendly vibe. Pull in at 9:30 p.m. and Van Halen will be cranked up and drinks will be flowing. Pull in at 11:00 p.m. and just about everyone will be asleep. If you love to kayak or SUP, try to get a waterfront site and you can launch just steps away from your campfire.

---------------- **Craft Brews and Kernels** ----------------

Fisher's Popcorn claims to be world famous, and the tourists who flock to Delaware's beaches certainly adore this place. It's been turning out handmade caramel popcorn since 1937, so make sure to drop by for a sample. And bring a tub back to the campground for snacking.

According to the Brewers Association, there are currently twenty-seven craft breweries packed into this small state. You can create your own personalized pub crawl at brewtrail.com. Dogfish Head Craft Brewery is one of the oldest and offers a free "Quick Sip" tour or longer, more in-depth experiences. Other hot spots include Crooked Hammock Brewery and 3rd Wave Brewing Company.

----------------- **Farm to Fork in Delaware** -----------------

Once you fall down the rabbit hole of family-owned farms in Delaware, you may never want to come out. There are so many amazing agricultural experiences to be had, but here are just a few of our favorites.

The Lavender Fields at Warrington Manor

Wander through the lavender fields and butterfly garden, then bust your budget at the adorable shop filled with soaps, body spray, pet products, and delicious lavender cookies.

Hopkins Farm Creamery

This dairy has over 1,000 cows, but more importantly it has an ice cream shop that produces all of the flavors on-site with the freshest ingredients available. One-hour farm tours end with a free scoop of freshly churned ice cream.

Goat Joy

What camping vacation is complete without a bit of cuddle time with some goats? Goat Yoga is the main attraction at this farm, but if you aren't into yoga, just schedule a goat social. You can also learn how to milk a goat, if that happens to be on your bucket list.

Cape Henlopen State Park

▷ Lewes, Delaware

▷ destateparks.com

▷ RV and Tent Sites, Cabin

For such a small state, Delaware has an excellent system of state park campgrounds, and this one is located right on the beach. Way back in the seventeenth century, William Penn declared that the "land and natural resources" of Cape Henlopen State Park should be forever reserved for the "common usage of the citizens." We think he had RV owners and tent campers in mind for sure! Campsites may be small, but opportunities for recreation abound. Fish from the beach or pier, or go clamming or kayaking just steps from your site. A bike loop also threads its way around the campground. Most importantly, take time to relax and enjoy the Atlantic Ocean and Delaware's beautiful sand beaches. The campground was renovated in recent years and offers water and electric hookups, a modern laundry facility, and a well-stocked camp store. The best part about this campground may be that it is open year-round. Adventurous campers look for mild winter weekends to pack up their tents or hitch up their RVs and go!

ALSO GREAT

Killens Pond State Park

▷ Felton, Delaware

▷ destateparks.com

▷ Cabins, Tents, RV Sites

Like Cape Henlopen, the campground at Killens Pond is open year-round. Adventurous RV owners head here for winter camping trips and often have the place to themselves. During the summer months, kids love heading to the on-property water park (for a modest additional fee) that has 54-foot waterslides. The pond is always beautiful, but may be at its loveliest during peak foliage.

Best Beaches in Delaware

If you are camping in Delaware, you'll want to soak in the sand and the sea. There's plenty of opportunity to rent gear, so consider trying surf fishing, paddle boarding, or kayaking even if you don't personally own the equipment.

Rehoboth Beach

This beach is hopping during the peak summer months, so don't come here looking for peace and quiet. Rehoboth has guarded beaches and a boardwalk with tons of live music and other free entertainment.

Delaware Seashore State Park

Want to try your hand at crabbing or clamming? Then this is the beach to visit. Four-wheel drive vehicles can even cross the dunes for some surf fishing (permit required).

Lewes Beach

Lewes calls itself "the first town in the first state," and visitors will enjoy a beautiful beach paired with iconic, historical sites like the Harbor of Refuge Lighthouse.

· *Maryland* ·

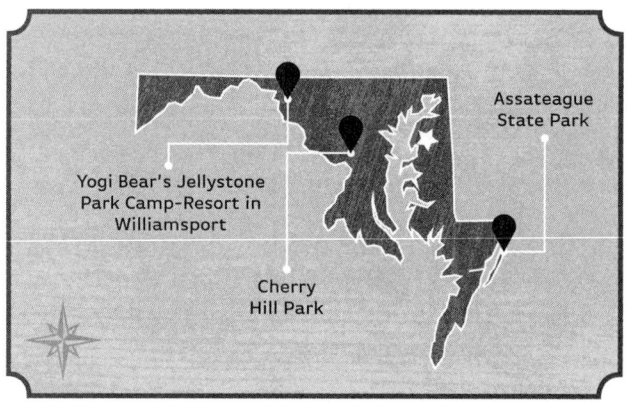

Yogi Bear's Jellystone
Park Camp-Resort in
Williamsport

Assateague
State Park

Cherry
Hill Park

Maryland is the first place we camped as a couple decades ago, and we still return again and again. It's one of our country's smaller states, but Maryland's unique geography offers visitors the opportunity to enjoy coastal plains to the east and the Appalachian Mountains to the west. The vibrant cities of Baltimore and Washington, DC, are there when you're in the mood for an urban camping adventure. Maryland truly offers a snapshot of everything we love about camping. It is home to one of our favorite state parks, one of our family's most beloved campground resorts, and one of the country's most famous urban campgrounds. Oh, and it has crabs—steamed hard shells, fried soft shells, or sautéed crab cakes. Nothing says Maryland like an Old Bay–infused blue crab dinner.

BEST IN STATE

Yogi Bear's Jellystone Park Camp-Resort in Williamsport

▷ Williamsport, Maryland

▷ jellystonemaryland.com

▷ RV and Tent Sites, Lodges, Cottages, Bungalows, Luxury and Rustic Cabins

Rentable hot tubs delivered to your spacious RV site or cabin rental...need we say more? This is family-style resort camping at its best. This Jellystone manages to have off-the-hook amenities like huge waterslides, laser tag, and jumping pillows while still offering campers large, semi-private sites that are not stacked right on top of each other like they are at so many other RV resorts. Mini golf is free, and so are many other activities like outdoor movie nights and family kickball. But it also offers a bunch of fun add-on items for a small extra fee. You can rent golf carts, hammocks, pool cabanas, and more. If you want to blow your kids' minds, schedule a personal visit from Yogi or Cindy Bear. Our kids love it here and always place it near the top of their list of all-time favorites. Hey Boo-Boo! We hope to see you again soon.

-------------------- **Before you go...** --------------------

▷ **Read:** *Misty of Chincoteague* by Marguerite Henry. This YA novel is worth a read no matter your age. Based on a true story, the book explores the unique world of coastal Maryland and its fabled wild ponies. Siblings Paul and Maureen have their hearts set on buying Phantom, a wild pony that avoided capture for two years of the annual roundup. The book is a classic and will bring Assateague and Chincoteague to life long before your own camping trip.

Assateague State Park

▷ Berlin, Maryland

▷ dnr.maryland.gov

▷ RV and Tent Sites, Tiny Home Rentals by Assateague Cottage

Assateague State Park has one of the most magnificent oceanfront camp-grounds in the country. It's also one of our personal favorites. We've been camping here since we were sweethearts in the 1990s. The park is on an island that's basically a spit of sand running north to south just below Ocean City, Maryland. The mostly spacious sites have no water or sewer hookups, and electric hookups are available in only one loop, which is notoriously difficult to book. Our favorite sites are nestled right up against the dunes where you are just steps away from spectacular views of the sunrise over the Atlantic Ocean. Wild horses roam freely here, and it is one of life's great pleasures to wake up and see them grazing on your site. Just make sure you pack your food away and keep it locked up tight. The park also offers clean bathhouses with hot showers—which is why we give it the nod over the neighboring campground at the National Seashore. Avoid mosquitoes by visiting in the fall.

Cherry Hill Park

▷ College Park, Maryland

▷ cherryhillpark.com

▷ RV and Tent Sites, Log Cabins, Glamping Pods, Yurt, Rental Houses

Our family adores this clean and well-managed resort campground and its incredible location just outside of our nation's capital. We are genuinely thankful that we can get our RV so close to downtown DC, which is only a twenty-to-thirty-minute drive away from the campground. The Metro line is so close that you don't even have to take your own car or truck into the town. Many urban campgrounds near big cities are just parking lots with RV hookups—but not Cherry Hill. This is a real campground with trees, shade, and wide-open spaces for walking the dog and going for a morning walk with a cup of coffee in your hand. A loud multilane highway sits right next to the campground, but otherwise this place is pretty close to perfect. After a long day of sightseeing on the National Mall, coming back to Cherry Hill is pure bliss. The pools and playground are large, and the indoor hot tub is a big hit with our kids. Having a Starbucks right up the road is also pretty clutch.

---------- **Historical Sites to Visit in Maryland** ----------

Antietam National Battlefield

Guided tours by park rangers will bring "the bloodiest day in American history" to life. Artillery firing demonstrations are regularly scheduled.

Harpers Ferry National Historic Park

Step back in time and explore a historic town that was at the center of the Civil War. Living history events abound, and ranger programs will teach visitors about the pivotal moment when John Brown raided the arsenal, was captured by General Lee, and became a martyr for the abolitionist cause.

Harriet Tubman Underground Railroad National Historic Park

Learn more about the life of this abolitionist icon in the region where she was born a slave. The new visitor center has an educational film and permanent exhibits, along with rotating programs and seminars.

ALSO GREAT

Elk Neck State Park

▷ North East, Maryland

▷ dnr.maryland.gov

▷ RV and Tent Sites, Cabins

Elk Neck State Park offers a classic family state park camping experience with stunning views of the Chesapeake Bay. The topography of this state park is varied and includes marshlands, woodlands, and sandy beaches. Some of the 250-plus sites are shaded and private, while others are stacked closely together out in the open—so choose wisely. This is a great park for kayaking and swimming, and paved roads are also good for bike riding.

Assateague National Seashore

▷ Berlin, Maryland

▷ nps.gov

▷ RV and Tent Sites

The campground at Assateague National Seashore is every bit as beautiful as the campground at the neighboring state park—maybe more so. So our friends always ask why we choose to camp at the state park each year. The answer is because the state park has clean modern bathrooms with hot water and the national seashore has pit toilets and cold water. The NPS campground does have the advantage of being open all year long, though—so hopefully we'll get there for a winter camping adventure one of these weekends!

Castaways RV Resort & Campground

▷ Berlin, Maryland

▷ castawaysrvoc.com

▷ RV and Tent Sites, Cottages

The East Coast definitely wins the prize for resort camping because of hot spots like Castaways RV Resort & Campground. Campers love swimming, crabbing, and fishing on the campground's bay beach, and pups love playing on Bark Beach, a designated spot just for them. The on-site Jackspot Tiki Bar is a great place for a cold drink on a hot day, and the food at the Bay Breeze Cafe is tasty and can be delivered right to your site.

--- What Makes a Maryland Crab So Special, Anyway? ---

You can find crab at seafood shops and restaurants up and down the East Coast, but Maryland natives swear their blue crabs are just better. There's some science behind this. Blue crabs are only in season from April through November, and apparently the Maryland crabs need more fat stores to get through winter hibernation. This leads to a more buttery, rich-tasting meat.

The traditional way of preparing crabs is also different in Maryland. In this state, they are always steamed, never boiled. Then the ubiquitous Old Bay is sprinkled directly on the crabs, instead of infused in boiling water.

You'll find the largest, fattest hard shell crabs in September and October. Soft shells will be sporadically available from mid-May through September. And if you don't like to work for your supper, crab cakes are available on lunch and dinner menus throughout the state.

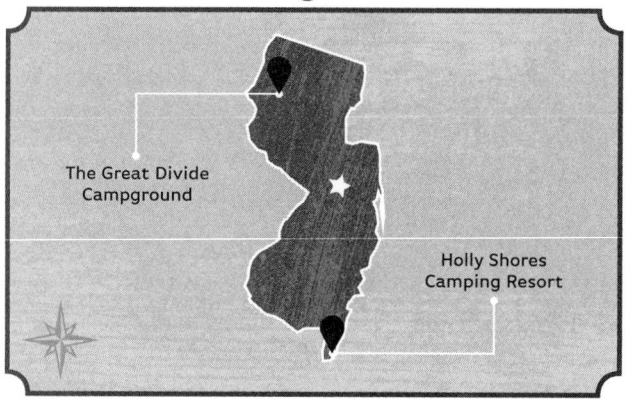

New Jersey

The Great Divide Campground

Holly Shores Camping Resort

We live in New Jersey, so we can pick on it just a little bit. For the last decade or so, we've headed out of state for most of our camping adventures. But that doesn't mean there isn't anything worthwhile to explore in our tiny and much-maligned home state. Cape May became one of our country's most famous seaside vacation destinations in the nineteenth century, and we still think it's a darling place for a family trip. There are quite a few well-reviewed campground options and miles of beautiful beaches. We particularly enjoy Cape May Point State Park, which has a historical lighthouse and miles of nature trails.

If you head north to the Highlands and Skylands region, you may have trouble believing you are in New Jersey at all. Gorgeous rolling hills and preserved farmlands provide plenty of opportunities for outdoor activities. Visitors enjoy hiking, kayaking, and fishing at places like High Point State Park and the Delaware Water Gap.

Of course, we have our fair share of urban areas with New York City to the east and Philadelphia to the west. The good news is that there are some great campgrounds in New Jersey that will serve as base camps for those city adventures. Be aware that, unfortunately, the New Jersey State Park system is woefully underfunded and under resourced. The state park campgrounds are largely ignored and mostly rustic.

---------------- **The Monarchs Are Coming!** ----------------

Every year tens of thousands of monarchs migrate over 2,500 miles to their winter home in Mexico. Cape May is the perfect place to witness this phenomenon starting in late September and continuing through October. If you visit during this time, check out the educational programs New Jersey Audubon Society offers, including tagging demonstrations and conservation talks.

BEST IN STATE

The Great Divide Campground

▷   Newton, New Jersey

▷   campthegreatdivide.com

▷   Cabins, Yurts, Conestoga Wagons, RV Rentals, RV and Tent Sites

The Great Divide Campground offers a classic camping experience less than 60 miles away from New York City. It strikes the perfect balance between RV resort and rustic retreat. There are plenty of shady sites for tent campers and RV owners, plus a quirky array of rentals for those in search of a glamping experience. The cabins are cute and the Conestoga Wagons are cuter. Those with large families or multifamily groups should check out the park model rentals. Kids will enjoy the Olympic-sized pool and the robust activity schedule, while adults traveling sans kids will enjoy live music and hiking trails right next to the campground. Every weekend at The Great Divide is a themed weekend, so be prepared for Golf Cart Karaoke, Back to the '70s, and Zombie Invasion, among other themes. It is possible to kick back and relax at this campground, but introverts may want to camp elsewhere.

----------------- **Ready for a Big Year?** -----------------

New Jersey is famous for its bird diversity. Seriously. Every year the Audubon Society holds the World Series of Birding in this state. Here are some great spots for bird watching in the Garden State. Remember to bring your insect repellent, because where there are birds, there are bugs.

✧ Edwin B. Forsythe National Wildlife Refuge

✧ Island Beach State Park

✧ Cape May Point State Park

✧ Great Swamp National Wildlife Refuge

✧ Sandy Hook in Gateway National Recreation Area

Holly Shores Camping Resort

▷ Cape May, New Jersey

▷ hollyshores.com

▷ Tiny Houses, Cabins, Safari Glamping Tents, RV Sites

Holly Shores has been family owned and operated since 1968, and the vibe here is always warm and welcoming. This resort-style campground near downtown Cape May is quirky and filled with one-of-kind South Jersey charm. We love to visit in the fall when the beaches are still beautiful but touristy summer crowds have declined. Holly Shores also stretches out the summer vibes by keeping its pool open until the end of September. This campground has been making RV owners smile for over fifty years, and now it is welcoming glampers in its tiny houses and safari glamping tents. Come back to the campground after a long day at the beach and cool off in the pool or soak in one of the hot tubs and grab a cold drink at the snack bar. Still have some energy left? Play a game of shuffleboard or grab some ping-pong paddles before you head back to your site for a campfire.

ALSO GREAT

Seashore Campsites & RV Resort

▷ Cape May, New Jersey

▷ sunrvresorts.com

▷ RV and Tent Sites, Cottages, Rental Houses

Seashore is every bit as good as nearby Holly Shores, but there are fewer options for glamping and unique accommodations. Proximity to Cape May is excellent and sites are mostly wooded and private. The pool and man-made lake are great for swimming on days when the ocean is rough, and resort amenities like a fitness room and tennis courts are available for all guests.

The Jersey Diner

New Jersey loves to call itself The Diner Capital of the World, and plenty of publications claim that it has more diners than any other state. It seems plausible since we have spent a good chunk of our lives in our home state's diners. Order breakfast at any hour of the day and save room for the desserts that are typically displayed in spinning showcases. This might be the perfect place to try a pork roll, egg, and cheese sandwich—a Jersey original.

Philadelphia South/Clarksboro KOA

▷ Clarksboro, New Jersey

▷ koa.com

▷ RV and Tent Sites, Deluxe and Rustic Cabins, Glamping Tents

This campground, which was recently acquired by KOA, is a diamond in the rough. When we visited, a major expansion was underway and lovely new common areas with grills and games had recently been added near the fishing pond. This is good news for campers who want to visit Philadelphia, which is only twenty minutes away. Deluxe cabins are cozy, and glamping tents are semi-private and nicely shaded.

High Point State Park

▷   Sussex, New Jersey

▷   state.nj.us

▷   Tent Sites, Cabins

The Skylands Region in Northwest New Jersey is filled with rolling hills and may just be the prettiest part of the state. Fifty campsites are nestled along Sawmill Lake and provide a back-to-basics camping experience. No RVs are allowed, but a limited number of cabins are available. Make sure to climb to the top of High Point Monument—the highest point in the state. The Cedar Swamp Trail should also not be missed.

---------- Camping Outside of New York City? ----------

It's not what most people picture when they think of camping, but there is actually a campground located just a few miles from Manhattan. Liberty Harbor RV Park in Jersey City is basically a parking lot, but you would be hard pressed to find a more affordable way to visit the Big Apple than in your own RV. There's a grassy area for tent camping as well, but you would have to be a hardy soul to sleep through the nighttime noises of the city.

New York

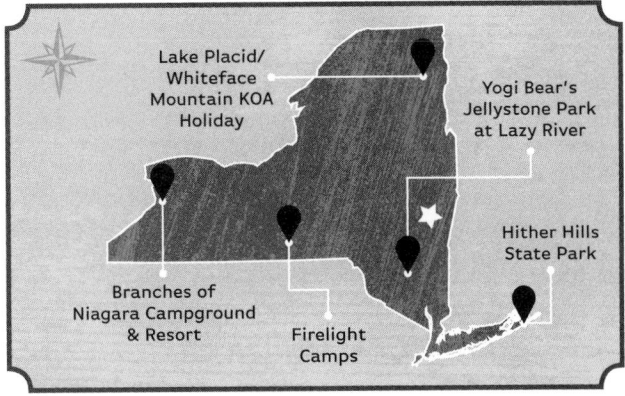

New York has an unbelievable range of camping opportunities, ranging from resorts near Niagara Falls to rustic state parks in the Finger Lakes to urban campgrounds outside of New York City. Our opinion is that New York is one of the more underrated camping destinations in America. Each region has its own unique beauty, with tons of opportunity for outdoor adventure. The Adirondacks alone is over six million acres, which is bigger than the Great Smokies, Yellowstone, Glacier, Grand Canyon, and Yosemite national parks combined. Between the Finger Lakes, Lake George, Lake Placid, and the Catskills, you could return to New York year after year and have a new camping adventure every time.

Before you go...

▷ **Read:** *Niagara: A History of the Falls* by Pierre Berton

BEST IN STATE

Firelight Camps

▷ Ithaca, New York

▷ firelightcamps.com

▷ Luxury Safari Tents

Firelight Camps is located deep in the heart of New York State's lush and Dionysian Finger Lakes region. Nestled at the edge of Buttermilk Falls State Park and just a few short minutes away from Cornell University and downtown Ithaca, this "camp" features fully furnished safari tents and communal areas for live music and games like bocce ball and gigantic chess. A locally sourced breakfast is provided by co-owner and culinary director Emma Frisch, who is the author of *Feast by Firelight: Simple Recipes for Camping, Cabins, and the Great Outdoors*, a ravishing "great outdoors" cookbook that was photographed on-site. Emma and husband Bobby provide guests with an exquisite glamping experience in an idyllic setting. After hiking in Buttermilk Falls, come back to camp and grab a cold drink from the full service bar or reward yourself with homemade s'mores around the communal campfire, which is lit every morning and night. Feeling sore? Book a massage at the August Moon Spa, just steps away from camp.

---------------------- **Empire Pass** ----------------------

If you are going to state park hop in New York, crunch the numbers and see if an Empire Pass is worth the purchase. For around eighty dollars, this pass will get you a year of unlimited day-use entry at dozens of New York State Parks, historic sites, and recreational facilities. New York State Parks also accept the National Park Service's Every Kid in a Park pass. So if you have a fourth grader in the family, make sure you sign up for that program online before you visit.

Lake Placid/Whiteface Mountain KOA Holiday

▷ Wilmington, New York

▷ koa.com

▷ RV and Tent Sites, Camping Cabins, Deluxe Cabins, Glamping Tents

This award-winning KOA is located at the base of Whiteface Mountain, just fifteen minutes away from downtown Lake Placid. We call this base camp option number one for any serious outdoor adventure in New York State's vast and magnificent Adirondack Park. Epic fly fishing and hiking opportunities abound just minutes from the campground—and more adventurous souls will walk right from their sites down to the Ausable River for Instagram-worthy cliff diving or lazy summer swimming and picnicking. The campground has a recreation room, sports center, snack bar, mini golf, pool, and a gorgeous main lodge—yet it still manages to have the tranquil feeling of a deeply wooded and relaxing state park. So yes campers, sometimes you can have it all. The 1932 and 1980 Olympics were held in Lake Placid, and the area is filled with Olympic legend and lore. During the fall, peak foliage is just as magical and colorful as it is anywhere in neighboring New England.

Yogi Bear's Jellystone Park at Lazy River

▷ Gardiner, New York

▷ lazyriverny.com

▷ RV and Tent Sites, Group Lodges, Cottages, Cabins, Bungalows

Our three boys jump for joy when we camp at this Jellystone Park, an elite resort-style campground that manages to maintain plenty of rustic charm. Summertime means playing baseball, basketball, or ga-ga ball until you are ready to cool off in the pool or hit the waterslides. Fall means pumpkin painting, trick-or-treating, and braving the "trail of terror" with older kids and adults who don't mind a good scare. Little ones will be better off traversing the "not so-scary trail" during daylight hours. Yogi Bear and friends roam through the campground during all seasons and make scheduled appearances for morning flag salutes and pancake breakfasts. You may not want to leave this campground during your stay because the activities calendar is guaranteed to be packed, but if you do, make sure to visit nearby Lake Minnewaska for a spectacular hike. Stop by a farmer's market on your way back or grab a locally sourced lunch in New Paltz, where the hipsters hang.

> --- **A Walk on the Wild Side: Camping in New York City** ---
> Okay, so Liberty Harbor RV Park isn't actually in New York City...but it is right across the Hudson River in Jersey City. It's not your typical camping location, but we love a good urban campground. Park your RV or pitch your tent (yes, the park has tent sites!) and then hop on the PATH to explore the Big Apple.

Hither Hills State Park

▷ Montauk, New York
▷ parks.ny.gov
▷ RV and Tent Sites

Do you like to fall asleep to the sound of waves breaking just steps away from your campsite? Then pack up your tent or RV and get yourself to Hither Hills State Park post haste. Beachfront campgrounds in the Northeast are few and far between, and this one is truly a gem. Anglers will love casting a line into the sparkling Atlantic, and surfers will find some of the best waves on the East Coast. All campers should be careful swimming in the consistently rough waters. This 190-site campground is very simple, because who needs fancy amenities when the ocean is just over the dunes? There are also no water, electric, or sewer hookups at the campsites, but the bathhouses are clean and the showers have hot water. Options for hiking, biking, and bird-watching abound in and around the park—and Montauk is filled with hip shopping and dining options, but we recommend that you spend as many long, lazy days at the beach as you can.

Branches of Niagara Campground & Resort

▷ Grand Island, New York

▷ branchesofniagara.com

▷ Cabins, RV and Tent Sites

Niagara Falls is magnificent—and while the Canadian side wins the popularity contest, the New York side is still well worth a visit. There are many camping options in the area, but Branches of Niagara Campground & Resort is our clear favorite. Its cozy, lakefront log cabins are perfectly situated for a romantic getaway. Families are also welcome, and kids will love the robust recreation program, which includes zip-lining, kayaking, fishing, nature shows, arts and crafts, and wagon rides. The log cabin–style general store, bathhouse, and activity center are all immaculately clean, and the young staff is well trained and friendly. When we visited, a young staffer asked us if the bathhouses met our expectations as we walked out one night. "Why yes, they certainly did," was our reply! We spent hours each day swimming in its man-made lake (where dogs were also welcome) and in its heated pool. The bugs were bad during our mid-July visit—but nobody's perfect, right? Next time we will head back in the fall for peak foliage and warm campfires during chilly nights.

------- **Enjoy a Michigan While Visiting New York** -------

You might be confused to see Michigan hot dogs on menus all over upstate New York. We were too. Ask about the history of these steamed beef hot dogs smothered in a tomato-based meat sauce and you will get a different story from everyone. You'll also get a different version at almost every joint in the Adirondacks. Some will have onions; some will be smothered in yellow mustard. Some are sweet; some are tangy. The important thing is to taste as many as possible to narrow down your own personal Michigan hot dog style, so you can recreate the magic back at the campground.

ALSO GREAT

Collective Governors Island (Collective Retreats)

▷ Governor's Island, New York City

▷ collectiveretreats.com

▷ Glamping Tents and Outlook Shelters

Waking up in a glamping tent with a view of the Statue of Liberty is actually a real thing you can do—but only at Collective Governors Island, which is just a short boat ride away from Manhattan and Brooklyn. This unique property offers lots of natural space, but it is a bit rougher around the edges than pictures suggest. If you go looking for a one-of-a-kind adventure, you will have a blast. But if you want quiet and tranquility, head out further from the city.

Posh Primitive

▷ Chestertown, New York

▷ poshprimitive.com

▷ Glamping Tents

Looking to cuddle up with your sweetie under a Pendleton blanket on a handcrafted timber bed deep in the woods of the Adirondack Park? Then Posh Primitive has a "canvas cabin" for you. Each one is graced with rustic antiques, handcrafted local furniture, a woodstove, and seasoned firewood so you can stay toasty warm on a cool summer night.

---- **Drive It: Whiteface Veterans Memorial Highway** ----

This toll road takes you to the top of New York State's fifth highest peak, Whiteface Mountain, and offers views of Vermont and Canada on a clear day. The entrance fee to the highway is included with the Olympic Sites Passport, which we highly recommend purchasing if you are visiting Lake Placid.

Herkimer Diamond KOA Resort

▷ Herkimer, New York

▷ herkimerdiamond.com

▷ RV and Tent Sites, Treehouse, Astronomy Lodges, Cabins

Love stargazing? Then this is where you should camp next. Its astronomy lodge looks like something out of a children's adventure book. Take turns looking through the telescope and exploring the constellations on the lodge's observation deck. Waterfront RV sites along the West Canada Creek are also perfect for tubing, trout fishing, and falling asleep to the sound of rushing water. A treehouse rental is also available.

Moose Hillock Camping Resort

▷ Fort Ann, New York

▷ moosehillock.com/new-york

▷ RV and Tent Sites

Moose Hillock is our top pick for the Lake George region. You will love the huge, wooded campsites, and kids will love Aloha Beach—its gigantic tropical and pirate-themed swimming pool with waterslides. Abundant organized activities make this feel like an old-fashioned summer camp from the 1960s. The sound of live music fills the air twice a week, and there is a Saturday evening chapel service if the spirit moves you to attend.

Watkins Glen State Park

▷ Watkins Glen, New York

▷ parks.ny.gov

▷ Tent and RV Sites, Rustic Cabins

The Gorge Trail at Watkins Glen State Park (which winds its way over, under, and through nineteen waterfalls) is one of the prettiest places in New York's under-appreciated Finger Lakes region. The campground offers over 300 tent and RV sites, and most are spacious and tucked into lush woods. Rustic cabins are also available. Camp here if you are seeking a peaceful back-to-nature experience. Amenities are sparse, but wineries and fine dining are nearby.

Letchworth State Park

▷ Castile, New York

▷ parks.ny.gov

▷ Tent and RV Sites, Cabins, Family Lodge

The Genesee River spills over three spectacular waterfalls in the heart of this park, which is known as the "Grand Canyon of the East." Shady and private RV sites are ample, and the cabins are cozy and Instagram-worthy. For an unforgettable family vacation, rent the Maplewood Lodge, which is adjacent to the NYS Snowmobile Trail System. No snowmobile? No problem. The park has 66 miles of hiking trails. Bring comfy socks.

------------ **Tips for Visiting Niagara Falls** ------------

✦ Avoid weekends and holidays. Tuesdays, Wednesdays, and Thursdays are the quietest days of the week at this very popular destination.

✦ Go early in the morning. The park doesn't usually get crowded until after 11:00 a.m. If you get there early, you can zip through popular attractions like Maid of the Mist and Cave of the Winds with little to no wait.

✦ Buy the Discovery Pass. Niagara Falls State Park is free to enter, but many of the attractions require an entrance fee. The Discovery Pass will save you money if you are planning on enjoying Maid of the Mist, Cave of the Winds, Aquarium, Discover Center, Trolley Tour, and Adventure Theater.

✦ Bring your passport. People love to debate whether the Canadian or American side of the falls is better. Walk from America into Canada over the Rainbow Bridge and form your own opinion.

· *Pennsylvania* ·

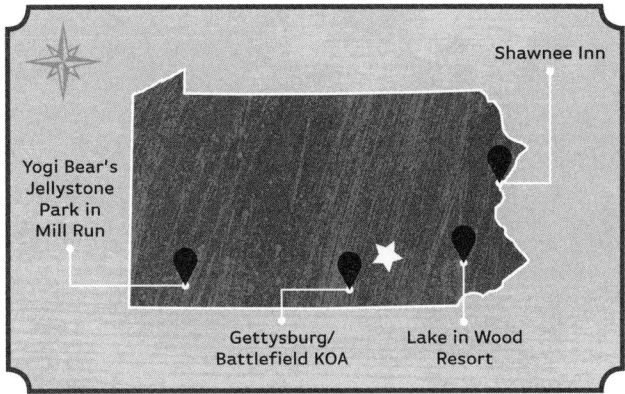

Pennsylvania makes it easy to camp with an abundance of state parks, well-appointed resorts, and waterfront U.S. Corps of Engineers campgrounds. Folks like us in neighboring states find ourselves visiting quite often, especially for quick weekend getaways. Whether we are touring Philadelphia, Pittsburgh, Gettysburg, or the Poconos, we have always found at least one—but often more—amazing campground options.

The majority of campgrounds in this region of the country will be open from April through October or mid-November. However, Pennsylvania does have some year-round camping options that set it apart from the mid-Atlantic pack. The Delaware Water Gap/Poconos KOA is open year-round and close to popular skiing destinations. Otter Lake Camp Resort provides an indoor heated pool for those brave enough to camp in the winter months. Residents and visitors could easily camp year after year in Pennsylvania, discovering one new gem after another.

BEST IN STATE

Shawnee Inn

▷ Shawnee on Delaware, Pennsylvania

▷ shawneeinn.com

▷ Glamping Tents

The Shawnee Inn offers glamping tents in two unique locations on its lovely property. Its "island glamping" is truly a great escape—guests must paddle out to the island by canoe. But they will be greeted by a camp attendant and luxurious amenities when they arrive. The island has electricity and shared bathrooms with showers, and the glamping tents come with locally made soaps and shampoos. Glampers can relax and unwind in the privacy of their tents, or they can socialize around the communal campfire under the stars. If it gets chilly at night, just crank up the heater in your tent—and make sure to get up in time for a hot breakfast cooked on a cast iron skillet over hot coals. If you want easier access to the amenities at the main inn (such as the hot tub and pool), you might choose a glamping tent in the quiet Riverside section and enjoy a glass of wine while taking in views of the Delaware River.

Lake in Wood Resort

▷ Narvon, Pennsylvania

▷ lakeinwoodcampground.com

▷ RV and Tent Sites, Tree House, Double-decker Bus, Yurt, Cabins, Caboose

Lake in Wood is one of the best campgrounds in America. We had a seasonal site here a few years back, and it was our home away from home. The campground is deeply wooded and filled with shade and rolling hills. Sites are spacious for a private campground, and the campground has many distinct sections with different features. We loved the clean, heated indoor and outdoor pool area and the huge rolling lawn that winds its way down to the lake. It's a great place for a game of catch. The lake is small and unremarkable, but the rest of the campground is so charming that you won't care. Lake in Wood specializes in weird and wacky outdoor accommodations, such as the caboose and double-decker bus rentals, which makes it our kind of place. The only thing our boys ever complained about here was the "no kids in the hot tub rule," which we loved! Don't forget to get a scoop or two of hand-dipped ice cream. It's reasonably priced and the kids line up for it on summer nights.

Gettysburg/Battlefield KOA

▷ Gettysburg, Pennsylvania

▷ koa.com

▷ RV and Tent Sites, Camping Cabins and Deluxe Cabins

This bucolic and cheerful campground is located only minutes away from one of the Civil War's most famous sites. History buffs will love the proximity to all that Gettysburg has to offer, and campers of all ages and inclinations will love this campground's cozy and secluded location. We visited in April, and the wooded areas that surround this KOA were filled with colorful wildflowers. Our boys loved the jumping pillow and games in the common area near the camp store. We spent hours playing mini golf, carpet ball, life-size checkers, and Connect Four—all of which were a welcome reprieve after spending our mornings touring battlefields and other NPS sites. The nature trail that cuts up into the woods above the campground makes for a lovely ramble. Bring a cup of coffee and contemplate the quiet in one of Pennsylvania's most beautiful and sylvan sections.

Yogi Bear's Jellystone Park in Mill Run

▷ Mill Run, Pennsylvania

▷ jellystonemillrun.com

▷ Bungalows, Cabins, Family Lodges, Tree House, RV Rentals, RV and Tent Sites

This campground is an absolute treasure. It is nestled into a cozy corner of the beautiful and underrated Laurel Highlands region of Pennsylvania. There is so much to do here that you may forget to leave, but that would be a mistake because Frank Lloyd Wright's iconic Fallingwater is less than four miles away. We suggest you go and take a tour of this iconic home even if that means ripping your kids away from the waterslides, playgrounds, and laser tag at the campground. Yogi and his friends also appear regularly, and you are pretty much guaranteed to see them at Cindy Bear's Kountry Kitchen if you get there for breakfast on a weekend morning. The food is also legitimately good. Not campground good—but diner or breakfast joint good. We also love the wide variety of accommodations at this Yogi. We stayed in the family lodge that sleeps sixteen—a perfect place for a family reunion or multifamily trip. RV sites are also nice, and there are cabins galore (and a super cute tree house) for those who want a memorable glamping experience.

ALSO GREAT

Leonard Harrison State Park

▷   Wellsboro, Pennsylvania

▷   dcnr.pa.gov

▷   Tent and RV Sites

For those looking for a more rustic camping experience, look no further than this gem that is located on the eastern rim of Pennsylvania's Grand Canyon. The park is surrounded by rigorous hiking opportunities—so bring comfortable boots and a camera to get a gorgeous waterfall photo at the bottom of the Pine Creek Trail.

Philadelphia/West Chester KOA Holiday

▷ Coatesville, Pennsylvania

▷ koa.com

▷ Glamping Safari Tent, RV and Tent Sites, Deluxe Cabins and Camping Cabins

This pretty KOA is nestled alongside the banks of the Brandywine River, making it a perfect place for those who like to fish, kayak, or SUP. And while it may not actually be that close to Philadelphia, it is very close to Longwood Gardens and Winterthur—both breathtaking Dupont properties that shouldn't be missed.

Yogi Bear's Jellystone Park Camp-Resort in Quarryville

▷ Quarryville, Pennsylvania

▷ jellystonepa.com

▷ Cabins, Cottages, Lodges, RV and Tent Sites

Jellystone Quarryville is a fast-paced, almost high-octane kind of campground! The fun here never stops, and we actually never left the campground during our last visit. Our boys spent hours playing in the gigantic pool and water park area, and we played laser tag every night. Most RV sites here are spacious and shaded. This campground is huge, so treat yourself and rent a golf cart for the weekend. You won't regret the splurge.

Falling in Love with Fallingwater:
A Frank Lloyd Wright Treasure

Mill Run, Pennsylvania

Where Is Fallingwater Located?

Fallingwater is located southeast of Pittsburgh, just over the border from West Virginia and Maryland. It's most certainly an A-list attraction if you are visiting Pittsburgh, but also if you're just heading through Pennsylvania on I-81. Fallingwater is located in the beautiful region of the Laurel Highlands, which surprises people with its natural beauty. The area is an outdoor enclave with a plethora of biking, hiking, tubing, and rafting opportunities nearby.

Before You Go to Fallingwater

Visitors need to purchase tickets for house tours in advance of arrival. In fact, tickets for the guided tours, which are the only way to see the interior of the house, are not even available on the day of visit. Tickets sell out in advance on virtually every single day from May through November. If you do miss out on buying tour tickets, note that a limited amount of grounds passes are available each day for walk-ups. You can tour the grounds and see the house from the outside.

Available Tours at Fallingwater

Our family enjoyed the standard guided house tour for people ages six and up. Adult tickets were $30 and youth were $18. At the time of purchase, I cringed at paying over $100 to bring my kids to a pretty house. However, after the tour we felt like the price was an amazing value. The tour guide was engaging and knowledgeable, and the experience was priceless. Seeing how much effort goes into preserving the house and grounds was eye-opening to say the least. There are also many in-depth tours of the Fallingwater house, where visitors can see spaces not accessible on the main tour.

Additional Information about Visiting Fallingwater

▷ Know in advance that you will not be able to take any photos during the Fallingwater tour. After the tour, you can walk down to a viewpoint and get a selfie in front of the iconic house and waterfall.

▷ The surrounding grounds are beautiful and worth spending time exploring.

▷ You'll probably want to bring a picnic lunch. The cafe served tasty, but very pricey, food.

▷ The gift shop was worth browsing. There were so many beautiful items from local artisans, and the prices seemed reasonable to us. It felt like the type of gift shop where you can find unique, special holiday presents for everyone on your list, kids included.

▷ Check out the membership options before buying your tickets. One of the membership levels gives you reciprocal membership to thirty other Frank Lloyd Wright homes. It may be worth the money to get that membership depending on your travel plans.

The Dos and Don'ts of Dragging Your Kids to Gettysburg Military National Park

We love national parks. And our kids do, as well. But you know those stories of children getting dragged around to battlefields by their boring parents? They probably originated in places like Gettysburg. On our first visit, we made the mistake of saving money on the guided tours and just buying an audio tour from the gift shop. Don't be like us. Gettysburg, and most other historic sites, are brought to life by ranger programs, living history demonstrations, and guided battlefield tours. Plan ahead, and history will come to life.

Start with the Film, Cyclorama, and Museum experience.
These tickets are timed and if you get an early start, it will help the rest of the day flow a bit more smoothly. The whole experience should take about an hour.

Pick a battlefield tour option.
Gettysburg is unique in that it has a couple of different ways you can explore with a licensed battlefield guide. You can reserve a car tour, bus tour, or bicycle tour. The weirdest part is that the guide drives *your car* if you choose the car tour option. Bikes are available to rent from local outfitters if you choose a bicycle tour.

Choose the ranger programs you wish to attend.
Look at the online schedule ahead of time to get the most value out of your visit. The ranger programs run all day and vary from guided hikes to inter-active programs using your personal devices. Definitely plan on visiting the Soldiers' National Cemetery where Lincoln gave his famous address. From Memorial Day to Labor Day, it plays "Taps" at 7:00 p.m., which is a very moving experience.

The
SOUTH

THE BEACH

FORT WILDERNESS

THE LAKE

GREAT SMOKY MOUNTAINS

• Alabama •

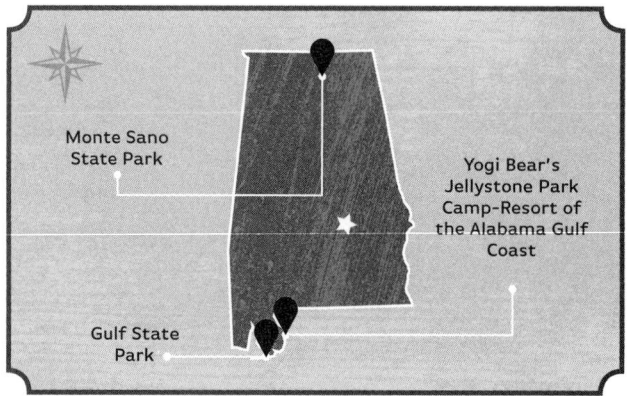

Monte Sano
State Park

Yogi Bear's
Jellystone Park
Camp-Resort of
the Alabama Gulf
Coast

Gulf State
Park

Thousands of Civilian Conservation Corps workers built an amazing state park system in the 1930s, and camping enthusiasts in Alabama are still reaping the results. Hikers will find amazing vistas at Cheaha State Park, beautiful waterfalls at Desoto State Park, and paddling paradise at Gulf State Park. But along the way, they'll also find stone bridges, rock walls, pavilions, and boardwalks built decades ago and immaculately maintained by the state park system.

We also love the small but vibrant city scene in Alabama. Places like Huntsville and Birmingham are perfect for those long weekend getaways in the spring and fall. Settle in at a nearby campground, then head in for the day to explore historical monuments, museums, and restaurants. By evening, you can be back roasting marshmallows around the campfire.

--------------- **Drive It: Talladega Scenic Drive** ---------------
This 26-mile drive will take you to Cheaha Mountain, Alabama's highest point at 2,407 feet above sea level, and ends in the beautiful Talladega National Forest.

BEST IN STATE

Gulf State Park

- ▷ Gulf Shores, Alabama
- ▷ alapark.com
- ▷ Cottages and Cabins, RV and Tent Sites, Lodge Room

Gulf State Park is an absolute favorite among Alabama's legions of campers and outdoor recreation lovers, and it is one of the finest state parks in the country. Almost two million visitors come here each year to swim and play on the sugary sand beaches and fish on the spacious pier. The campground on Lake Shelby has many of the qualities of a first-class RV resort, at a fraction of the price. There are almost 500 campsites here, and almost all of them have concrete pads and full hookups. Campers with kids love the huge pool and splash pad area, which is for the exclusive use of registered campground and cabin guests. The cottages and cabins here are an absolute delight, and they put to shame many of the state park lodging offerings in other parts of the country. The campground at Gulf State Park should serve as a model for other state parks that want to improve their facilities in the decades to come. We would love to see state park offerings like this in New Jersey where we live—but for now we will have to hitch up and head down south to Alabama to experience public camping like this.

Yogi Bear's Jellystone Park Camp-Resort of the Alabama Gulf Coast

- ▷ Elberta, Alabama
- ▷ jellystonegulfcoast.com
- ▷ Cabins, RV and Tent Sites

Yogi and his friends strike a perfect balance at this Jellystone Park. Campers can find peace and quiet at this campground and off-the-hook family fun and amenities. Many private campgrounds with lots of amenities and shared common spaces pack campers in like sardines—but not here. Many of the RV sites here look like state park sites, with plenty of elbow room and lots of shade. Cabins are also cute and offer lots of privacy and shade. Boo-Boo cabins are basic without bathrooms, and Cindy Bear and Yogi Bear cabins offer more space along with bathrooms and kitchens. There are so many fun activities here that it is hard to know where to start—how about with the Water Wars Wagon Rides or Flashlight Freeze Tag? You can count us in every time! There is also a basic pool and splash pad at this park and a pretty two-acre fishing pond that is packed with bluegill, bass, and catfish. Many folks pack a picnic lunch and spend the afternoon at the lake—not a bad way to spend a summer day—and a pretty awesome place to spend a summer vacation.

-------- Civilian Conservation Corps in Alabama --------

The New Deal's Civilian Conservation Corps—or CCC—left its physical mark on state and national parks across the country in the 1930s, and Alabama has many well-preserved examples of this unique moment in American history. Here are some CCC treasures to track down in Alabama's state parks.

⬦ Tour the CCC museum at DeSoto State Park.

⬦ Stay in one of the beautiful CCC-built cabins in Monte Sano State Park.

⬦ Visit remnants of old CCC living quarters along the Old First Quarters Trail at Muscle Shoals Reservation.

⬦ Paddle through the three freshwater lakes at Gulf Shores State Park that the CCC connected by digging trenches between them.

⬦ View the waterfall that flows over the dam built by the CCC at Chewacla State Park.

Monte Sano State Park

▷ Huntsville, Alabama

▷ alapark.com

▷ Cabins, RV and Tent Sites

Monte Sano means "mountains of health" in Spanish, and this state park lives up to its name with plenty of fresh air and spectacular mountain vistas. Azaleas bloom in the springtime, and fall colors are an absolute delight. This classic state park sits at an elevation of 1,600 feet, which is pretty darn tall for an Alabama mountain. Once you drive up to the top of the mountain, you will find a heavily wooded campground and a bluff with mountain views. Most sites are large and well shaded, and fifteen have full hookups, fifty-nine have water and electric, and twenty-one are primitive. But the real star of the show at Monte Sano State Park may be the eleven original CCC-constructed stone cabins. Built in the 1930s, each cabin features a working fireplace, a screened-in porch, and bathrooms and kitchens. As if they weren't delightful enough, they also sit upon a bluff with excellent mountain views. Hiking and biking trails are popular, and the park has a superfun eighteen-hole disc golf course. Monte Sano is also the home to the North Alabama Japanese Garden, which is every bit as relaxing as it sounds. The park also has its own planetarium that takes things completely over the top. Just dreaming about Alabama's state park system picks me up when I'm feeling blue.

ALSO GREAT

Cheaha State Park

▷ **Delta, Alabama**

▷ **alapark.com**

▷ **Cabins, Chalets, Hotel, RV and Tent Sites**

Cheaha's stunning stone cabins and chalets were built by the Civilian Conservation Corps in the 1930s and are almost one hundred years old. Camping in them is a timeless and classic experience that few campgrounds in the country can offer. Even if you own an RV or love to tent camp, consider a romantic getaway in one of the bluff-side or deluxe cabins here. Alabamians have also invested in this state park with their tax dollars, and it shows. The Upper and Lower Campgrounds have many awesome new, improved sites with full hookups. There is also a modest hotel in this state park, so feel free to invite your noncamping friends.

---------------------- **Before you go...** ----------------------

▷ **Watch:** *Fried Green Tomatoes*, which takes place in Birmingham, Alabama.

▷ **Read:** *To Kill a Mockingbird* by Harper Lee, set in the fictional town of Macomb, Alabama.

DeSoto State Park

▷ Fort Payne, Alabama

▷ alapark.com

▷ Cabins, Log Cabins, Rustic CCC Cabins, Mountain Chalets, RV and Tent Sites

This may be the best state park for cabin rentals in the entire south—the log cabins are cozy, the rustic CCC cabins are historical, and the mountain chalets are Instagram-worthy. And did we mention that the RV sites are shady, private, and easy to back into? All of these delightful accommodations are situated on a lush mountaintop with wildflowers and rushing waterfalls that will delight all five of your senses. Alabama is such a sweet state for camping, and this state park is one of the top reasons why.

Gunter Hill Campground/U.S. Army Corps of Engineers—Alabama River Lakes

▷ Montgomery, Alabama

▷ recreation.gov

▷ RV and Tent Sites

Gunter Hill Campground has amazing RV sites that are paved and level and back up to the woods or directly to the Alabama River. The sites are so big that they almost look like long driveways. This allows campers to have an unusual amount of privacy, peace, and quiet. Big rigs that struggle to find sites at other public campgrounds can easily fit into these delightful sites. Fishing, boating, hiking, and hunting opportunities are ample at this excellent U.S. Army Corps of Engineers campground.

------------------- **A Day in Huntsville** -------------------

Camping at beautiful Monte Sano State Park? Here are the best things to do in nearby Huntsville:

✦ Tour the U.S. Space & Rocket Center, and learn about our nation's aerospace history through rocket displays and hands-on demonstrations.

✦ Explore the Huntsville Botanical Garden, which has beautiful gardens and sculptures, plus plenty of family-friendly programs and activities.

✦ Enjoy living history exhibits at the Alabama Constitution Hall Park.

✦ Take a walking tour of the Twickenham Historic District and soak in the antebellum architecture.

✦ Dive into the emerging craft beer scene on the Downtown Huntsville Craft Beer Trail, where ten stamps on a card will get you a free Trail Boss bottle opener.

· Arkansas ·

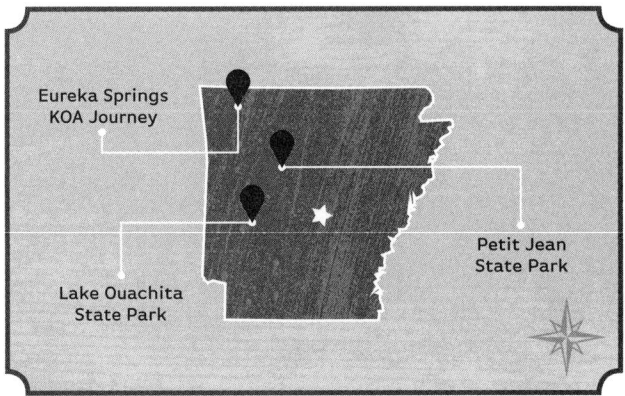

We can safely say that Arkansas was not on our road tripping bucket list when we started camping about a decade ago. Well, that was only because we had no idea that the Natural State might just be the single most underrated camping destination in the whole country. In fact, we suspect that the folks in Arkansas might deliberately be keeping their beautiful state parks and well-appointed campgrounds a secret from all of us outsiders.

The secret has slowly leaked out over the years from the many podcast guests and Facebook group members who have raved about their amazing camping adventures in Arkansas. Petit Jean State Park and Lake Ouachita are breakout favorites for long weekend getaways. Hot Springs and Bentonville are great examples of charming small towns with both public and private campground options right outside the city limits. Top it off with a great urban camping option in Little Rock, and Arkansas checks off the boxes for virtually every type of camper out there. Visitors take note—the only natural attraction that doesn't get rave reviews from our camping community is Crater of Diamonds State Park. Apparently the search for gems is a lot less exciting (and profitable) than many anticipate.

BEST IN STATE

Lake Ouachita State Park

▷ Mountain Pine, Arkansas

▷ arkansasstateparks.com

▷ RV and Tent Sites, Deluxe Cabins and Camping Cabins

Arkansas (aka the Natural State) is one of the most underrated camping states in the country, and Lake Ouachita State Park is one of its crown jewels. Lake Ouachita is Arkansas's biggest lake and measures in at a whopping 40,000 acres. Swimming, fishing, and kayaking opportunities abound in its crystal-clear waters, which are surrounded by Ouachita National Forest. The campground is relatively small but has large, beautiful sites, and some even offer full hookups, which is almost unheard of for a state park. Sites in Loop B and Loop C have nice gravel pads, and most sites there have views of the lake. Tent campers will want to reserve a site in Loop A along the edge of the peninsula that juts out into the lake. Glampers will love the full service cabins with outdoor seating that have all of the amenities right down to linens. If you don't have your own kayak, consider renting one (or larger options like the 29-foot party barge with an upper deck and 150-horsepower motor!) from the marina where prices are reasonable and service is friendly. Once here, you may never want to leave, but then you would be missing the quirky charms of Hot Springs, which is less than half an hour away.

- - - - - - - - - **Drive It: Mount Magazine Scenic Byway** - - - - - - - - -

This 20-mile drive brings you to the top of Mount Magazine, the highest peak in Arkansas. There are plenty of places to stop along the way for hiking, swimming, and enjoying a picnic lunch.

> ------------- **Petit Jean State Park Hiking** -------------
> ▷ 7 Hollows Trail, 4.4 miles
> ▷ Cedar Falls Trail, 1.9 miles
> ▷ Rock House Cave and Lookout Trail, 4 miles
> ▷ Bear Cave Trail, 1.1 miles

Eureka Springs KOA Journey

▷ Eureka Springs, Arkansas

▷ koa.com

▷ RV and Tent Sites, Deluxe Cabins, Camping Cabins

This cute-as-a-button campground wins high marks for cleanliness and good customer service. The RV sites are also level and fairly spacious. The cabins look brand new, and many offer privacy and views of the woods. Looking for a back-to-nature glamping experience? Check out the yurt that is surrounded by deep and lush Ozark forest. The KOA "journey" designation suggests that this campground makes a great stopover on the way from one destination to another, but there is charm enough here to make a longer stay enjoyable. The pool, playground, and dog park areas are small but tidy, and they are plenty inviting after a long day of exploring Eureka Springs, which is only twelve minutes away.

Petit Jean State Park

▷ Morrilton, Arkansas

▷ arkansasstateparks.com

▷ Lodge, Cabins, RV and Tent Sites

Petit Jean was the first state park in Arkansas, and it set the gold standard for the rest of the beloved park system. It is located on Petit Jean Mountain, adjacent to the Arkansas River and situated between the Ouachita Mountains and the Ozark Plateaus.

Many features in the park were built by the Civilian Conservation Corps (CCC), so Petit Jean showcases lots of the classic architecture of the New Deal. Visitors love the rustic lodges and structures built from native stone and timber. The campground is located at the northern end of the state park and is made up of four loops in total. It has a total of 125 campsites (27 of which are pull-through), and all have water and electric hookups. A few have full hookups, a notable state park accomplishment. Petit Jean State Park also has lodge accommodations, cabins, and yurts.

ALSO GREAT

Downtown Riverside RV Park

▷ North Little Rock, Arkansas

▷ downtownriversidervpark.com

▷ RV Sites

We love urban campgrounds and would love to see more of them pop up in cities across the country. Downtown Riverside RV Park isn't much of a campground at all, but its location right on the banks of the Arkansas River is astonishing—and so are the views.

Wanderlust RV Park

▷ Eureka Springs, Arkansas

▷ wanderlustrvpark.com

▷ RV Sites and Cabins

This is another great base camp for exploring the sweet city of Eureka Springs. It's only 3 miles from downtown, and guests can catch the Blue Route trolley that runs right past the campground. Deer often wander through the park in the early morning hours and just before dark.

The Small Towns of Arkansas

Eureka Springs

Shop the artsy downtown, visit Thorncrown Chapel, and take a ghost tour at the Crescent Hotel.

Bentonville

Visit the Crystal Bridges Museum of American Art, established by the daughter of Walmart founder Sam Walton.

Hot Springs

Enjoy the historic architecture of Bathhouse Row, then learn more about this former haven for illegal gambling at the Gangster Museum of America.

Florida

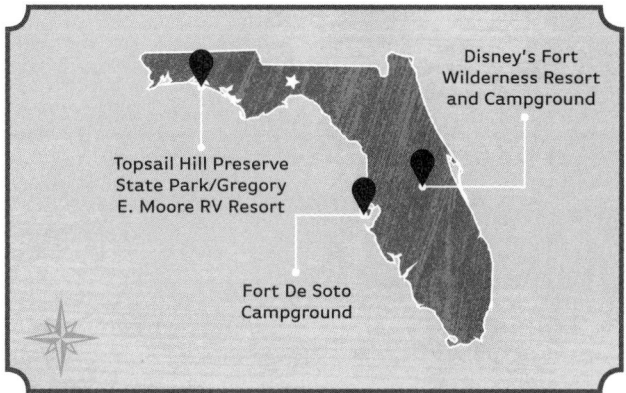

The most important thing you need to know about camping in Florida is that everyone is doing it between the months of December and April. There are times when folks cannot find a single campsite in the whole state during the season when an additional one million snowbirds head south to enjoy the mild winter. However, if you plan ahead, you can enjoy some of the best camping in the United States in this southern state.

The Florida state park system is ridiculously popular on account of both the desirable locations and modern, though varied, amenities. Reservations can be made up to eleven months in advance, and camping enthusiasts boot up their laptops and try to snag spots the second they become available. There are other public camping options available as well. County parks, national forests, and national preserves offer less competitive booking opportunities. Everglades National Park has two campgrounds open to RVs and tent campers. Just remember to stock up on the bug spray before your adventure.

Private campgrounds and resorts are also abundant in the Sunshine State. Fort Wilderness at Walt Disney World may just be the most popular and most loved campground in the entire country. There's also places like Beverly Beach Camptown RV Resort, Camp Gulf, and Bluewater Key RV Resort, where you can pay a pretty penny to camp just steps from the beach.

BEST IN STATE

Fort De Soto Campground

▷ Tierra Verde, Florida

▷ pinellascounty.org

▷ RV and Tent Sites

Fort De Soto Campground is a perennial favorite for native Floridians and for the snowbirds that flock down to the Sunshine State every winter. And it's easy to see why. Simply put, this is one of the most beautiful campgrounds we have ever seen. The campground is located in Fort De Soto Park, part of the Pinellas County Park System. There are 238 campsites spread out over three loops, and each loop has distinctive characteristics and rig and pet limitations. The great news is that all three loops offer back-in waterfront sites and spacious interior pull-throughs. Even though the pull-through sites don't back up to the water, they are nothing to scoff at. They are lush and large, with an appeal of their own, especially if the waterfront sites are all booked. Plus, some have good views, even if they aren't right on the water. Every site at Fort De Soto Campground has water and electric (30 amp and 50 amp) hookups, with dump stations easily accessible from each area. They don't have sewer, but that would be a rare find in a county park along the water. We did not want to leave Fort De Soto. The beaches were beautiful, and the water was warm, even in January. This is a magical camping experience, pure and simple.

------------------ **Florida RV SuperShow** ------------------

Thinking about buying an RV? One of the biggest RV shows in the country takes place every January in Tampa, Florida. The Florida RV SuperShow displays over 1,500 RVs on 26 acres of property. Plus, the live entertainment includes bagpipe bands and magicians. It's a bucket list event for RV enthusiasts.

Topsail Hill Preserve State Park/Gregory E. Moore RV Resort

▷ Santa Rosa Beach, Florida

▷ floridastateparks.org

▷ Cabins, RV and Tent Sites

Florida State Parks are known for their fabulous campgrounds, but Topsail Hill Preserve State Park takes it to another level. The campground is large with 156 RV sites, and every single RV site has full hookups and concrete pads. Seriously. A state park with full hookups! On a perfect beach with crystal clear waters. See why everyone loves this place? There are also tent sites with water and electric, plus thirty-two cabins and bungalows. It's important to note that the RV sites, tent sites, and cabins are all in designated areas, so you won't be able to park your RV next to friends in a cabin. The campground is beautifully maintained with paved roads throughout. Topsail Hill Preserve State Park delivers on the tropical scenery with plenty of Florida vegetation and palm trees. It is also affordable. The only catch is that you actually have to find an open campsite to book. The reservation window is eleven months, and the park sells out during the most popular times of the year. Cancellations do happen, so if at first you don't succeed try, try again!

-------- **10 Tips for Camping at Fort Wilderness** --------

1. Book up to 499 days in advance by calling (407) 939-3463.

2. Splurge on a premium campsite.

3. Request to be near the Meadows area for easy access to most of the campground amenities.

4. Make reservations at the Hoop-Dee-Doo Musical Revue.

5. Roast marshmallows at Chip 'n' Dale's Campfire Sing-A-Long.

6. Eat breakfast at the Trail's End Restaurant.

7. Watch the evening fireworks from the Fort Wilderness beach.

8. Rent a golf cart and go "looping" to enjoy the decked out Disney-fied campsites.

9. Take the boat to the Magic Kingdom.

10. Shop for all your souvenirs at the Trading Posts, which have the best Disney merch on the whole property.

Disney's Fort Wilderness Resort and Campground

▷ Orlando, Florida

▷ disneyworld.disney.go.com

▷ RV and Tent Sites, Cabin Rentals

You can camp at Walt Disney World? We get this question quite often when sharing our epic Fort Wilderness adventures. The answer is a resounding yes, there is actually a camping resort *in* Disney World. And Fort Wilderness is as amazing as you would expect a Disney campground to be. We think it is one of the best campgrounds in the country. The Fort (as it is affectionately known by regulars) is located on the Walt Disney World property in Orlando, Florida. The campground borders Lake Buena Vista, which means you can take boat transportation to the Magic Kingdom. You can also easily access the other resorts near the Magic Kingdom. But please know that The Fort *is* officially a Disney resort property, so you get all the benefits of staying on-site at Disney World. These include early dining reservations, extra magic hours, and complimentary MagicBands. There are partial, full, preferred, or premium campsites. There are also designated pet-friendly loops. The campground is organized around three main locations. The Outpost Depot is the entrance of the resort and also the transportation hub for accessing other Walt Disney World locations. The Meadows Depot is in the middle of the property and hosts a pool and recreation area as well as a trading post. The Settlement Depot is at the other end of the resort and has dining options, entertainment, a trading post, and the boat docks. Fort Wilderness has an incredibly natural feel considering this is Disney World. The wildlife is legendary. Wild turkeys wander through your site, and folks regularly report seeing deer, armadillos, peacocks, and rabbits. There are towering cypress and pine trees on pristinely clean and manicured grounds. This is our happy place. It could be yours too.

---------------- Drive It: Seven Mile Bridge ----------------

The modern version of this marvel was built in the late twentieth century and connects Knight's Key to Little Duck Key. Portions of the original bridge, completed in 1912, are still open to cyclists and pedestrians.

ALSO GREAT

Bahia Honda State Park

▷ Big Pine Key, Florida

▷ bahiahondapark.com

▷ RV and Tent Sites, Cabins

Bahia Honda State Park is located in Big Pine Key, Florida. It's one of Florida's southernmost state parks and a jewel of the Keys. It offers beautiful beaches, stunning sunsets, and world-famous snorkeling. Birders are particularly fond of this state park. There are also plenty of boat excursions available on-site for campers to explore the reefs and waterways. Tent campers often complain about the noise from the nearby bridge, but RV owners think this campground is the cat's meow. Some sites have direct access to the water, making this a paradise for kayakers and SUP lovers.

Lazydays RV Resort

▷   Seffner, Florida

▷   lazydays.com

▷   RV Sites and RV Rentals

Lazydays RV Resort is a really fun place to camp, especially if you want to spend a few days RV shopping at its adjacent dealership, which is one of the largest in the country, or if you are in town for the Florida RV SuperShow. The campground has 300 full hookup RV sites and an excellent screened-in pool and hot tub area. We enjoyed eating at the on-site Exit 10 Restaurant and Pub—it has great food and a road trip theme that fits the resort perfectly. Downtown Tampa is about fifteen minutes away.

Beverly Beach Camptown RV Resort

▷   Flagler Beach, Florida

▷   beverlybeachcamptown.com

▷   RV and Tent Sites, Cabins

Beverly Beach Camptown is located directly on the Atlantic Ocean half-way between St. Augustine and Daytona Beach. RV sites bump right up to a beach wall, and the sand is just a few steps away. Go RVing filmed a television commercial here—it's that beautiful! Cabins are also available, and two of them are oceanfront. The campground is divided into three sections—Camper's Village is located across Highway A1A so we prefer the Oceanview and Beachfront sections for easier access to the beach.

Camping in the Keys

Whether you are looking for luxury, natural beauty, or a combination of both, there's a perfect campground for you in the Florida Keys.

Bluewater Key RV Resort

Located on Key West, this is simply one of the most luxurious RV resorts in the entire country. Many of the large, paved lots include private tiki huts and boat ramps.

Boyd's Key West Campground

This waterfront resort is a bustling bastion of amenities and activities with a pool, tiki hut, fishing pier, kayak rentals, and more.

Bahia Honda State Park

This campground on Big Pine Key grants you access to one of the most beautiful beaches in southern Florida. This is the perfect location for your snorkeling, fishing, or kayaking adventures.

Long Key State Park

This state park offers oceanfront camping with virtually no amenities except for clean bathhouses. If you want to do nothing but sit in the sand and stare at water, this is the place for you.

John Pennekamp Coral Reef State Park

Full hookups are available at this popular state park, which offers access to two beaches. The full roster of activities in the park includes guided hikes and a glass-bottom boat tour that departs from the visitor center.

Georgia

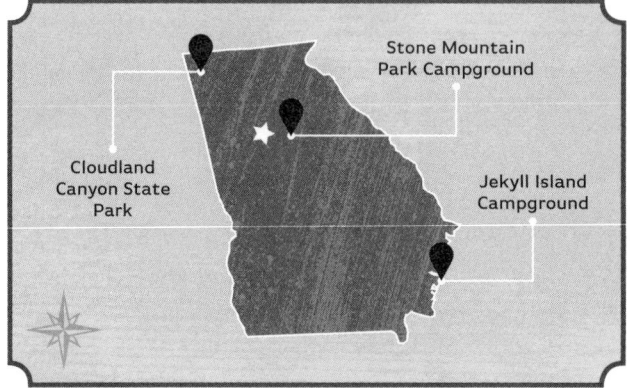

Stone Mountain Park Campground

Cloudland Canyon State Park

Jekyll Island Campground

Georgia doesn't necessarily have many well-known camping meccas, but residents will tell you there is an abundance of amazing getaways for both weekend warriors and destination campers—as long as you can successfully break free from the traffic-choked areas around Atlanta. Spring and fall are the most popular times of the year to enjoy a camping escape, and those in the know often avoid summer on account of the heat and humidity.

The state park system—forty-eight properties in total—is unique, diverse, and sufficiently funded. Stone Mountain Park Campground is about as close to a resort as state parks get. You can camp in the north Georgia mountains at places like Vogel State Park, or while away lazy days on Skidaway Island along the Georgia coast. You'll find cave tours in Cloudland Canyon and a cool spring water swimming pool at F.D. Roosevelt State Park. Bike trails, horseback riding, and hiking are prevalent throughout the Peach State. Just make sure to book those campsites thirteen months in advance when reservations open, because—like we said—the locals are fully aware of the great camping options all around them.

BEST IN STATE

Stone Mountain Park Campground

▷ Stone Mountain, Georgia

▷ stonemountainpark.com

▷ RV and Tent Sites, Safari Tents, Yurts, and RV Rentals

Stone Mountain Park Campground is about thirty minutes from downtown Atlanta (depending on traffic, of course), but it feels like it is many worlds away. This is no regular state park—it actually feels more like a hybrid between a stunningly beautiful state park and a luxury RV resort. It has sites that can accommodate big rigs, and 250 of them offer full or partial hookups. Additionally, there are almost 200 other sites that are reserved for tent campers and those with pop-ups. Is this Georgia's best campground for tent campers and RV owners? We would answer that question with a resounding yes. In fact, it is probably one of the best campgrounds in the entire country. Glampers also delight in Stone Mountain's lakefront yurt rentals, safari tents, and RV rentals. The amenities at the campground are off-the-hook for a state park. They include a nice pool, horseshoe and sand volleyball courts, and a recently renovated playground—and this is all just in the campground. The state park proper has dozens of other events and activities that will keep families occupied for days at a time.

Jekyll Island Campground

▷ Jekyll Island, Georgia

▷ jekyllisland.com

▷ RV and Tent Sites

If you want to take an RV or tent camping trip to Jekyll Island, this campground is your only choice. Thankfully it's a good one. Much like Stone Mountain, this campground feels like a hybrid between a state park and a private campground. It is actually owned by the state but is not part of

Georgia's excellent state park system. Sites are not large and private like they are at many state parks, but the location is excellent and the campground is wooded and shady. It has 144 RV sites that are all full hookup, and it offers tent camping sites as well. There are no cabins or yurts, so glampers will need to look for a house rental or hotel nearby. The campground is popular and offers monthly rentals, which are snapped up by snowbirds in the winter—so book early! The island itself is gorgeous with many beaches to choose from. Best among them is Driftwood Beach, which is close to the campground. The beach is filled with the skeletons of old trees that have been exposed by erosion. This creates a spooky look for photos and a natural playground that will keep your kids occupied for hours while you chillax on the beach.

------------ Charming Northeastern Georgia ------------

Northeastern Georgia is full of quaint towns like Blairsville, Helen, and Hiawassee. The hiking, shopping, and dining experiences make for the perfect weekend escape, especially in the fall when foliage colors start to pop. Here are some recommendations for exploring historic Blairsville.

- ✧ Visit Vogel State Park and check out the ranger program. It's designed for children ages six to twelve and has three different badge levels to work through.
- ✧ Hike the falls. There are three beautiful waterfalls near Blairsville: Helton Creek Falls, Trahlyta Falls, and DeSoto Falls.
- ✧ Stand on the observation deck at Brasstown Bald, Georgia's highest peak. Visitors can take a shuttle to the top or hike on a paved path.
- ✧ Ride on the Blue Ridge Scenic Railway and enjoy a four-hour journey through the hills of north Georgia.
- ✧ Pick your own at Mercier Orchards. Pick fruit, ride on a tractor, eat lunch, and stock up on fresh farm produce and baked goods to bring home from your camping trip.

Cloudland Canyon State Park

▷ Rising Fawn, Georgia

▷ gastateparks.org

▷ Cottages, Yurts, Tents, and RV Sites

Cloudland Canyon State Park campground is located on the western edge of Lookout Mountain and is only thirty minutes from downtown Chattanooga across the state line in the great state of Tennessee. There are closer camping options if you want proximity to Chattanooga, but none are as beautiful as this. Mountain biking is popular here, and so is hiking. There are 30 miles of biking trails and 64 miles of hiking trails. The excellent views on the shorter Overlook Trail and the steep descent into the canyon on the more challenging Waterfalls Trail are among the most popular. Fishing, cave exploration, disc golf, and horseback riding are also options in the park for those who love outdoor adventure. The campground is mid-sized and offers RV and tent sites that are large, private, and shaded. Larger rigs can fit in many of the water/electric sites. Glampers will also enjoy the park's cozy cottages with screened-in porches and the quirky yurts with large decks and Adirondack chairs.

ALSO GREAT

Conestoga Wagon Camping at The Rock Ranch

▷ The Rock, Georgia

▷ therockranch.com

▷ Conestoga Wagon Rentals

If sitting around a crackling campfire and sleeping in a Conestoga wagon are not on your bucket list, they should be. And the Rock Ranch is the place to do it. Each wagon sleeps eight, and a glorious hot dog dinner with lemonade and s'mores is available for a few additional gold coins.

Skidaway Island State Park

▷ Savannah, Georgia

▷ gastateparks.org

▷ Cabins, Tent and RV Sites

The campground at Skidaway Island State Park is an absolute delight and can serve as the perfect base camp for exploring Savannah and the Georgia coast. The only thing you won't like about it is how hard it is to book a site. The campground is on the small side (eighty-seven sites), incredibly beautiful (Spanish moss abounds), and almost perfectly located (about twenty minutes from charming downtown Savannah). What's not to love?

------- **What to Do When Camping on Tybee Island** -------

✦ Tybee Island Light State and Museum: Tour Georgia's oldest and tallest lighthouse and learn about the Euchee Tribe and Fort Screven.

✦ Tybee Island Marine Science Center: Check out the schedule for the Walks, Talks, and Treks one-hour programs exploring the local ecosystem.

✦ Fort Pulaski National Monument: Take a guided tour to truly appreciate the role of this fort in the American Civil War.

✦ McQueens Island Historic Trail: Bring your own bikes or rent some to explore these 6 miles, often referred to as the Rails-to-Trails by locals.

River's End Campground & RV Park

▷ Tybee Island, Georgia

▷ riversendcampground.com

▷ RV Sites, Tent Sites, Cabins

Looking for a beachy, relaxing campground just half a mile from the beach on Tybee Island and an easy drive from historic and beautiful Savannah? Then make sure to check out River's End Campground & RV Park. Cabins are clean and simple, tent sites are excellent (but not private), and RV sites are more than adequate. The community room has a fireplace and is a cozy spot on a rainy day.

-------------- **Georgia's Largest State Park** --------------

F.D. Roosevelt State Park is located an hour and a half south of Atlanta and is a favorite escape for the locals who manage to fight through the legendary traffic. There are 42 miles of hiking trails and a spring-fed swimming pool built by the Civilian Conservation Corps in the 1930s.

· *Kentucky* ·

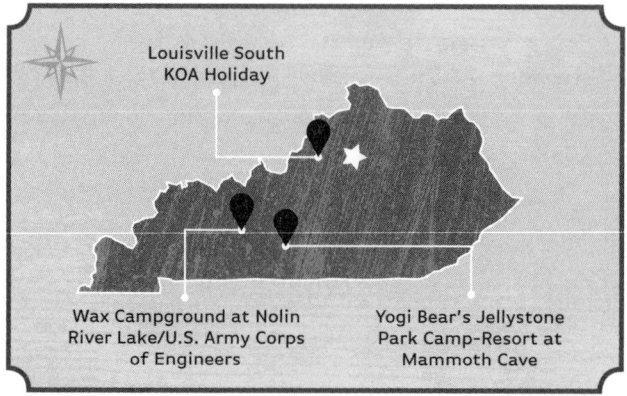

Louisville South
KOA Holiday

Wax Campground at Nolin
River Lake/U.S. Army Corps
of Engineers

Yogi Bear's Jellystone
Park Camp-Resort at
Mammoth Cave

Kentucky is a bit of an underground rock star in the camping community. You probably won't find Kentucky destinations on many top-ten travel lists, but when you start asking around you'll find that the state is beloved for its many natural—and man-made—gems. Mammoth Cave National Park is a bucket list destination for many Americans, with over a half a million people visiting every year to experience the world's longest recorded cave system. There's also 53,000 acres above ground for hiking, horseback riding, and rafting. There is a campground for every type of camper—the nearby Jellystone offers resort amenities; the KOA is a quieter, family-friendly option; and the NPS campground provides a quiet, rustic retreat.

If you want to explore the Kentucky Bourbon Trail, you can easily do that RVing, tenting, or cabin camping along the way. There are great family-owned campgrounds like the Louisville South KOA and the Elkhorn Campground that put you right in the heart of distillery country. My Old Kentucky Home State Park in Bardstown is a local treasure, with a small campground that offers convenient access to popular state park attractions like the Federal Hill Mansion House tours and the Stephen Foster Story outdoor drama.

BEST IN STATE

Yogi Bear's Jellystone Park Camp-Resort at Mammoth Cave

▷ Cave City, Kentucky

▷ jellystonemammothcave.com

▷ Cabins, Cottages, Bungalows, RV and Tent Sites

An off-the-hook Jellystone Park with tons of fun family activities located just minutes away from an epic national park that is also a UNESCO World Heritage Site? Sign us up now. After a morning of exploring Mammoth Cave's underground trails, you will love heading back to this Jellystone Park for swimming, waterslides, pedal carts, mini golf, jumping pillows, and the campground's own sandy beach and 2.3-acre lake. Yogi and his friends can also be seen throughout the park and are available for bear hugs and fun photo ops. We do always like to emphasize that Jellystone Parks are not just for little kids. Teenagers will love the huge inflatable sports park on the lake (known as the Wibit!) and will also spend hours playing softball, basketball, and volleyball. A wide variety of RV and tent sites are available, and they can accommodate the biggest of rigs and the smallest of tents. This Jellystone also has over ninety cabins, making it a perfect place for glampers who don't own an RV and don't want to sleep in a tent. The Cindy Bear Cottage and Ranger's Retreat look pretty darn cozy to us!

Louisville South KOA Holiday

▷ Shepherdsville, Kentucky

▷ koa.com

▷ Camping Cabins, Deluxe Cabins, RV and Tent Sites

Start your journey on the Kentucky Bourbon Trail in the Louisville area, and book yourself a nice site or cabin at this excellent KOA with mature and shady trees. Kids will love the large common area with ga-ga ball, a jumping pillow, horseshoes, and more. Everyone will love taking a dip in the pool at the end of a hot Kentucky day. There is also a stocked catch-and-release catfish pond. On summer nights, fireflies fill the air and so does the sound of laughter from the outdoor movie theatre. In recent years, many of the RV sites have been upgraded and include patio sites with a dining table and chairs and an extra-large fire ring. Nature trails ring the campground, and every KOA has a dedicated dog park so everyone (including your beloved pup) will have room to roam. If you finish your book while you are there, leave it behind and grab a new one at the book exchange in the camp store.

Wax Campground at Nolin River Lake/ U.S. Army Corps of Engineers

▷   Clarkson, Kentucky

▷   recreation.gov

▷   RV and Tent Sites

If you want to visit Mammoth Cave and camp in a peaceful and natural setting, then this Corps of Engineers park might be perfect for you. Wax Campground is located on the tranquil shores of Nolin River Lake and is surrounded by rolling hills. Canoe and kayak lovers will enjoy hitting the water and utilizing the campground's easily accessible launch points. But just make sure you bring plenty of groceries and supplies, as the campground is in a fairly remote location with few shops around. Most sites here offer water and electric hookups so you can run your RV's air-conditioning during the hot summer months. Tent campers might choose to stay here during the shoulder seasons when the heat and humidity are milder.

ALSO GREAT

Mammoth Cave Campground

▷ Mammoth Cave, Kentucky

▷ nps.gov

▷ RV and Tent Sites

Looking for a quiet, rustic base camp for exploring Mammoth Cave National Park and don't need the hookups and kid-friendly amenities that the Jellystone provides? The wooded, shady sites offered by the NPS at the Mammoth Cave Campground are spacious and affordable. The visitor center is also a short walk away.

The Elkhorn Campground

▷ Frankfort, Kentucky

▷ elkhorncampground.com

▷ RV Sites

The Elkhorn Campground is a charming mom-and-pop operation deep in the heart of Bourbon Country. The Elkhorn creek provides a relaxing soundtrack to long summer nights, and you can wet a line right from the comfort of your own camp chair next to your RV. Here, guests are treated as family members, and many return year after year.

---------------------- **Before you go...** ----------------------

▷ **Read:** *American Pharaoh: The Untold Story of the Triple Crown Winner's Legendary Rise* by Joe Drape

▷ **Watch:** *Secretariat*, a 2010 movie about a Triple Crown winner and famed racehorse

A Quick Guide to Mammoth Cave National Park

Where to Camp
▷ Yogi Bear's Jellystone Park Camp-Resort at Mammoth Cave
▷ Horse Cave KOA
▷ Mammoth Cave Campground
▷ Wax Campground (U.S. Army Corps of Engineers park)

Where to Stock Up
Cave City is 6 miles from the main entrance of Mammoth Cave National Park and is the place to grab groceries and other provisions.

Regularly Scheduled Ranger Programs
▷ Coffee with a Ranger
▷ Porch Talk
▷ Heritage Walk
▷ Junior Ranger Nature Track
▷ Echo River Springs Walk
▷ Sloan's Crossing Pond Walk
▷ Evening Program at the Amphitheater

Cave Tours
It's imperative to research cave tours ahead of time to find the right ones for your family. You'll also want to make reservations in advance, as the most popular tours fill up not only during the summer months but also during the spring when local schools visit for field trips. There are age restrictions for many of the tours. Strollers and child backpack carriers are prohibited on all cave tours, so plan accordingly.

Easy Cave Tours for the First-Time Visitor

▷ Frozen Niagara Tour, 0.25 mile

▷ Mammoth Passage Tour, 0.75 mile

▷ Discovery Tour, 0.75 mile (unguided)

Moderate Cave Tours for the Adventurous Visitor

▷ Historic Tour, 2 miles

▷ Domes and Dripstones Tour, 0.75 mile

▷ Gothic Avenue Tour, 1 mile

Strenuous Cave Tour for the Bold and Brave Visitor

▷ Violet City Lantern Tour, 3 miles by lantern

Caves Outside of the National Park

▷ Cub Run Cave

▷ Diamond Caverns

▷ Hidden River Cave

▷ Onyx Cave

▷ Outlaw Cave

Additional Activities Outside the National Park

▷ Dinosaur World

▷ Kentucky Action Park

▷ Kentucky Down Under Adventure Zoo & Mammoth Onyx Cave

▷ Hidden River Cave and American Museum

▷ Diamond Caverns

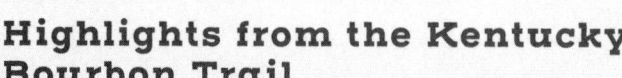

Highlights from the Kentucky Bourbon Trail

It's virtually impossible to visit all the famous distilleries along the Kentucky Bourbon Trail. Here is a selection that won't disappoint. Many are surprisingly family-friendly and offer engaging tours and wonderful outdoor spaces to let off some steam.

Boundary Oak Distillery

This distillery is about twenty-five minutes south of Louisville and just minutes from Abraham Lincoln's birthplace. Boundary Oak is family-friendly with outdoor music and food trucks in the summer season. The tasting bar allows visitors to sample bourbon in all the stages of production. This distillery stands out for small batch commemorative collections paying tribute to famous military figures and regiments. Try the Patton Armored Diesel, the Blackhorse 1901, or the Lincoln Straight Bourbon.

Evan Williams Bourbon Experience

Evan Williams was one of Kentucky's first commercial distillers. It is known for straight and single barrel bourbon whiskeys. Be sure to make reservations in advance for tours. The Traditional Tour & Tasting is one hour and includes three bourbon tastings. The Sweet & Neat Tour will teach you why chocolate and bourbon are a match made in heaven. And the Speakeasy Tasting Experience will transport you back to the days of Prohibition in Louisville.

Castle & Key Distillery

In 1887, distiller Colonel Edmund Haynes Taylor Jr. built what became known as the birthplace of bourbon tourism. The distillery originally included a castle, springhouse, and sunken gardens. It fell into disrepair over the next century, but it's once again open for business. Try the Restoration Release Gin, Restoration Release Vodka, Castle & Key Rye, and Castle & Key Bourbon.

Buffalo Trace Distillery

Started in 1775, Buffalo Trace is the oldest continuously operating distillery in the United States. It was even allowed to operate during prohibition in order to make whiskey for "medicinal purposes." Bring the whole family to this place. The videos and exhibits get kids excited about the science behind the official spirit of America. They can even sip limestone water and come up with a personalized flavor profile for a mash! Check out all the tours before you visit to decide what would suit your crew the best. Some of the most popular include the Trace Tour, the Hard Hat Tour, and the Ghost Tour.

Maker's Mark

You won't want to miss touring what is probably the most recognizable bourbon brand on the market. Technology hasn't made its way to this distillery—the bottles are still hand dipped in that iconic red wax and bottle labels are cut on a hand-operated printing press. Popular tours include the General Distillery Tour, Maker's Immersion, Behind the Bar, and the Heritage Tour.

Louisiana

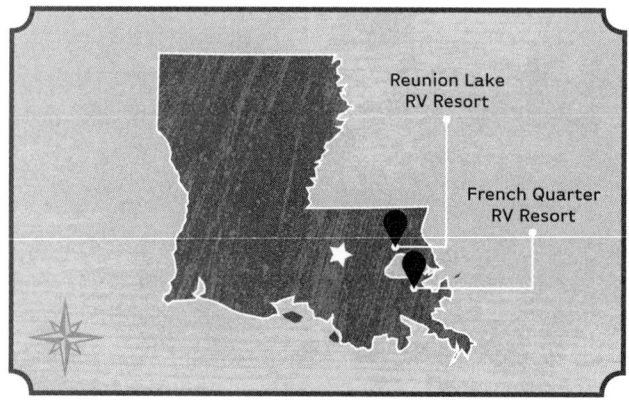

Camping in Louisiana is about so much more than getting within spitting distance of New Orleans. But for people like us visiting from far away, we can't imagine traveling all that way and not soaking in the magic of the Big Easy. We've highlighted some great options for camping and touring the city, featuring an urban campground smack in the middle of the action and also a beautiful state park close enough for a day trip but far enough to escape for some peace and quiet.

And then there are all the other outdoor attractions in the Bayou State. The state park system offers wonderful opportunities for hiking, biking, and fishing. The coastal wetlands provide the perfect opportunity to enjoy a guided kayak tour or become an amateur birder. The high temperatures and rainfall make summer the least popular season for camping in Louisiana. The shoulder months of April, May, October, and November are most likely to bring you those camping conditions—warm days and cool nights.

BEST IN STATE

Reunion Lake RV Resort

▷ Ponchatoula, Louisiana

▷ reunionlakerv.com

▷ RV Sites

Many RV owners want the same types of resort-style amenities and activities that travelers get when they check into luxury hotels, and they are willing to pay for them. Over the last decade the campground industry (particularly in the Northeast and the South) responded by building true resort-style campgrounds like Reunion Lake RV Resort. This is a gated resort with concierge-level service and facilities. Kids and adults love the lazy river and family pool. But if it gets too noisy or crowded, just head on over to the adult pool with a swim-up bar and the friendly bartenders will be happy to mix your favorite drink. If it gets unbearably hot, rent yourself a poolside cabana with a ceiling fan and your own personal attendant to bring drinks and food. The lake is also a great place for a refreshing dip or kayak ride. The Float Lake Obstacle Course is fun for older kids and adults who are still young at heart. RV sites are mostly pull-throughs that are out in the open with minimal shade. Bring a screen room or plan on using your RV's awning to create a cool and comfortable place to kick back with a book or just watch the world go by.

---------------------- **Before you go...** ----------------------

▷ **Read:** *A Streetcar Named Desire* by Tennessee Williams and *Interview with the Vampire* by Anne Rice. *Confederacy of Dunces* by John Kennedy Toole is also one of our favorite books of all time. Let's face it—a lot of great literature is written about New Orleans.

---------- **New Orleans Jazz & Heritage Festival** ----------

Most folks think the time to visit New Orleans is during the Mardi Gras season, when more than 1.4 million visitors descend upon the city for parades and festivities. We, however, have a soft spot in our hearts for another annual attraction— the New Orleans Jazz & Heritage Festival. Maybe it's because this was the destination for our first official road trip as a couple decades ago, or maybe it's because the entire city comes alive with amazing music of every genre and you don't even have to actually buy tickets to the outdoor festival to be immersed in live performances. Don't let anyone tell you that a visit to Preservation Hall is too "touristy." Sitting on the floor just feet away from some of the best musicians in the city will be a travel highlight that sticks with you forever.

French Quarter RV Resort

▷   New Orleans, Louisiana

▷   fqrv.com

▷   RV Sites, On-site Condo Rental

We've said it before and we'll say it again: We love urban camping. Getting our RV close to great American cities like Charleston and Philadelphia is always a thrill and our favorite way to visit these kinds of iconic destinations. The French Quarter RV Resort is located only a few blocks from the French Quarter proper, and it serves as a good example of what many urban RV parks can and should look like. Some folks might take one look at this place and dismiss it as not much more than an expensive parking lot, but we see so much more. The location is absolutely incredible, and the twenty-four-hour gated security makes this a safe and comfortable place to sleep right near the action. You can stroll to the French Quarter for food, drinks, and live music then walk or catch an Uber back to your site. The park has a cute little pool, hot tub area, gazebo with bar facilities, and a small but functional fitness room in the club-house area. The staff is also excellent and knowledgeable about all things New Orleans. If you want to take an RV trip to the Big Easy, this is the way to do it.

ALSO GREAT

Fontainebleau State Park

▷ Mandeville, Louisiana

▷ crt.state.la.us

▷ RV and Tent Sites, Lakefront Cabins, Lodge Rooms

Fontainebleau State Park is an awesome place to camp when it is warm and dry, although it can get soggy and swamp-like after a good rain. The sites are large and private, and the campground has direct access to the north shore of Lake Pontchartrain. Lovely walking trails can be found throughout the park, and lodge and cabin options are excellent and affordable for those without tents and RVs. New Orleans is also within striking distance for a day trip.

Lincoln Parish Park

▷ Ruston, Louisiana

▷ rustonlincoln.com

▷ RV and Tent Sites

The small campground at Lincoln Parish Park is a bit of a hidden gem, but it's well worth a visit if you are passing by this lovely part of the Pelican State. Sites are located right near the lake, and the walking trails in the park are excellent. The mountain biking here is unparalleled and draws enthusiasts from all over the state and beyond. The park rangers are super friendly here and go out of their way to make everyone feel welcome and comfortable.

Bayou Segnette State Park

▷ Westwego, Louisiana

▷ lastateparks.com

▷ RV and Tent Sites, Cabins

The campground at Bayou Segnette State Park is grassy and parklike with big back-in sites and wide open spaces that are great for games of catch or Wiffle ball. Everything about this place is peaceful and relaxing. Dog owners love the mile-long walking trail that winds through a pretty swamp area that is wooded and filled with shade—making it a perfect place to take your pooch for a stroll on a hot summer day. All traveling campers *love* the laundry room with free washers and dryers. We have never seen free washers and dryers at a campground before—so let us all pause and reflect on how awesome this is! The newly built waterfront cabins are also pretty darn amazing and have beautiful bayou views from their spacious front decks. These units have full kitchens and bunk beds that make them a great choice for families without RVs. The location of Bayou Segnette State Park is also convenient. Downtown New Orleans is only twenty-five to thirty minutes away, depending on traffic. If you don't want to camp in the city at the French Quarter RV Resort, then this is an obvious and excellent choice.

---------- **A National Park Experience in NOLA** ----------

New Orleans Jazz National Historical Park has a visitors center right in the heart of the action on North Peters Street. Drop in and chat with the rangers about the various self-guided walking tours exploring iconic places like Canal Street, Lafayette Square District, and more. There's even a free self-guided audio tour you can enjoy from your phone. If you are visiting with kids and looking for family-friendly activities, this is a great place to start. Pick up a ranger program booklet to earn a badge and check the schedule for events like Family Friendly Fridays.

Baton Rouge KOA Holiday

- ▷ Denham Springs, Louisiana
- ▷ koa.com
- ▷ RV and Tent Sites, Camping Cabins and Deluxe Cabins

This is a comfortable and well-managed KOA that serves as a quality base camp for visiting the Baton Rouge area. The pool and hot tub are nice, and the entire park is clean and well kept. The staff goes out of their way to welcome campers and make them feel like they are home. The game room is great for rainy days, and the mini golf course is brand new. Great regional food is within walking distance of the campground. Ask for recommendations at the front desk.

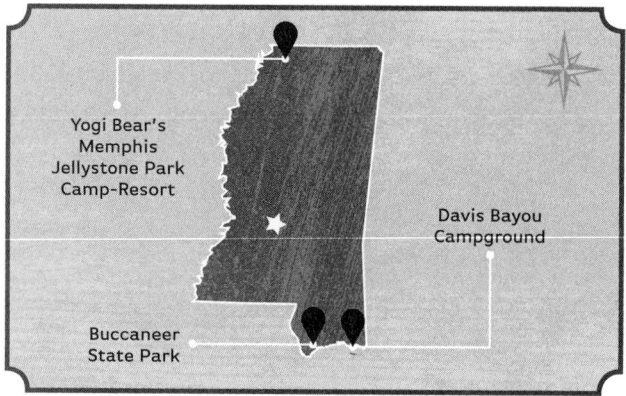

Mississippi

- Yogi Bear's Memphis Jellystone Park Camp-Resort
- Davis Bayou Campground
- Buccaneer State Park

From the Gulf Islands National Seashore to the Natchez National Historical Park, the state of Mississippi packs in its fair share of natural beauty and historical landmarks. Although the state parks offer many outdoor recreation opportunities along with a handful of lovely camping options, they should look to neighboring Alabama and Georgia for some inspiration on sprucing up the campgrounds and adding more modern amenities to welcome the next generation of campers.

-------------------- **Before you go...** --------------------

▷ **Watch:** *Elvis Presley: The Searcher*, a two-part HBO documentary chronicling the life of the King

▷ **Read:** *A Time to Kill* by John Grisham if you're looking for a page turner, or *As I Lay Dying* by William Faulkner if you never actually read it in high school

BEST IN STATE

Buccaneer State Park

▷　Waveland, Mississippi

▷　mdwfp.com

▷　RV and Tent Sites

The name may make this sound like a cheesy third-rate theme park, but this top-notch state park is anything but cheesy. It is rich in history (think smugglers, pirates, and Andrew Jackson) and has a magnificent waterfront setting and modern amenities throughout. Buccaneer State Park's structures and facilities were completely destroyed by Hurricane Katrina in 2005, but by November of 2013 the park had been completely reconstructed. The lovely campground offers spacious and level sites with full hookups. Seventy water and electric sites are also available on a grassy field with stunning views of the Gulf of Mexico. The sites are sparse and unreservable, but they have water and electric with a dump station nearby. Families love cooling off at the Buccaneer Bay Water Park, which is available to all campers for an additional fee. The wave pool is a blast, and the two giant waterslides will keep the kids occupied for hours. New Orleans is about an hour away if you want to head into town for jazz and gumbo.

Davis Bayou Campground

▷　Ocean Springs, Mississippi

▷　nps.gov

▷　RV and Tent Sites

We are huge fans of national seashores (like Cape Hatteras) and national lakeshores (like Sleeping Bear Dunes) and think that they are too often overlooked by NPS units with "national park" designations. Gulf Islands National Seashore stretches out across 150-plus miles along the northern coast of the Gulf of Mexico in Florida and Mississippi, with a wide variety of coastal and marine habitats. It also has some of the coolest camping options in America. Ever tried "boat-in" backcountry camping? Well, neither have we, but it is an awesome option for boat owners with adventurous spirits. Tent and RV owners also have an excellent option for camping at this NPS unit. The Davis Bayou Campground is an absolute delight. It is clean and well kept and has spacious shady sites surrounded by live oaks and pine trees. The campground is adjacent to a saltwater marsh and is in a great spot for those who love birdwatching. Downtown Ocean Springs is a short bike ride away and has good eats and fun and funky coastal shopping.

Yogi Bear's Memphis Jellystone Park Camp-Resort

▷   Horn Lake, Mississippi

▷   memphisjellystone.com

▷   RV and Tent Sites, Deluxe Cabins

It's called the Memphis Jellystone, but this superclean and superfun park is actually located 5 miles away in Horn Lake, Mississippi. If you want to visit Memphis with your family and indulge in its legendary food, music, and history, then this might be the base camp that makes everybody happy. Take trips into the city in the morning and enjoy the family-friendly amenities at the park in the afternoon. The pool and inflatable waterslides will help everyone cool off on a hot summer day, and the volleyball, basketball, and ga-ga ball courts will keep your kids occupied for hours at a time. The RV sites are spacious, level, and nicely manicured, and the cabin options are comfortable and well equipped. Jellystone Parks typically do a great job with the quality levels of their cabins, and this park is no exception. Our boys always love the loft cabins because they give them their own private clubhouse/fort area that is hard for us adults to squeeze into! Tent sites here are not private, but they are excellent. They have water and electric hookups, dedicated level pads for tents, picnic tables, and raised fire pits. Any kind of camping family will love this Jellystone, and it would make a great place to camp with friends or have a family reunion.

------- **The National Heritage Areas of Mississippi** -------

Mississippi Delta National Heritage Area

Celebrating the region where blues, gospel, and rock 'n' roll took root and blossomed, this national heritage area has forty recommended destinations to visit including the GRAMMY Museum, Delta Blues Museum, and Tate County Heritage Museum. See all forty places at msdeltatop40.com.

Mississippi Gulf National Heritage Area

This region is composed of the six southernmost counties of Mississippi identified as having unique historical and ecological landmarks and destinations. There are thirty-nine cancellation stations to stamp your National Parks Passport throughout the area, including the Biloxi Lighthouse, Gulf Islands National Seashore Davis Bayou, and Waveland's Ground Zero Hurricane Museum.

Mississippi Hills National Heritage Area

This area is located in the northeastern part of the state and celebrates the unique cultural intersection of the Delta and Appalachia. This is where musicians like Elvis, Jerry Lee Lewis, and Howlin' Wolf were born. And this is where writers like William Faulker, Tennessee Williams, and John Grisham became storytellers. The passport program includes twenty-two locations to get stamped.

ALSO GREAT

Tishomingo State Park

- ▷ Tishomingo, Mississippi
- ▷ mdwfp.com
- ▷ Cabins, RV and Tent Sites

Tishomingo State Park, which is nestled among the foothills of the Appalachian Mountains, offers a classic camping experience beloved by generations of Mississippians. The campground occupies a lovely spot on the edge of Haynes Lake, but it is not in prime condition and should be refurbished for future generations to enjoy. But it is still worth camping here! Outdoor recreation, including hiking and canoeing, is excellent. There is also a large pool near the cabin area—a rare sight at a state park.

------------ **Drive It: Natchez Trace Parkway** ------------

The Natchez Trace Parkway passes through three states—Mississippi, Alabama, and Tennessee—but most of the 444 miles are in Mississippi. Starting in Natchez and running through Jackson and Tupelo, this is a great way to see the state and soak up some history, from Native American populations who lived there for thousands of years to the Kaintucks who floated supplies down the river in the 1800s. There are plenty of camping options along the route, including public options like Natchez State Park, Rocky Springs, and Jeff Busby campgrounds.

Persimmon Hill Campground at Enid Lake/ U.S. Army Corps of Engineers

▷   Oakland, Mississippi

▷   mvk.usace.army.mil

▷   RV and Tent Sites

Like so many U.S. Army Corps of Engineers parks, this one is clean and has large, level sites with water views. Campers love the cute little beach area for swimming, and outdoor enthusiasts love the Persimmon Hill Multi-Purpose Trail for walking, jogging, and biking. The park tends to be packed with RVers, but tent campers are also welcome. A nice playground will keep the little ones occupied, and parents with teenagers should remember to pack a basketball. Campers with kayaks and canoes will have a blast here. There is a boat ramp located right inside the campground.

The Birthplace of...

There seems to be an outsized number of famous people who were born in the Magnolia State. Here are some of the most famous childhood hometowns to visit:

- Elvis Presley—Tupelo, Mississippi
- William Faulker—Oxford, Mississippi
- Oprah Winfrey—Kosciusko, Mississippi
- B.B. King—Itta Bena, Mississippi
- Eudora Welty—Jackson, Mississippi

North Carolina

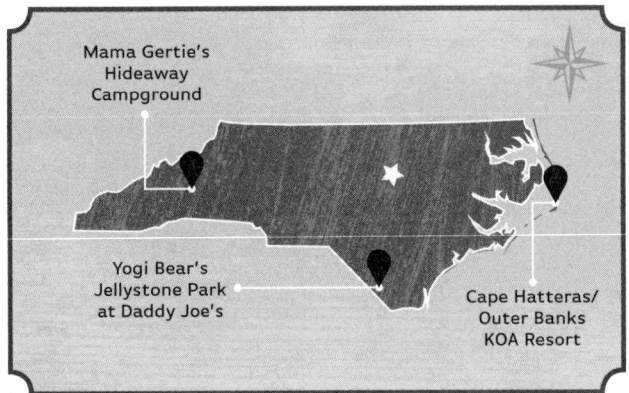

With both beach and mountain camping galore, we find ourselves returning to North Carolina again and again. The Outer Banks are a longtime favorite of ours. We vacationed near Cape Hatteras for years in rentals prior to buying our pop-up camper, and it was one of the very first places we camped as a family. There aren't dozens of campground options on this spit of sand, but the ones that exist are perfect for spending lazy days wandering back and forth between the beach and the pool.

Head west to find another one of our favorite destinations—Asheville. Spend the days hiking in Pisgah National Forest, then eat your fill of barbecue and listen to live bluegrass music at your pick of dive bars. Of course, you can also head to the mountains and camp in the Cherokee area, often referred to as the "quiet side" of the Smokies. Far from the hustle and bustle of places like Gatlinburg and Pigeon Forge, the North Carolina side of Great Smoky Mountains National Park has some of our very favorite family hikes in the entire country.

BEST IN STATE

Mama Gertie's Hideaway Campground

▷ Swannanoa, North Carolina

▷ mamagerties.com

▷ RV and Tent Sites, Camping Cabins

We enjoyed a magical stay at Mama Gertie's a few years back. The rear bed of our pop-up camper was hanging directly over a gurgling stream behind our site. We fell asleep each night to the gentle sound of that stream and we have been recommending Mama Gertie's for Asheville-area stays ever since. Since we camped there, it has added breathtaking new mountain view sites to accommodate large RVs. The setting here is gorgeous, but the amenities are limited—no playground and no pool—and while kids are welcome, this will probably not be their favorite campground. But that's okay, mom and dad count too, right? The location is also excellent. Mama Gertie's is less than twenty minutes from Asheville (depending on traffic—yes there is traffic in Asheville) and less than ten minutes from Black Mountain. Folks come here to visit Asheville for its food, culture, and craft beer. But we always implore them to take a drive into Black Mountain too. It's like a mini Asheville with tons of charm and great food of its own.

Yogi Bear's Jellystone Park at Daddy Joe's

▷ Tabor City, North Carolina

▷ taborcityjellystone.com

▷ RV Sites, Cabins, Yurts, Tents

There are about a hundred things to love about this award-winning Jellystone Park, and it's hard to know where to start. So let's begin with ice cream. The Creamery at Daddy Joe's is an on-site ice cream shop that serves homemade ice cream and organic coffee from a local roaster. But this Yogi is not a one-trick pony. The campground is an absolute delight. The RV sites are spacious, and you can choose between a sunny site, a shaded and thickly wooded site, or a quad buddy site that you can share with three other families. All of the sites are large and affordably priced. In season, there is an outdoor pool, and an indoor pool is open year-round. Little kids will love getting hugs from Yogi and friends, and older kids will love playing baseball, basketball, and volleyball. There is also a dedicated bike track for kids and parents to cruise around on and several stocked fishing ponds. Day trips into Wilmington, North Carolina, and Myrtle Beach, South Carolina, are within easy reach—but this is destination camping at its best. When you go you won't want to leave the campground. There is enough to do right on-site to keep your family happy for an entire week.

------------- The Quiet Side of the Smokies -------------

Tennessee has Gatlinburg and Pigeon Forge, but North Carolina has Cherokee, a quieter gateway town to the most-visited national park in the country. Quiet doesn't mean dull and boring, however. There is plenty to see and do around Cherokee, and some of our favorite family hikes are in the North Carolina side of Great Smoky Mountains National Park. Here are some of the best things to do on the quiet side.

▷ *Visit the Oconaluftee Visitor Center* and get some handpicked activities from the rangers.

▷ *Tour the Mountain Farm Community and Mingus Mill* to see a collection of historic log buildings that have been gathered together from around the Smokies.

▷ *Hike the Oconaluftee River Trail* that runs for 1.5 miles (3 miles round trip) along the banks of the river.

▷ *Tube and splash in the waterfalls at the Deep Creek Area.*

▷ *Hike the Kephart Prong Trail*, one of our favorite family hikes, and enjoy the wooden foot bridges and remains of an old CCC camp.

Cape Hatteras/Outer Banks KOA Resort

▷ Waves, North Carolina

▷ koa.com

▷ RV and Tent Sites, Camping Cabins, Deluxe Cabins, Vacation Rentals

There is little to no shade at this campground, and the RV and tent sites are small and lack privacy. But if you can get past those things, you are in for a magical stay if the weather is good. The Wright Brothers came here for good reason—it can be windy at any time of year. We come back here again and again for good reason too. The beaches are beautiful, the water is great for fishing or surfing, and the campground is packed with amenities that we love. In fact, some of the best surfing on the East Coast happens right in front of this campground. The pool complex is also one of the best pool campgrounds in the country. Kids love the zero-entry side, and adults love the lap lanes and spacious hot tub. We spend our days here going back and forth between the beach and the pool and our nights grilling back at our site and playing Wiffle ball in the sand. If you can't get a site here, try Camp Hatteras next door—most folks think it's just as good.

---------- **Asheville and Pisgah National Forest** ----------

Many of our early family vacations were in the Asheville area, so it holds a special place in our hearts. There's something about hiking during the day and listening to live music at night that feels just about perfect to us. If you like hip, artsy cities nestled in gorgeous mountains, put a camping trip to Asheville on your list.

Some of our favorite hikes include Looking Glass Rock Trail and Balsam Mountain Nature Trail. We also enjoy leisurely drives on the Blue Ridge Parkway and fast rides down Sliding Rock, landing in a pool of ice-cold water. Then we end the day at Jack of the Wood, an Irish pub with great live bluegrass.

ALSO GREAT

Smokemont Campground/Great Smoky Mountains National Park

▷ Cherokee, North Carolina

▷ nps.gov

▷ Tent and RV Sites

Beautiful, natural, no frills Great Smokies camping at its best. Mountain streams, rivers, and hiking trails abound at this classic campground near the border of North Carolina and Tennessee. Most sites are shaded and private, and some fit larger RVs. Tent campers and small RV owners will have the most options. Plan on disconnecting during your stay. Internet service isn't a thing in these woods.

--------------- **Camping on the Outer Banks** ---------------

The Outer Banks is basically a 200-mile sandbar off the coast of North Carolina, but people flock to this popular vacation destination from up and down the East Coast. There are camping options for everyone, from the rustic campgrounds in the national seashore to the resorts in Avon. Whether you have hookups or not, be prepared for the elements when visiting the Outer Banks. The wind can whip up at all times of the day, thunderstorms roll in and out with virtually no warning, and there is little shade to protect you from the hot summer sun. Yet we return again and again for fabulous beach getaways.

Cherokee/Great Smokies KOA Holiday

▷ Cherokee, North Carolina

▷ koa.com

▷ RV and Tent Sites, Deluxe and Camping Cabins

The Cherokee KOA is the perfect base camp for exploring the North Carolina side of the Smokies. At least it was for us. We loved tubing in the chilly waters of the Raven Claw River and then hightailing it to the hot tub to warm up after each run. The indoor pool and hot tub were also nice after dark. One of our all-time favorite hikes, the Kephart Prong Trail, is a short drive away.

Davidson River Campground

▷   **Pisgah Forest, North Carolina**

▷   **pisgahhospitalitypartners.com**

▷   **RV and Tent Sites**

The Davidson River Campground offers a simple but classic summer camping experience in Western North Carolina's Pisgah National Forest. Leave your technology at home and bring fishing poles, bikes, tubes, and bathing suits for long days on the river and quiet nights in the woods. The town of Brevard is nearby if you need food and supplies.

Oklahoma

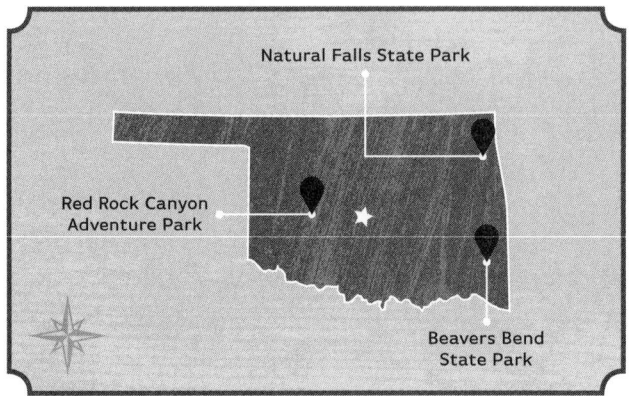

Natural Falls State Park

Red Rock Canyon
Adventure Park

Beavers Bend
State Park

Even though it is officially considered a southern state by the U.S. Census Bureau, Oklahoma feels like a state that straddles the South, the West, and the Midwest, bringing elements of all those regions together in one place. There are flat plains with tall oil wells dotting the landscape and cattle grazing in large herds. Then there are also the mountains and hills of the Ozarks and Red River Valley. The state park system has well-appointed campgrounds no matter which region of Oklahoma you are exploring. However, these treasures are well-loved by locals, so make sure you reserve early. Reservations are available eleven months in advance of the first day of your stay.

Stephanie's grandmother was born and raised on a pecan farm in Oklahoma. Distant relatives used to arrive in New Jersey every summer with heaps of fresh pecans that would be immediately frozen and used to make pies on Thanksgiving, Christmas, and Easter. In our opinion, picking up some pecans from a place like the Nut House on Route 66 should be at the top of your list when visiting Oklahoma.

BEST IN STATE

Beavers Bend State Park

▷ Broken Bow, Oklahoma

▷ travelok.com

▷ Rustic and Modern Cabins, RV and Tent Sites, Lakeview Lodge

Beavers Bend State Park is beautiful and worth visiting during any season, but the fall foliage is absolutely spectacular. There are so many things to love about this state park that it can be hard to figure out where to start. How about with the diverse glamping options for non-RV and tent campers? There are almost fifty comfortable cabins with kitchenettes located in a prime spot right along the Mountain Fork River, and some of them are even pet-friendly. The forty-room Lakeview Lodge is also a glamper's delight. It is nestled along the shores of Broken Bow Lake, and every single room has a view of the water. So how about the campground? It's pretty darn special too. It has over 400 sites, and it is an easy walk down to the water from most of them. Go for a refreshing dip there or take a kayak out on the lake for some gorgeous paddling. Fishing and hiking are also top-notch.

Natural Falls State Park

▷ Colcord, Oklahoma

▷ travelok.com

▷ Yurts, RV and Tent Sites

Most of the RV sites at Natural Falls State Park are huge and could easily fit two RVs on them. Seven of the forty-four sites even have full hookups. Camp here on a warm summer night and you will hear the sounds of kids playing catch and of burgers and dogs sizzling over charcoal grills. The sites are big enough to set up a game of bocce ball or invite a bunch of friends over for a campfire. This Oklahoma gem also features a 77-foot waterfall that can be viewed by hikers from a railed observation platform, and a second observation deck that has seats so you can kick back and enjoy the relaxing sound of water cascading down across the rocks. There is also a basketball court and a volleyball court for the older kids and a playground for the little ones. Glampers will love the spacious and well-equipped yurts. They come with microwaves, small fridges, air conditioning and heat, electrical outlets, and a coffee maker. Make sure to spend some time in the forest here—it is packed with dense trees and wildflowers and makes for a perfect place for a quiet summer stroll.

------------ **Visit the Center of the Universe** ------------

Who knew that the center of the universe is in Tulsa, Oklahoma? Find the small, concrete circle on Archer Street, stand in the middle and make a noise, then listen as the sound is echoed back to you. Folks swear that you could stand in the middle, blow a foghorn, and those standing on the outside of the circle wouldn't hear a thing. Bring your own foghorn and test out the legend.

Red Rock Canyon Adventure Park

▷   Hinton, Oklahoma

▷   redrockcanyonadventurepark.com

▷   RV and Tent Sites

Red Rock Canyon Adventure Park used to be known as Red Rock Canyon State Park, until the state almost sold it because of budget cuts. But the deal never went through, and instead it was leased out to an individual for fifty years. This decision was quite controversial among some Oklahomans, but thankfully the park remains, same as it ever was, and is open to the public. The road leading to the entrance is steep and winding, and larger rigs over 40 feet may have a bit of trouble getting in. But most folks will be just fine. The red rock of the canyon is gorgeous and changes color throughout the day and as the sun sets. Hiking and fishing are excellent here, and the canyon walls are never far away. There is also a large swimming pool for hot summer days. A handful of sites here have full hookups, and over forty of them have water and electric. There are also twenty-six primitive sites that are perfect for tent campers. The park also has an interesting history. During the 1849 California Gold Rush, the road became a famous stop for weary travelers looking for fresh water and a safe place to let their cattle graze before plunging further west on their quixotic quest for riches.

ALSO GREAT

Route 66 RV Park

▷ Elk City, Oklahoma

▷ elkcityrvpark.com

▷ RV Sites

Located right off historic Route 66 and within walking distance of the Historic Route 66 Museum, this park makes for a sweet little stop for weary travelers of the Mother Road. The staff and ownership are as sweet as a slice of cherry pie from a Route 66 diner—count on them welcoming you with open arms and guiding you right to your site. This park is clean and simple, but its location makes it great. Stock up on groceries and supplies for the rest of your trip right across the street from the park.

Yogi Bear's Jellystone Park Camp-Resort at Lake Eufaula

▷ Eufaula, Oklahoma

▷ jellystoneok.com

▷ RV Sites, Cabins and Cottages

For off-the-hook family camping fun in eastern Oklahoma, look no further than Yogi Bear's Jellystone Park at Lake Eufaula. The RV sites and cabins all have views of the lake, and the sandy beach is just steps away from your site. The dominating features at this Jellystone are the gigantic inflatable obstacle course, slides, and water trampoline that are located right off the beach. Your kids will play here for hours, and we think you will want to get in on the action too!

Twin Fountains RV Resort

▷ Oklahoma City, Oklahoma

▷ twinfountainsrvresort.com

▷ RV Sites

This modern and luxurious RV resort is a terrific base camp for exploring Oklahoma City. It even offers a free limo shuttle for destinations within 3 miles of the resort—and there are plenty of good ones, like the Oklahoma City Zoo, The National Cowboy & Western Heritage Museum, and the Tinseltown Theatre. The clubhouse here has a fireplace and comfortable couches and recliners, and the on-site restaurant, The Semper Fi Bar & Grill, has excellent burgers and wings.

--------- **Favorite Hikes in Featured State Parks** ---------

Beavers Bend State Park

▷ Lookout Mountain Loop: A shady and moderate 2.9-mile loop trail.

▷ Lakeview Lodge Trail: A 3.5-mile loop trail with some scenic views of the lake.

Natural Falls State Park

▷ Dripping Springs Trail: A 1-mile loop that brings you to a 77-foot waterfall.

▷ Bear Trail: This 0.1-mile trail is not really about hiking, it's about getting to the scenic waterfalls and splashing in the water.

Red Rock Canyon Adventure Park

▷ Red Rock Canyon Rim Trail: A 3.9-mile loop trail with beautiful views of the red canyon walls.

▷ Rough Horsetail Nature Trail: A short but fun 0.6-mile loop trail that offers a great opportunity for families to scramble over the red rocks.

Route 66 Highlights in Oklahoma

Oklahoma is a favorite state for Route 66 enthusiasts. Four hundred miles of the Mother Road pass through here, and it has the longest drivable stretch of any Route 66 state. Here are some of the most iconic attractions to check when visiting.

Blue Whale of Catoosa

2600 Rte 66, Catoosa, OK 74015

This is one of the most iconic roadside attractions on all of Route 66. Although there's nothing really to *do* here, the picture is worth the stop.

Will Rogers Memorial Museum

1720 West Will Rogers Boulevard, Claremore, OK 74017

Will Rogers is as iconic as Route 66, and this museum has displays and exhibits that explore the life of America's "philosopher cowboy."

Golden Driller

Tulsa Expo Center, 4145 E 21st Street, Tulsa, OK 74114

It's hard to get a good picture of this 76-foot statue that hearkens back to when Oklahoma considered itself the "oil capital of the world," but it's worth the effort.

Pops

660 OK-66, Arcadia, OK 73007

How can you not stop at a place that has 700 types of soda and a 66-foot-tall neon soda bottle out front? Visit at night to watch the LED lights change color.

Round Barn

107 OK-66, Arcadia, OK 73007

The Round Barn was bought and restored by the Oklahoma Historical Society and houses a collection of Route 66 memorabilia and, of course, a gift shop.

South Carolina

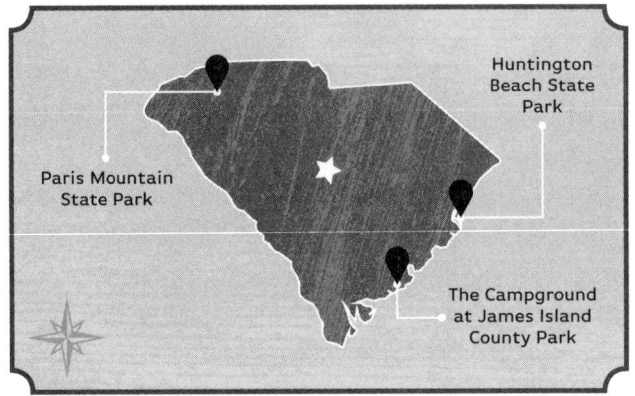

We, like so many people, had our first South Carolina camping experience in Myrtle Beach. We ended up returning again and again, discovering that while we truly did love a good spring or fall vacation along the strip, there were plenty of other amazing locations in the Palmetto State. We started heading a bit farther south to Charleston, which has some of the best urban camping options in the whole country (we can't ever decide between James Island County Park and the Mount Pleasant KOA). After many trips to the Low Country, we realized that South Carolina had even more to offer up to the north, where visitors will find the charming city of Greenville and the beautiful Blue Ridge Mountains.

There are plenty of amazing RV resorts peppered throughout the state, but the real South Carolina claim to fame is the well-funded state park system, with an abundance of campgrounds, lodges, and cabins, plus an easily navigable booking system. Many of the parks were built by the Civilian Conservation Corps (CCC) more than eighty years ago, and the South Carolina State Park system prides itself on continually updating and modernizing the amenities, while keeping the spirit of outdoor experiences intact.

TOP PICKS

The Campground at James Island County Park

⊳ Charleston, South Carolina

⊳ ccprc.com

⊳ RV and Tent Sites, Cottages

The campground at James Island County Park may be the best county-run campground in America. We wish we had campgrounds like this back in New Jersey, but sadly, we don't. The RV sites at James Island are large, private, attractive, and have full hookups at county park prices. This is an absolutely lovely place to take a bike ride or an evening stroll before settling in around the campfire. The campground is nestled into a quiet section of this vast and entertaining park where getting bored is never an option. Head to the rock climbing wall in the morning and then cool off in the Splash Zone Waterpark in the afternoon. The playground is gigantic and will keep littles occupied for hours. Traveling with a pup? Head to the gigantic doggy park and let them run off leash and meet some new friends. If you don't feel like driving, take the round-trip shuttle service into one of America's hippest and most historic cities—and make sure you bring an appetite. Charleston is our favorite food city in the South, and we are willing to bet it will become yours too.

Huntington Beach State Park

⊳ Murrells Inlet, South Carolina

⊳ southcarolinaparks.com

⊳ RV and Tent Sites

Trying to choose a favorite campground in the Myrtle Beach area is like trying to choose a favorite child. Your answer will change on a daily basis depending on your mood and how everyone is behaving. Huntington Beach State Park earns top spot for us because it is located directly on the beach and because it is quieter and (a little bit) prettier than Myrtle Beach State Park. We also love the sites themselves—some are shaded and private and many have full hookups. There are also a handful of spots for rigs longer than 35 feet. The park itself is incredibly well run and is filled with things to do and see. Check out birds and alligators along the causeway and take a self-guided audio tour of Atalaya—a national historic landmark that will sweep you into its storied past after taking just one step inside. You can also take a tour with a naturalist or enjoy a hike with a ranger who will teach you about the wildlife and the coastal landscape. But most importantly, you can spend your days swimming in the deep blue waters of the Atlantic and your nights enjoying campfires under the stars with the sound of breaking waves in the near distance.

Paris Mountain State Park

▷ Greenville, South Carolina

▷ southcarolinaparks.com

▷ RV and Tent Sites, Primitive Cabins, Group Lodging

The city of Greenville in northwestern South Carolina is currently hipper than Elvis singing "Suspicious Minds" in Vegas in 1968. Thankfully, there is a beautiful state park campground less than twenty minutes away from its downtown. The roads into the campground are narrow and twisty, so larger RVs should take caution or consider the Traveler's Rest KOA nearby. But tent campers, cabin dwellers, and small RV owners will delight in the natural beauty of this park and the affordability of its campground. Paris Mountain has over 15 miles of hiking and biking trails, and swimming and fishing are also options for those who love the great outdoors. The CCC-built Park Center is also worth a visit, as are the ranger-led programs. Or just use this lovely campground as a base camp for exploring the foodie scene in downtown Greenville. Farm-to-table options are abundant and so are craft roasters and breweries. Gorgeous state park camping right outside of a hip urban location? Sign me up again and again!

ALSO GREAT

Mount Pleasant/Charleston KOA Holiday

- ▷ Mount Pleasant, South Carolina
- ▷ koa.com
- ▷ RV and Tent Sites, Camping Cabins, Deluxe Cabins

This delightful KOA is located on the privately owned 377-acre Oakland Plantation, whose history predates the Civil War. We loved kayaking on the lake and spotting alligators resting in the sun along the shore. Our boys also spent hours swimming in the pool and playing basketball while we were able to relax and read at our deluxe patio site. Proximity to downtown Charleston is very good, and there is also excellent food nearby.

Myrtle Beach State Park

- ▷ Myrtle Beach, South Carolina
- ▷ southcarolinaparks.com
- ▷ RV and Tent Sites, Cabins

We spend our winters in New Jersey dreaming of places like Myrtle Beach State Park, where spring starts early and summer ends late. The smell of fragrant oak, myrtle, poplar, and magnolia trees fills the air here, and the sound of gently crashing waves is never far away. The sites here are almost all shady and private, providing a welcome respite from the hustle and bustle of downtown, which is only a few miles away. A variety of charming cabins are also available—just steps away from the beach.

Hunting Island State Park

▷ Hunting Island, South Carolina

▷ southcarolinaparks.com

▷ RV and Tent Sites, Cabin Rental

When it comes to ravishingly beautiful camping right on the beach, South Carolina wins the contest, at least on the East Coast. Hunting Island State Park has over 5 miles of sandy beaches that will seduce you into coming back again and again. The campground here is simple and straightforward, featuring nice big sites with water and electric, many with shade. And they're all close to the beach. We have always loved beach camping the best. How about you?

Spotlight on Myrtle Beach Campgrounds and RV Resorts

Myrtle Beach is one of our country's most popular RV destinations, and people often have trouble picking a campground because there are just too many to choose from. Here's a quick guide to the best options (in addition to Myrtle Beach State Park and Huntington Beach State Park featured previously), whether you are looking for a pirate-themed resort or a rustic state park.

Myrtle Beach KOA
The Myrtle Beach KOA is a wooded retreat a few blocks inland from the beach. A beach shuttle runs during the day. The campground is located just a short walk to the boardwalk, mini golf, zip-lining, and the Skywheel. This KOA has a pool, splash pad, second heated pool, playground, jump pad, golf cart rentals, camp store, game room, and snack stand.

Ocean Lakes Family Campground
This beachfront campground is just south of the Myrtle Beach board-walk and is a quick drive to many popular activities. There is a 2-acre family fun center with pools, waterslides, sun deck, cafe, lazy river, and splash zone. It's more of a camping city than a campground. With 859 campsites and 2,566 annual lease sites, it's the largest campground on the East Coast and one of the largest in the country. If you want a beach vacation at a campground with every possible on-site amenity, this is your spot.

Pirateland Family Camping Resort
Pirateland is located directly south of Myrtle Beach State Park, so you can enjoy the amenities of a resort, plus the activities and natural beauty at the State Park. The campground has a themed waterpark, indoor pool, eighteen-hole mini golf, paddle boat and kayak rentals, playgrounds, and

recreation room. Pirateland is family resort camping with an emphasis on kid-friendly fun.

10 Things to Do in Charleston

We love urban camping, and we love urban camping in Charleston most of all. It is truly one of our favorite family vacation destinations in the country, and here are some our favorite things to do there:

Palmetto Carriage Works Tours

There are quite a few options for carriage tours in Charleston, but this one is our favorite. The tour guides are fun and informative. You can tour the barn and visit the animals, plus the company is transparent about the welfare of its horses.

Charleston Pirate Tours

Learning about the history of pirates in Charleston from a costumed pirate with a parrot on the shoulder? Yes, please. Tour guides Sabrina and Eric will take you through the oldest parts of the city and make the golden age of piracy come alive. This two-hour walking tour starts at the Powder Magazine Museum and includes a visit to the Old Exchange Building and Provost Dungeon.

Old Exchange Building and Provost Dungeon

This is one of the most historically important buildings in Charleston, so even if you don't do the Pirate Tour, put it on your agenda. There are two floors of exhibits, plus a twenty-five-minute guided tour of the Provost Dungeon, which was used as a British military prison during the Revolutionary War. You can also see the only publicly viewable part of the original city wall in the dungeon.

Charleston City Market

The artisans and entrepreneurs of the Charleston area have some of their best wares on display here. Yes, there is a fair share of touristy trinkets. But there is also a variety of beautiful sweetgrass baskets, fresh roasted coffee, and other local delights.

Fort Moultrie

This fort was the first on Sullivan Island and had a storied military history from the Revolutionary War through the Civil War and beyond. It has been restored to display artifacts from the major periods of American history. Visit Fort Moultrie before you head out to Fort Sumter.

Fort Sumter

The first shots of the Civil War were fired here, and you can't visit Charleston without taking the ferry boat out to Fort Sumter. Book the first ferry boat of the day, and you'll get to participate in the flag raising ceremony. Also make time to explore the exhibits at the national monument.

USS *Yorktown*

Located at the Patriot's Point Naval and Maritime Museum in Mount Pleasant, the USS *Yorktown* was the tenth U.S. Naval Aircraft Carrier and served in WWII and Vietnam before being decommissioned in 1970. There are multiple self-guided walking tours available, and you can get audio sets for an additional fee. Tours #1 and #3 are a great combination. Tour #1 will lead you through the living quarters of the ship, while Tour #3 will take you up to the flight deck and through all the control rooms and officer quarters.

Magnolia Plantation and Gardens

There are so many plantation tours available in the Charleston area, but the Magnolia Plantation has two things that stand out: the trolley tour and the award-winning gardens. The dark stain of slavery can easily be overlooked on a visit to some of the area plantations, but this one does a good job of acknowledging all aspects of its history. Magnolia Plantation has a Slavery to Freedom Tour, which focuses on the slave dwellings, the history of the Gullah, and their contributions to Low Country culture.

Charleston RiverDogs Minor League Baseball Game

Minor league games are a fantastic way to soak in local flavor, and the RiverDogs is a particularly great option. The food choices include chicken and waffles served in a dog bowl and macaroni and cheese with pulled pork and okra. Bellyitcher Ale is the signature ballpark beer specially made by the local Rusty Bull Brewing Company.

Bulls Island with Coastal Expeditions

Bulls Island is an uninhabited island 3 miles off the coast of South Carolina that is part of the Cape Romain National Wildlife Refuge. You'll have to take your own boat to get there, or you can hop on the Coastal Expeditions ferry, which offers half- or full-day trips to the island. It's a 1.5-mile hike from the dock to the beach, so wear appropriate clothes, a hat, sunscreen, and bug spray. Bring plenty of water and snacks. Then have an absolutely magical day on your almost-private island beach.

• Tennessee •

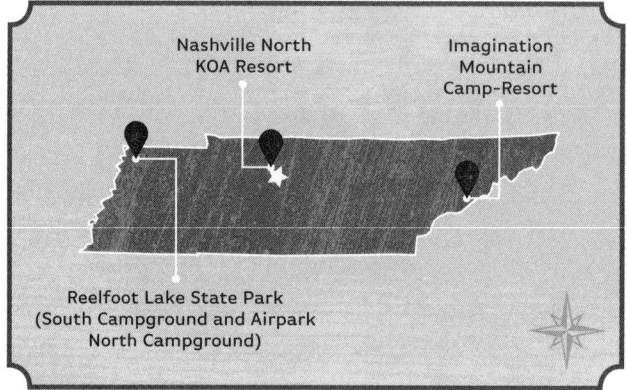

Nashville North KOA Resort

Imagination Mountain Camp-Resort

Reelfoot Lake State Park (South Campground and Airpark North Campground)

Many folks have their first Tennessee camping experience by visiting Great Smoky Mountains National Park. The Smokies is the most visited NPS site in the country, welcoming over twelve million guests every year. Luckily, there is a wide selection of wonderful campgrounds on the Tennessee side of the park, ranging from rustic retreats to well-appointed resorts.

However, there are many other camping destinations worth a visit in the Volunteer State. We love exploring urban destinations with our RV, and there are a handful of great camping options that are only a quick Uber ride away from downtown Nashville. In fact, some of these campgrounds are just a few miles from the legendary Grand Ole Opry. If you are on an urban camping kick, there's also Memphis to explore. For a more mellow city adventure, check out Chattanooga.

In addition to the popular national park and splashy cities, Tennessee is full of many more opportunities for magical camping getaways. Residents adore Land between the Lakes National Recreation Area, and many return year after year to stay at one of its many campgrounds and enjoy the

170,000-acre recreational area. Or check out Defeated Creek Park, where you'll find a 12,000-acre lake and over 381 miles of shoreline.

BEST IN STATE

Imagination Mountain Camp-Resort

▷   Cosby, Tennessee

▷   imaginationmountaincamping.com

▷   Cottages, Cabins, Yurts, RV Rentals, RV and Tent Sites

Choosing a "top pick" on the Tennessee side of Great Smoky Mountains National Park is a difficult task—so just consider Imagination Mountain a starting point and take a look at the sidebar on page 143 for other equally awesome options. But man oh man did we love Imagination Mountain. The family that runs the campground is kind and helpful, and the streamside setting is absolutely magical. Our boys played in the stream behind our site for hours each day and spent more time in its crystal-clear water than they did in the campground's excellent heated saltwater pool. Max, Theo, and Wes also spent an inordinate amount of time in the rustic camp store, which has a beautiful ice cream parlor with shakes and hand-dipped cones and cups. RV and tent sites are beautiful, but the sites are a bit tight to get into for larger rigs. The cabins and yurts also make a great option for those who want a family-friendly glamping experience for a reasonable price. Don't worry if you get a rainy day—the upstairs game room is the best we have ever seen at an American campground.

---------------------- **Before you go...** ----------------------

▷   **Listen:** *Dolly Parton's America*, a podcast series hosted by Jad Abumrad and produced by WNYC Studios.

Nashville North KOA Resort

▷ Goodlettsville, Tennessee

▷ koa.com

▷ RV and Tent Sites, Camping Cabins, Deluxe Cabins

Located just fifteen minutes from downtown Nashville and less than ten minutes from the Grand Ole Opry, this KOA is our top pick for a visit to Music City. The campground even offers its own free shuttle service to downtown—which makes it perfect for those campers who want to see Nashville and not stress out about traffic and parking. On Thursday nights (May through September) it also brings the music and BBQ right to the campground with live performances and food trucks. The kids can play ladder ball or hit up the playground while you relax and enjoy good food and good tunes. But if the Opry is in session while you are visiting, you *must* get tickets and go. We saw Darius Rucker, Wynonna Judd, and Little Big Town—all in one night! The campground is clean and well kept, and the RV sites and cabins are more than adequate. There is road noise nearby, so we would not recommend tent camping here. Please promise us you'll stop by Hattie B's Hot Chicken while you are in town. We are frequent flyers whenever we visit Nashville.

Reelfoot Lake State Park (South Campground and Airpark North Campground)

▷ Tiptonville, Tennessee

▷ tnstateparks.com

▷ Cabins, RV and Tent Sites

We can thank a series of violent earthquakes way back in 1811 and 1812 for backing up the Mississippi River and creating the stunning landscape of 18,000-acre Reelfoot Lake, which the state of Tennessee likes to call a "flooded forest." This is a boating and birdwatching heaven, so bring your canoe or kayak and a set of binoculars. The South Campground offers eighty-six paved RV and tent sites that all have electric and water hookups. The camp store here is tiny, so bring all the supplies you need for enjoying the park. Fishermen and women will love the fish cleaning house for preparing the day's catch. Glampers will rejoice to find seven gorgeous cabins with fully modern conveniences right on the shore of the lake. Cabins have either two or three bedrooms with full kitchens and can sleep six to ten people. Airport North Campground is much smaller but also has excellent sites in a lovely shaded setting. Join a naturalist for a Deep Swamp Canoe Tour or Eagle Tour and revel in the natural beauty of one America's most beautiful state parks.

ALSO GREAT

Under Canvas Great Smoky Mountains

▷ Pigeon Forge, Tennessee

▷ undercanvas.com

▷ Glamping Tents

The luxurious glamping tents at Under Canvas GSM form a little storybook village where guests can breathe in fresh mountain air and enjoy daily housekeeping and organic soaps. Packages include an adventure with concierge service. Whether you choose fly fishing, zip-lining, or a Jeep safari, this camp will send you on your way with a boxed lunch and have dinner waiting when you get back to your tent.

Piney Campground at Land between the Lakes

▷ Dover, Tennessee

▷ landbetweenthelakes.us

▷ Cabins, RV and Tent Sites

The Land between the Lakes is a 170,000-acre natural wonderland (and National Recreational Area) situated between Kentucky Lake on the west and Lake Barkley on the east. Piney Campground serves as a great base camp for exploring this region and there is plenty to do right at the campground as well, including swimming, fishing, and archery.

-------------- **The Firefly Event Lottery** --------------

Synchronous fireflies live in the Smokies and are only one of a handful of species known to synchronize their flashing patterns. This natural phenomenon occurs for a few weeks out of the year from late May to early June. In order to manage the crowds that descend on the park for this popular event, there is a parking ticket lottery that visitors must enter. The lottery opens (and closes) every year in April, and can be found at the recreation.gov website.

Graceland RV Park & Campground

▷ Memphis, Tennessee

▷ graceland.com

▷ RV and Tent Sites, Camping Cabins

This campground is simple, clean, and comfortable—and its location in Memphis, on Elvis Presley Boulevard, is spectacular. Graceland is right across the street, but we think it should be schnazzed up and made worthy of the King. Suspicious minds might worry about the neighborhood around the park, but they shouldn't. The campground boasts twenty-four-hour security.

More Camping Options Near Great Smoky Mountains National Park

Great Smoky Mountains National Park is the most visited NPS site in the country and one of the most popular places to camp. It's comparable to Myrtle Beach in that first-time visitors are often overwhelmed by the number of campgrounds. Here are some more favorites, in addition to our featured picks:

Gatlinburg

Gatlinburg is arguably the most popular tourist hub in the Smokies. It's known as the gateway to GSMNP, and the main visitor's center, Sugarlands Visitor Center, is just minutes from downtown. Some of the most famous hikes and drives are near the main drag as well, like the Roaring Fork Motor Nature Trail and Chimneys Picnic Area.

Some folks love to be right in the middle of the action, and others will cringe at the seemingly endless T-shirt and fudge shops. If you want a quiet getaway, Gatlinburg may not be your best option in the Smokies. However, if you love to mix your hikes with amusement park rides and aquarium visits, check out these campgrounds.

▷ **Greenbrier Campground:** The Little Pigeon River runs around the Greenbrier Campground, offering guests a swimming hole, private beach, and on-site trout fishing. There are full hook-up sites, some with water access and some wooded options, plus tent sites and cabins. Campers rave about the pet-friendly policies and cleanliness. Greenbrier offers plenty of recreation for families, including volleyball, ga-ga ball, badminton, bocce ball, and corn hole. The campground is less than a half mile from the Greenbrier entrance to GSMNP.

▷ **Anchor Down:** Located about forty-five minutes north of Gatlinburg, this RV resort opened just a few years ago, and the word about it spread quickly. The campground is on the shores of Douglas Lake, and the sites are legendarily Instagrammable. Many have large, custom stone fireplaces with water and mountain views. Anchor Down also has all the resort amenities you could want, including a pool and lake beach with swimming and inflatables. There are many options for watercraft rentals.

Pigeon Forge

People seem to either love or hate staying in the Pigeon Forge area of the Great Smoky Mountains. If you want to be surrounded by nonstop action, this is the place for you. Parents of teens particularly like the fact that their older kids can use the trolley and get around independently. And Dollywood. Need we say more?

▷ **Pigeon Forge KOA:** This family-owned KOA opened in 1966 and is practically legendary in the area. The campground is right off the main drag, and a trolley will take you into town and even to Dollywood, right up the road. It has all the amenities you would expect in a KOA—pool, hot tub, snack bar, dog park. Plus it has some extras like a waterslide, outdoor cinema, and fun train. Some visitors complain about the tight sites and general hustle and bustle, but this is just not a campground for anyone looking for peace and quiet. Come here if you want to be in the heart of the action.

▷ **Riveredge RV Park & Log Cabin Rentals:** Riveredge RV Park & Log Cabin Rentals has beautifully manicured sites and landscaping just 1.5 miles from Dollywood. The RV sites are all full hookups with fire rings, cooking grates, and picnic tables. There's a pool, kiddie pool, hot tub, and splash pad to enjoy after a day of sightseeing. Even the people who love this campground note the smaller site size. Staying here is about location, location, location, combined with an impeccably clean campground.

▷ **River Plantation RV Resort:** River Plantation RV Resort is a bit farther north of the downtown Pigeon Forge area, more toward Sevierville.
There are a variety of site options, from pull-throughs to riverfront
back-ins. Amenities include two pools, a lazy river, splash pad, playground, basketball court, and fitness center. You'll also find lots of outdoor games like corn hole, ga-ga ball, and pickleball.

Townsend

Townsend is located in an area often referred to as "the quiet side of the
Smokies." People who loathe the touristy commercialism of Gatlinburg and
Pigeon Forge often stay here when visiting Great Smoky Mountain National
Park. Don't let the nickname fool you. Even though Townsend is quiet, there
is a ton to see and do in the area. Plus you are right near the Cades Cove
entrance to the park, a favorite area for many visitors.

▷ **Townsend KOA:** This is one of the most loved and recommended campgrounds in the Smokies, probably because it combines the best features of many different places. It's located right on the river and offers
on-site tubing and fishing. Plus, it has the amenities KOAs are known
for such as a pool, playground, and scheduled activities. The managers
create a warm and cozy family-friendly atmosphere, and people return
year after year.

▷ **Little Arrow Outdoor Resort:** The Little Arrow Outdoor Resort changed
owners in recent years and is developing that hipster glamping vibe
that is so popular right now. Framed as a "wilderness retreat," it offers
RV sites, tiny homes, cabins, tents, and even an Airstream rental. There
is a swimming pool, river access, and organized activities. Clean bathhouses get rave reviews from visitors.

Inside the Park: Great Smoky Mountain National Park Campgrounds

You can camp within the boundaries of Great Smoky Mountain National Park, but you have to realize two things. First, these campsites are highly competitive. Second, you'll have to be up for dry camping, since there are no hookups offered in the park.

▷ **Elkmont:** This beautiful campground is a family favorite on account of the riverfront sites. The sites are spacious with a picnic table and fire ring. The bathhouses have flush toilets, but no showers.

▷ **Cades Cove Campground:** While Elkmont is the perfect place to have the Smokies mountain river experience, Cades Cove Campground puts you in the middle of the most iconic wildlife and scenic loop. The campground has a nice camp store with supplies, souvenirs, and ice cream. You can also rent bikes on-site.

Texas

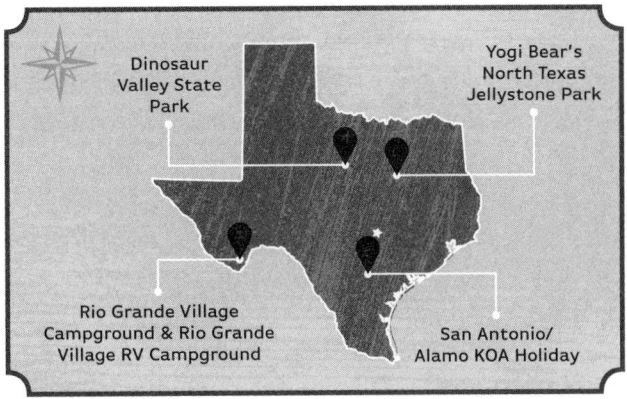

Dinosaur Valley State Park

Yogi Bear's North Texas Jellystone Park

Rio Grande Village Campground & Rio Grande Village RV Campground

San Antonio/ Alamo KOA Holiday

Everything is bigger in Texas, including the wide range of camping options. Good thing, because residents often complain that it takes them too long to drive out of state to go camping anywhere else. Starting north in the panhandle, you'll find lots of fun campgrounds along iconic Route 66. Places like Big Texan RV Ranch and Oasis RV Resort are popular favorites in Amarillo, where you may want to stop for the 72-ounce steak challenge at the Big Texan Steak Ranch and Brewery.

If you are looking for quick getaways or longer family vacations outside of cities like Dallas, Austin, and San Antonio, you have your pick of amazing private and public campgrounds. We stayed at the largest campground we've ever visited—North Texas Jellystone—outside of Dallas, which had everything from a water park to paintball to an on-site escape room. We also found a dizzying number of wonderful campground options in nearby Hill Country. Search for dinosaur tracks while camping at Dinosaur Valley State Park, or soak in a hot tub with a glass of wine at one of the RV resorts in Fredericksburg.

The Gulf Coast is another popular Texas camping destination, and you'll find plenty of places where you can actually camp right on the beach. Many of the beachfront sites offer primitive camping, but if you want electric hookups, popular spots like Galveston Island State Park and Mustang Island State Park have you covered.

And if you want to *really* get away from it all, there is no better camping destination than Big Bend National Park which the NPS website describes as "splendid isolation." It has been designated as an International Dark Sky Park, so if sleeping under the stars is your camping jam, put this place on your bucket list.

BEST IN STATE

Dinosaur Valley State Park

- ▷ Glen Rose, Texas
- ▷ tpwd.texas.gov
- ▷ RV and Tent Sites

Our trip to Texas was filled with delightful surprises, and our visit to Dinosaur Valley State Park was certainly one of them. Where else can you search for dinosaur footprints just steps away from your campsite? The Paluxy River winds its way through this park and offers up several perfect swimming holes for cooling off on a hot Texas day. The park is also filled with well-marked hiking and biking trails for those who love nonstop outdoor adventure. The campground at DVSP is small, and it can be difficult to nab a site—but it is well worth the effort. Sites are shady and private, and the facilities are clean and well maintained. Big rigs might take caution here, as some of the turns are tight and there are low-hanging trees. Tent campers and small RV owners love it, though—and not just because sites have electric hookups so you can run the air conditioning in the summer. Downtown Glen Rose is nearby and has a handful of really good restaurants and tons of Texas charm.

Rio Grande Village Campground & Rio Grande Village RV Campground

▷ Big Bend National Park, Texas

▷ nps.gov

▷ RV and Tent Sites

The Rio Grande Village Campground is a concessionaire-managed campground (run by a private company) within Big Bend National Park that is situated on the banks of the Rio Grande. Mexico's Sierra del Carmen Mountains can be viewed to the east and are spectacular at sunset. The campground has one hundred sites, and some can handle RVs up to 40 feet. There are no hookups at the sites, but the Rio Grande Village Store has supplies and is right outside of the campground. The Rio Grande Village Nature Trail starts in the campground next to site #18 and ends at a gorgeous bluff overlooking the Rio Grande. The Rio Grande Village RV Campground is located directly across from its big brother and offers twenty-four RV sites with full hookups. Big Bend National Park is massive and will require several days to explore in any kind of meaningful way. The park has scenic drives and hiking galore— and some of the darkest night skies in the country.

San Antonio/Alamo KOA Holiday

▷ San Antonio, Texas

▷ koa.com

▷ RV and Tent Sites, Camping Cabins, Deluxe Cabins

We are huge fans of urban camping and love campgrounds that put us close to the center of the action in our favorite cities. This KOA is only ten minutes from San Antonio, and the city bus (which is affordable and easy to use) stops right in front of its entrance. San Antonio is a lovely city, and this is a lovely campground that offers much more than proximity to the Alamo, the River Walk, and all points downtown. The pool area is nicely landscaped and provides a relaxing place to unwind after a long day of exploring the city. The fishing pier and playground areas are also relatively new and picture-perfect. Bike rentals are available for tooling around the campground or exploring the Salado Creek Nature Trail located on the west side of the property. Before you head for a bike ride along the creek, consider having breakfast at Fred's Fix'ins cafe. The Kampers breakfast is tasty, and the coffee is complimentary.

Yogi Bear's North Texas Jellystone Park

▷ Burleson, Texas

▷ northtexasjellystone.com

▷ RV Rentals, Cabins, Pirate Ship Suites, Bunkhouse Apartments, RV and Tent Sites

Our kids have not stopped talking about the North Texas Jellystone Park since we visited three years ago. It's gigantic (120 acres) and packed with all kinds of crazy amenities that will keep your kids busy from sunup to sundown. Little kids love the train rides and Hey, Hey, Hey Rides, and older kids love the laser tag and paintball. Pirate's Cove Water Park is located right next door, and registered guests at the campground receive discounted admission. You can walk directly over to the waterpark or ride a golf cart over and park it there. We do recommend renting a golf cart here if your budget allows, as the activities are spread far and wide. A wide variety of lodging options are available here, making this a great place to stay if you are new to the world of camping and want to give it a try without purchasing an RV or tent of your own. Downtown Burleson is right up the road and has cute restaurants and shopping.

---------------- **Remember the Alamo** ----------------

Let's rephrase that: Remember to take a guided tour when you visit the Alamo. This popular historical site is basically a bunch of plaques on crumbling stone walls, unless you join in on one of the fantastic guided tours that bring the Battle of the Alamo and the Texas Revolution to life. Then head to the River Walk for tacos.

---------------------- **Don't Miss It** ----------------------

You'll only find one gas station recommended in this book, and that's Buc-ee's. You haven't really experienced Texas until you've sampled the beef jerky, eaten the freshly prepared barbecue, and visited the legendarily clean restrooms at this gas station and travel center chain. Make sure you grab a bag of Beaver Nuggets for the road.

ALSO GREAT

Galveston Island State Park

▷ Galveston, Texas

▷ tpwd.texas.gov

▷ RV and Tent Sites, Lodges

Galveston Island State Park is just an hour away from Houston, but it feels remote and isolated. The camping options here are simple and amenities are few, but the beach and bay are just steps away from the campsites and the park has excellent biking, kayaking, and fishing options around every corner. Those who love sandy beaches will want to camp on the newly renovated ocean side, but those who love birding and fishing will probably like the bay side better.

Collective Hill Country

▷ Wimberley, Texas

▷ collectiveretreats.com

▷ Glamping Tents

Texas Hill Country, with its wineries, wildflowers, and antique shops, is the perfect place for the luxurious glamping experience that Collective Hill Country offers. The tents feature 1,500-thread-count linens and wood-burning stoves for heat on those chilly nights. Food is farm to table and the service is five stars. The staff will guide you to the best local adventures in Hill Country and make sure that everything in your tent is perfect for a relaxing and unforgettable getaway. As for the price? If you have to ask...

Mustang Island State Park

▷   Corpus Christi, Texas

▷   tpwd.texas.gov

▷   RV and Tent Sites

Birdwatchers and beach lovers delight at the miles of wide open beaches in and around Mustang Island State Park. Fishing and boating opportunities are also ample in both the Gulf of Mexico and the calmer waters of Corpus Christi Bay. The section of the campground with water and electric sites isn't much more than a parking lot, but tent camping sites are directly on the beach. Both RV and tent campers love falling asleep to the sounds of the surf crashing on the shore.

Drive It: Ross Maxwell Scenic Drive in Big Bend National Park

Big Bend National Park is one of the largest and least visited national parks in the country, with fewer than 500,000 visitors per year. The National Park Service claims that Big Bend has less light pollution than any other park unit in the lower forty-eight. Find the Sotol Vista Overlook off this scenic drive at sunset for amazing views of Santa Elena Canyon and then watch the night sky come to life.

Gulf Coast State Park Campgrounds

Sea Rim State Park

▷ 15 campsites with electricity, $20 nightly

▷ 75 primitive campsites, $10 nightly

Galveston Island State Park

▷ 20 campsites with electricity, $20 nightly

▷ 10 campsites with water, $15 nightly

Goose Island State Park

▷ 44 bayfront campsites with electricity, $22 nightly

▷ 57 wooded campsites with electricity, $18 nightly

▷ 25 tent sites with water, $10 nightly

Mustang Island State Park

▷ 48 campsites with electricity, $20 nightly

▷ 50 primitive campsites, $10 nightly

Lake Corpus Christi State Park

▷ 26 full hook-up campsites, $25 nightly

▷ 23 campsites with electricity, $20 nightly

▷ 59 campsites with water, $10 nightly

A Hill Country Getaway: Fredericksburg, Texas

Fredericksburg is a small town with big personality. Founded in the mid-1800s by German settlers, it offers a unique combination of German and Texan cultures. Add in wineries, craft breweries, and beautiful scenery, and you have yourself a fabulous vacation destination.

Fredericksburg is just about 80 miles east of Austin and 70 miles north of San Antonio, making it a popular weekend destination for residents from those cities, and that means you have to plan your campground reservations well in advance.

Best Time to Visit

Peak tourist season is from March through May when wildflowers bloom across the region. May is also peach season, and many visitors come for the Stonewall Peach JAMboree and Rodeo. Visit in October to experience Oktoberfest in this historically German town.

Outdoor Experiences

- Enchanted Rock State Natural Area
- Old Tunnel State Park
- Pedernales Falls State Park

Historical Attractions

- Lyndon B. Johnson State Park and Historical Site
- National Museum of the Pacific War
- Pioneer Museum
- Texas Ranger Heritage Center

Where to Eat

- Auslander German Bavarian Cuisine
- Otto's German Bistro
- Old German Bakery and Restaurant
- Opa's Smoked Meats

Where to Drink

- Pontotoc Vineyards
- Messina Hof Winery and Resort
- Fredericksburg Brewing Company
- Altstadt Brewery

Route 66: Texas

There's only about 180 miles of Route 66 in Texas, but some of the most iconic stops on the Mother Road are in this state.

▷ U-Drop Inn, Shamrock

▷ The Leaning Tower of Texas, Groom

▷ Cadillac Ranch, Amarillo

▷ Midpoint Café, Adrian

Virginia

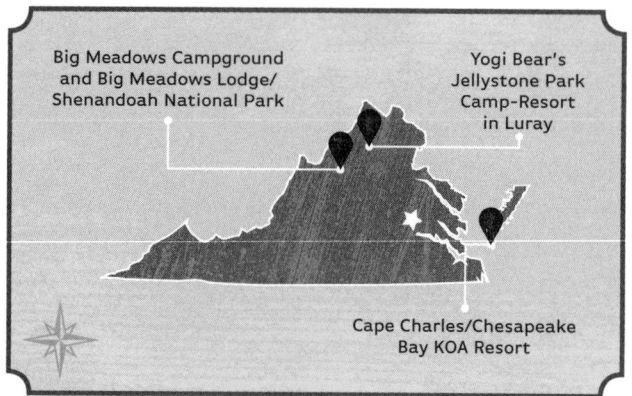

Big Meadows Campground and Big Meadows Lodge/ Shenandoah National Park

Yogi Bear's Jellystone Park Camp-Resort in Luray

Cape Charles/Chesapeake Bay KOA Resort

There are so many reasons to camp in Virginia, especially considering it is home to the oldest national park in the eastern part of the United States. Shenandoah National Park was established in 1935 and provides a much-needed natural retreat from the crowd-choked city of Washington, DC, just 75 miles away. There are so many wonderful camping opportunities in and around the park, and we are known to occasionally leave behind our tent and RV for the experience of spending a weekend at one of the beautiful lodges. Farther south, the Blue Ridge Parkway picks up where Skyline Drive leaves off and will take you to iconic locations like the Mabry Mill and the Blue Ridge Music Center.

In the mood for some sand and sun? Most people think of the popular Virginia Beach as the ultimate shore vacation spot in Virginia, but we prefer a quieter part of the coast just a bit north over the Chesapeake Bay Bridge and Tunnels. Cape Charles and the surrounding Chesapeake Bay area is just the perfect spot for our family to return again and again to relax and unwind. There are great private and state park camping options, depending on the types of amenities and environment you prefer.

BEST IN STATE

Yogi Bear's Jellystone Park Camp-Resort in Luray

▷ Luray, Virginia

▷ campluray.com

▷ Deluxe and Camping Cabins, Tent and RV Sites

We think that Jellystone Luray is one of the best family campgrounds in the country. The pools and waterslides are a blast, and most of the campground has stunning views of the Blue Ridge Mountains. It is rare to find a full-fledged resort campground located just minutes from the gates of a national park. Jellystone Luray is that rare campground. You can spend mornings hiking in Shenandoah National Park and afternoons relaxing at the pool or bounce pillow with your kids. Hey Hey Rides and photo ops with Yogi and Friends will charm younger campers, while laser tag and full-sized sports facilities will keep teenagers busy for hours at a time. Spend your evenings relaxing under the stars and enjoying a crackling campfire or watching a movie together in the campground's delightful outdoor theater. Food options at the campground are better than average, and mini golf is free.

Big Meadows Campground and Big Meadows Lodge/ Shenandoah National Park

▷ Stanley, Virginia

▷ nps.gov

▷ goshenandoah.com/lodging/big-meadows-lodge

▷ RV and Tent Sites, Lodge Rooms

There are five campgrounds in Shenandoah National Park, but Big Meadows is our favorite for several reasons. Some of the park's most popular hikes are nearby, including Dark Hollow Falls and Stony Man. The Byrd Visitor Center is within walking distance, as is a well-stocked camp store. Big Meadows has over 200 sites that are excellent for tents and smaller RVs, and dozens of deer can be seen in the evenings as families settle in for dinner and campfires. The amphitheater also offers excellent ranger-led programs and talks that educate campers about bear safety, the night sky, and local wildlife, among other topics. We also love the Big Meadows Lodge right next to the campground. Guest rooms at the lodge are fairly affordable, and the Great Room is a cozy and comfortable place to play a game of checkers, read a book, or relax and watch a spectacular sunset light up the park. There is live music on summer nights in the downstairs pub, and the snacks and beer will hit the spot after a long day of hiking. Campers are welcome to join along and can walk back to their tents or RVs after the show.

Cape Charles/Chesapeake Bay KOA Resort

▷   Cape Charles, Virginia

▷   koa.com

▷   RV Sites, Tent Sites, RV Rentals, Glamping Tents, Deluxe Cabins

The Chesapeake Bay KOA is one of our favorite places to bring the RV in the summer months. We love the sandy bay beach right in front of the campground, because it is perfect for swimming, kayaking, and SUPing. The water is warm and calm in the summertime, and the sunsets are truly spectacular. Grab dinner and drinks at the Jackspot Cafe and enjoy an outdoor table with a water view, or just order to go and bring your food right down to the beach. The pool area is also nice, and if it gets hot you can rent a cabana to stay made in the shade. Our kids spent hours swinging on the hammock porch at the edge of the beach, which gave us some time to read our books and relax with our toes in the sand. We think it is wise to rent a golf cart at this KOA because the camp store is a bit far away and we often found ourselves wanting hand scooped ice cream after grilling up dinner at our campsite.

ALSO GREET

Luray KOA Holiday

▷ Luray, Virginia

▷ koa.com

▷ RV and Tent Sites, Deluxe Cabins and Yurts

The Luray KOA is a charming and quiet alternative to Jellystone Luray. The RV sites are large and lovely, and so are the views of rolling hills and farmland that surround the campground. The central common area is a great place to meet other campers and play a game of frisbee or outdoor ping-pong.

Fancy Gap/Blue Ridge Parkway KOA Journey

▷ Fancy Gap, Virginia

▷ koa.com

▷ RV and Tent Sites, Deluxe Cabins and Camping Cabins

This delightful campground is carved into the side of a shady hill, and the elevation keeps it cool and comfortable during the hot summer months. The pet-friendly "backyard sites" are absolutely incredible for dog owners who want to give their pups extra room to roam. This KOA is also close to Mount Airy, North Carolina—aka Andy Griffith's Mayberry.

---------- **Hiking in Shenandoah National Park** ----------

Hiking is among the best things to do in Shenandoah National Park. It doesn't get much better for the casual day hiker or for families with young kids. You can reach spectacular summits in Shenandoah on relatively short round-trip hikes like Stony Man (1.4 miles round trip) and Hawksbill (2.8 miles round trip). You can also descend into the cool and shaded world of Dark Hallow Falls for a waterfall hike that is not to be missed (1.4 miles out and back). Our favorite hike in Shenandoah National Park is Bearfence Mountain (1.2 mile lariat). Climbing and scrambling through this trail's jumbled rocks has just the slightest whiff of danger, but it is oodles of fun. You'll feel accomplished and winded when you reach the top. Thankfully, there is an easy section of the Appalachian Trail that leads right back down to the parking lot.

More Shenandoah National Park Camping

Shenandoah River State Park Campground

Shenandoah River State Park Campground may be the perfect base camp for RV owners who want a bucolic setting without having to tow their RVs into the park. You can see Shenandoah National Park to the east, and rent a canoe or launch your own right inside the park. Sites are large, but they may be difficult to come by. Book well in advance to get a spot.

Matthew's Arm Campground

Matthew's Arm is located at mile marker 22.1 on Skyline Drive. The campground is pretty and close to a waterfall hike to Overall Run Falls. This is a perfect spot for tent camping, and there is a dump station for RV owners who want to camp inside the park. Matthew's Arm is the closest campground to the northern terminus of Skyline Drive and the gateway community of Front Royal.

Lewis Mountain Campground

Lewis Mountain Campground (located at mile marker 57.5) is the smallest campground in the park and almost looks like a smaller version of Big Meadows. However, reservations are first-come, first-served, and there is no dump station for RVs. If you are a tent camper and don't care about being near the lodge for dinner or drinks, then this might be the spot for you.

Loft Mountain Campground

Loft Mountain may win the prize for having the National Park Service's prettiest amphitheater with mountain views. This campground is absolutely gorgeous and has mountain views to the east and to the west. Two waterfall hikes are nearby. Make sure you catch a ranger talk while you are camping here. Loft Mountain is located at mile marker 79.5 on Skyline Drive. The campground does have a dump station and camp store on-site.

Other Favorite Shenandoah National Park Experiences

Cruise on Skyline Drive

Skyline drive is over 100 miles long with stretches that are breathtakingly beautiful. If you are looking for things to do in Shenandoah National Park, don't forget to just roll the windows down, put on some good music, and cruise. This classic American drive starts at Front Royal in the north, then deposits you onto the Blue Ridge Parkway at its southern terminus. We recommend pulling over at whatever overlooks catch your fancy. Take your time and breathe in the cool mountain air, particularly at sunset.

Grab Lunch or Dinner on the Back Deck of Big Meadows Lodge

The Spottswood Dining Room at Big Meadows Lodge is open to the public, and it is surprisingly easy (especially at lunch) to get a table on its gorgeous back deck. Your blackberry lemonade will taste better with mountain views.

Learn about the Park's History

The history of Shenandoah National Park is not without controversy. In the West, conservation often came well before development. But in the East, development came before conservation. The end result? In order to create Shenandoah National Park, over 500 families were displaced against their will. The permanent display in the Byrd Visitor Center tells this story without simplifying the human complexity of these events.

Become a Junior Ranger

This beloved program is available at NPS sites across the country, and it has a different flavor in each location. Ask at the front desk for a Junior Ranger booklet, and let your kids get to work. They will never forget the experience.

West Virginia

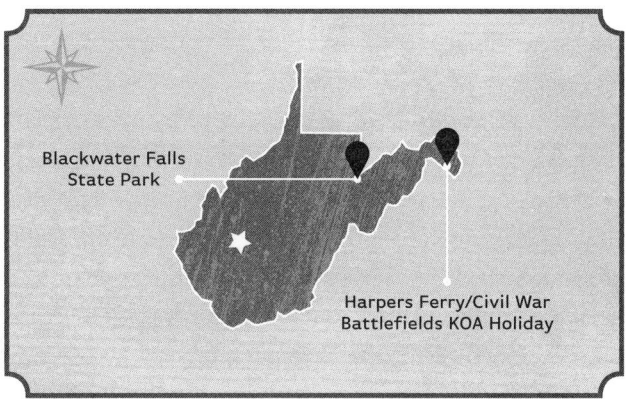

Blackwater Falls State Park

Harpers Ferry/Civil War Battlefields KOA Holiday

West Virginia seems to be a bit overlooked in favor of the more well-known neighboring camping destinations of Pennsylvania, Virginia, and Kentucky. But on our very first visit years ago, we learned that it is most certainly wild and wonderful. The state park campgrounds tend to lean to the rustic side and will give you that much-needed nature fix. On the other hand, many of the state parks offer great lodge options that will allow you to disconnect in more comfort. Whether you stay in a tent, RV, or cabin, be ready to embrace outdoor adventure in order to truly appreciate this beautiful part of the country.

In addition to rafting, hiking, and horseback riding, there's also a good amount of history to enjoy in West Virginia. Head up to the northern part of the state to visit Harpers Ferry and other famous Civil War battlefields.

BEST IN STATE

Blackwater Falls State Park

▷ Davis, West Virginia

▷ wvstateparks.com

▷ Cabins, Lodge, RV and Tent Sites

Blackwater Falls has something for every kind of camper or glamper. If you are a tent camper or RV owner, the campground is pretty darn good. It is clean and well kept, and most sites are spacious. Some sites may be unlevel, and many do not offer privacy, but the campground has classic charm and offers families an affordable back-to-nature camping experience. But we think the lodge and cabin options at Blackwater Falls (which are open year-round) are the real stars of the show. The Lodge has a retro feel with cozy guest rooms and a comfortable lobby with a fireplace. There is also an on-site restaurant and an indoor pool! The classic cabins and vacation cabins (with two bedrooms) would make for a lovely romantic retreat or a fun-filled family vacation. Opportunities for outdoor recreation abound at Blackwater Falls—hiking, biking, fishing, sledding, and cross-country skiing are all possible, depending on the season. Photographers travel far and wide to photograph the falls, which drop 57 feet into the Blackwater River and form the heart and soul of this iconic state park.

Harpers Ferry/Civil War Battlefields KOA Holiday

▷ Harpers Ferry, West Virginia

▷ koa.com

▷ RV and Tent Sites, Camping Cabins and Deluxe Cabins

Civil War buffs will delight in a camping trip to Harpers Ferry, and this KOA is our top pick for the region. This campground has a delightful setting and is just minutes away from Harpers Ferry National Historical Park, where visitors can participate in historic trades workshops or learn about the area's rich history on a guided hike with a park ranger. Back at the campground, families can play a game of mini golf, jump on the covered bounce pillow, or take a dip in the pool. Older kids love the indoor and outdoor basketball courts and game room—especially on a rainy day. Adults love Grapes & Grinds, the campground's specialty wine and coffee store. Start the day there with a piping hot cup of coffee and make sure you don't miss one of the afternoon wine tastings. There are a wide variety of tent and RV sites and plenty of cabins to choose from. If you are in a big rig, take turns slowly, as the campground has a few tight corners and it gets quite crowded during peak season.

ALSO GREAT

Tygart Lake State Park
- ▷ Grafton, West Virginia
- ▷ wvstateparks.com
- ▷ Cabins, Lodge, RV and Tent Sites

Yet another great West Virginia state park with a cute campground and awesome lodge and cabin options! The campground may be tiny, with only thirty-six sites, but the lake is large and lovely for those who enjoy swimming, fishing, and kayaking. Plan on eating at the restaurant in the lodge—the food is good and the views of the lake are even better.

Twin Hollow Campground and Cabins
- ▷ Gilbert, West Virginia
- ▷ twinhollowcampground.com
- ▷ Tent and RV Sites, Cabin Rentals

Love to camp and own an ATV or want to rent one? Then you might think you've died and gone to almost-heaven as you drive the country roads into

Twin Hollow Campground. From your cabin, tent, or RV site you have direct access to over 300 miles of ATV trails, and you can even drive into several small towns for lunch or supplies.

---------- **Earn the Junior Ranger Angler Badge** ----------

You've probably heard of the Junior Ranger badges, but some NPS sites also offer Junior Ranger Angler badges, and New River Gorge National Park in West Virginia is one of them. Ironically named, the New River is one of the oldest rivers in North America and offers plenty of fishing opportunities. There are dozens of public access points to catch bass, walleye, bluegill, carp, and channel catfish. You can download the Junior Ranger Angler booklet online before you visit, or stop in at the Canyon Rim or Sandstone Visitors Center to pick up a booklet.

Harpers Ferry

Harpers Ferry National Historical Park is a favorite destination for Civil War buffs. The famous location of John Brown's Raid, Harpers Ferry changed hands fourteen times during the war. Located at the confluence of the Shenandoah and Potomac Rivers, the park has plenty of natural beauty in addition to historical significance. You can pair a visit with nearby Antietam National Battlefield where 23,000 soldiers were killed, wounded, or missing after a single day of battle during the Civil War.

Ranger Programs
Crumbling buildings and battlefields come alive in the presence of these knowledgeable and gifted storytellers. Check the online calendar ahead of time, or head to the visitor's center to learn about the daily ranger programs at Harpers Ferry.

Living History Demonstrations
Most national historical sites have regularly occurring living history demonstrations. Harpers Ferry has regularly scheduled living history event weekends focused on topics like Civil War medicine and artillery demonstrations.

Historic Trades Workshops
These workshops offer a unique look into nineteenth-century life. Rangers trained in crafts like blacksmithing and cooking provide demonstrations for visitors. Most of these workshops require registration, and some also charge a fee, so visit the NPS website for more information.

Hikes
The Appalachian Trail runs through Harpers Ferry, and there are plenty of great hikes from which to choose. The Maryland Heights Loop is a popular one that offers beautiful views of the river, but you'll have to climb more than 1,000 feet in elevation to get there.

THE MIDWEST

Illinois

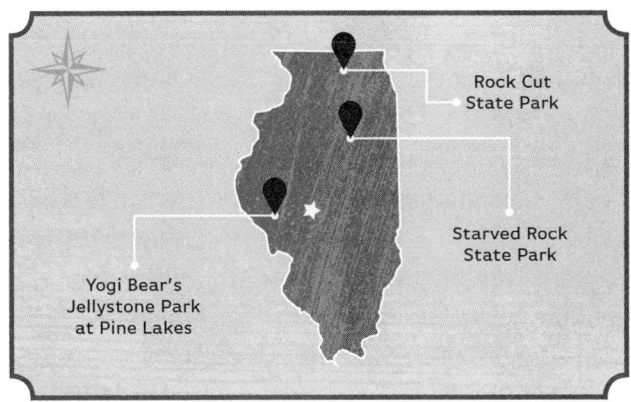

When we ask our friends in Illinois where they love to camp, they jokingly tell us Wisconsin. We get it. You folks in Chicago are close to amazing camping destinations to the north in Wisconsin and Minnesota and to the west in Iowa. However, Illinois does have its own camping treasures, so don't be so quick to head out of state. Rock Cut State Park is a favorite weekend getaway, and Starved Rock State Park is a gem. You can also find plenty of options along the first stretch of Route 66, if you are journeying down the Mother Road. Looking for a base camp to explore Chicago? We will send you out of state. Indiana Dunes State Park runs daily public transportation into the Windy City.

BEST IN STATE

Yogi Bear's Jellystone Park at Pine Lakes

▷ Pittsfield, Illinois

▷ jellystonepinelakes.com

▷   Cottages, Bungalows, Cabins, RV and Tent Sites

This top-ranked Jellystone Park is located in a rural part of west-central Illinois, and it offers a complete family vacation. Once you pull in, you really don't need to leave. Novice campers might look at the price of a Jellystone like this and wonder why it costs more than a state park or some other mom-and-pop campgrounds listed in this book, but once you come visit and see what is included, and what is available for nominal extra fees, it starts to feel like a bargain right quick. This Jellystone can be relaxing or exciting, or both, depending on what you want. RV and tent sites are pretty and well shaded, and the best of them are located right on the lake. Lakefront cottages and cabins are also available for those who want more of a glamping experience. All of the basic family-friendly amenities are here—the pool and playgrounds are nice, and so is the swimming beach. But that's just for starters. The jumping pillow and inflatable water playground will provide off-the-hook fun for hours on end—and the organized activities like kids' fishing derbies, dance parties, and outdoor movie nights will help you make great memories with your kids that they will talk about for years to come.

Rock Cut State Park

▷   Loves Park, Illinois

▷   illinois.gov

▷   RV and Tent Sites, Rustic Cabin

Rock Cut State Park is just 80 miles northwest of Chicago, close to the border of Wisconsin. Campers who live close to the Windy City often find themselves here for quick weekend getaways. The park, which has two lovely lakes, is peaceful and offers a great combination of back-to-nature experiences and easy-to-access local activities. A hiking trail circumnavigates Lake Pierce (the larger lake) and makes for a lovely stroll, particularly when the leaves are red and gold in the fall. The lake is also excellent for kayaking and fishing, and there is a sandy beach for swimming that has concessions and picnic areas. RV owners and tent campers love the campground, which has almost 300 sites. Some are wooded and private, and some are out in the open with a few shady trees, but all of them are spacious and relatively level. The campground is open year-round for those hearty souls (like us) who love winter camping. We also love taking in a minor league sports game when we are traveling, and there are two options near Rock Cut. The Rockford IceHogs are a few minutes away (go Hogs!), and the Beloit Snappers baseball team plays just over the border in Wisconsin (go Snappers!) only fifteen minutes away from the campground.

Starved Rock State Park

 ▷ Oglesby, Illinois
 ▷ illinois.gov
 ▷ RV and Tent Sites, Lodge Rooms, Cabin Rooms

The campground at Starved Rock State Park is plain and simple. There are some large sites out in the open and many medium- to large-sized sites that are tucked into the woods. If you camp here, you will probably not spend much time in the campsite proper, except for time around the campfire each night. But you will be located in the heart of the action at one of the prettiest state parks in the entire Midwest. The cabins and lodge rooms at the lodge in Starved Rock State Park are anything but plain and simple. This log built lodge is on the National Register of Historic Places, and its lobby and rooms are filled with a laid-back luxury that is more often found in our great National Park lodges. Most folks don't think of a state park lodge as a great place for a romantic getaway, but just take one look inside at the comfortable and cozy rooms and you will want to book one for an upcoming trip. If you want more privacy and space there are also authentic log cabins built by the CCC in the 1930s—they are in a slightly more remote section of the park right near the entrance to several hiking trails. No matter how you stay at Starved Rock, you will want to plan on spending your days exploring this park's canyons, waterfalls, and dramatic overlooks. Fishing, boating, and hunting opportunities are also available for those who love the great outdoors. Or just sit in the great room of the lodge and read a book by the fireplace. It's totally up to you.

---------- Lincoln Home National Historic Site ----------

Springfield, Illinois

Historic Springfield, Illinois, is a great weekend destination, and the nearby Springfield KOA Journey is a perfect, no-frills base camp. The Lincoln Home site can be toured in a half day, and then you will be free to explore the rest of Springfield, chock-full of history and iconic Route 66 attractions. Here are some planning tips:

- The Lincoln Home can be seen only by guided tour. Timed tickets are free but must be reserved on a first-come, first-served basis.
- Check out the Living History Events calendar in advance of your visit. These include performances of Lincoln's famous speeches and historical toy demonstrations.
- Build in time to watch the thirty-minute film on Lincoln's life, preferably before you tour the house.
- Walk through the historic four-block neighborhood that has been restored to its 1860s appearance.
- Fast forward in time and tour the Abraham Lincoln Presidential Library and Museum.

ALSO GREAT

Timber Ridge Outpost & Cabins

- ▷   Elizabethtown, Illinois
- ▷   timberridgeoutpost.com
- ▷   Treehouses, Cabins, Houses

Timber Ridge offers a variety of unique and on-trend glamping experiences in the heart of the Illinois Ozarks. The fully furnished treehouses are comfortable and come with plenty of outdoor space for a picnic or campfire. The Sassafras Ridge Log Cabin is perfect for families who love outdoor fun, and the Hickory Hollow log cabin is cute as a button for a quiet weekend away without the kids.

Lena KOA Holiday

▷ Lena, Illinois

▷ koa.com

▷ Camping Cabins, Deluxe Cabins, Tepees, RV and Tent Sites

Some campground owners just have that magic touch. Campers speak about the guest experience at the Lena KOA with reverence in their voices. Whether you are singing along with the staff at their annual luau or making a mess of yourself at a watermelon eating contest, you are pretty much guaranteed a good time at this KOA. Just don't forget to try your hand at the Poly Pong Table, okay?

Johnson-Sauk Trail State Recreation Area

▷ Kewanee, Illinois

▷ illinois.gov

▷ RV and Tent Sites, Cabin

The RV and tent sites set among the tall pine trees at the Chief Keokok are stunning, and when the wind starts to blow through them the sound is calming—and borderline mesmerizing. Located in the rolling hills of north-central Illinois, this state park is packed with options for outdoor adventure. There is also a single cabin for rent overlooking Johnson Lake. Make sure to bring your own bedding—if you can get a reservation!

Route 66: Illinois Highlights

Route 66 Starts Here Sign
78-98 E Adams Street, Chicago, IL 60603

A necessary photo op at the northwestern corner of Adams Street and Michigan Avenue.

Gemini Giant
S East Street, Wilmington, IL 60481

One of the few remaining Muffler Men, these giant statues were advertising staples along the Mother Road in the '60s.

Dell Rhea's Chicken Basket
645 Joliet Road, Willowbrook, IL 60527

Route 66 is dotted with legendary roadside restaurants, but this is one of the most famous. Get the fried chicken...obviously.

Funks Grove Pure Maple Sirup Farm
5257 Old Route 66, Shirley, IL 61772

The Funks have been tapping syrup in Illinois since the nineteenth century, and they love to share their family legends alongside the history of Route 66.

Henry's Rabbit Ranch
1107 Historic Old Route 66, Staunton, IL 62088

There's a giant fiberglass jackrabbit, Volkswagen Rabbits, and actual real furry rabbits at this ranch. This is the stuff Route 66 dreams are made of.

Indiana

Indiana Dunes State Park Campground

Yogi Bear's Jellystone Park Camp-Resort at Barton Lake

More than 80 percent of RVs are manufactured in Indiana, so you would think there would be some pretty great campgrounds in the state as well. Ironically, we've been hard pressed to find any amazing options in Elkhart County, often referred to as the RV Capital of the World. However, if you are looking to visit the area for some RV history, factory tours, and Amish baked goods, we do have some camping options that will do in a pinch.

To soak in the best camping that Indiana has to offer, you really have to travel north or south of Elkhart. To the north lies one of the newest NPS sites in the country, Indiana Dunes National Park, with great camping options both in the national park and next door in Indiana Dunes State Park. This is the perfect destination for a long weekend getaway or week-long family vacation at the beach.

And to the south, you have the greatly under-appreciated region of southern Indiana, where farmland turns into forest and rolling hills more often associated with neighboring Kentucky. Not far from the Ohio River, you'll find simple, rustic getaways like Lincoln State Park and also beloved

RV resorts like Lake Rudolph, located next door to Holiday World in Santa Claus, Indiana.

BEST IN STATE

Indiana Dunes State Park Campground

▷ Chesterton, Indiana

▷ in.gov

▷ RV and Tents Sites

Indiana Dunes National Lakeshore recently became Indiana Dunes National Park and made national news in the process. This newly birthed National Park has an appealing, rustic campground called Dunewood that has no electrical hookups and takes no reservations. But our top pick in the area is the Indiana Dunes State Park campground, which has direct access to the beach and electrical hookups at each site. A short and easy hike on Trail #4 leads you to the top of Mount Tom and then down onto the beach—which is the real star of the show here. We loved swimming in the clear warm waters of Lake Michigan in August and hope to make a return trip soon. The campground is delightful and has a well-stocked camp store (open in the summer), a playground, and heated restrooms. Additionally, it has paved roads, spacious sites, and ample opportunities to enjoy ranger-led programs. Indiana Dunes State Park regularly hosts theme weekends, including vintage camper rallies and birding festivals. The nature center is also excellent and has exhibits about the ecology of the area. Indiana Dunes National Park surrounds the state park and offers ample opportunities for even more hiking, swimming, bird watching, and ranger-led programs.

Yogi Bear's Jellystone Park Camp-Resort at Barton Lake

▷ Fremont, Indiana

▷ jellystonesbest.com

▷   RV and Tent Sites, Rustic Cabins, and Deluxe Cottages

Located near the crossroads of Indiana, Michigan, and Ohio, Yogi Bear's Jellystone Park Camp-Resort at Barton Lake is the perfect example of destination camping. Whether you are visiting for a weekend or an entire week, there are enough activities and amenities to keep you entertained right on-site. With three outdoor pools, an indoor pool, splash park, jump pillows, and volleyball court, it is virtually impossible to be bored at the Barton Lake Jellystone. Nevertheless, it also offers a full roster of daily activities beginning at 9:00 a.m. and running into the evening hours. If you let the kids get a hold of the activities schedule, they might just run you ragged here! We recommend grabbing hold of that schedule and choosing what works for everyone—because the kids are going to want to do everything! The lake is also a nice spot for fishing and kayaking, and we were glad to have all of our gear with us. The campground is located right off the highway, but once you are inside, it feels like you are a world away. But choose your site or cabin wisely—some are pretty close to the road.

ALSO GREAT

Prophetstown State Park

▷   West Lafayette, Indiana

▷   in.gov

▷   RV and Tent Sites

Prophetstown State Park is beloved by campers in Indiana because of its large, level, and lovely sites and beautiful setting surrounded by tall prairie grasses and abundant wildflowers. The park has an excellent paved bike trail and a large, modern playground for the lively little campers. Families will love the pool and waterslides at the popular Aquatic Center.

Turkey Run State Park

▷ Marshall, Indiana

▷ in.gov

▷ RV and Tent Sites, Cabins

Turkey Run State Park has excellent trails for hikers of every ability level. It also has a lovely campground. The sites are large, paved, and offer electric hookups—making this a real in-state favorite for RV owners. The bathrooms are kept remarkably clean considering how busy the campground can be. Make sure to grab dinner at the lodge inside the park where the food is tasty and affordable.

Two Great Campgrounds Near
Holiday World in Santa Claus, Indiana

Holiday World Theme Park and Splashin' Safari Water Park is a hugely popular family destination in southern Indiana. In fact, many families return year after year and stay at one of the nearby campgrounds. The good news is that there are options for both those who love resort camping and those who prefer to decompress at a beautiful state park after riding the coasters.

▷ *Lake Rudolph Campground and RV Resort*, located right next to Holiday World, has lodging rentals, tent sites, and RV sites. The campground has multiple pools, playgrounds, basketball courts, and a whole range of other amenities. This is the perfect place to gather with friends and family to enjoy a fun-filled getaway.

▷ *Lincoln State Park* is just minutes away and offers a whole different vibe, with 10 miles of hiking trails, boat rentals, and interpretative programs. A popular concert series takes place in the summer. There are cabins and cottages for rent, along with RV and tenting sites. Many of the campsites offer electric hookups.

Exploring the RV Capital of the World

Where to Camp

Elkhart Campground

25608 Co Rd 4, Elkhart, IN 46514

Elkhart Co./Middlebury KOA Holiday

52867 IN-13, Middlebury, IN 46540

What to Do

▷ Tour the RV/MH Hall of Fame and Museum. Enjoy the amazing display of RVs and motor homes dating back to the 1920s.

▷ Take an RV manufacturer tour. Jayco, Grand Design, Thor Motorcoach, and many other manufacturers offer scheduled factory tours for the public. Many require advance reservations, so visit their websites to learn more.

▷ Shop at the Shipshewana Auction & Flea Market. This is the largest flea market in the Midwest, so bring your souvenir money and do your best to stay on budget.

▷ Eat at the Rise'n Roll Bakery & Deli. Make sure to visit the original location in Middlebury for a complete selection of goodies. Also make sure to leave with a couple dozen donuts for later. Locals call them Amish Crack.

Vintage Trailer Madness

Looking to learn more about vintage trailers? Warning! These three books could lead to a lifelong obsession!

Trailerama by Phil Noyes
This kitschy coffee-table book is bursting with photos, advertisements, brochures, and magazine covers of vintage trailers. We can get lost in this one for hours.

The Illustrated Field Guide to Vintage Trailers: 100s of Popular, Rare, and Unique Trailers Identified by Bob Thompson and Carl Jameson
If you are contemplating becoming an aficionado of vintage trailers, then this delightful field guide is a must. The A–Z format and detailed illustrations make this book feel authoritative.

Airstream: The History of the Land Yacht by Bryan Burkhart and David Hunt
When it comes to vintage trailers, Airstreams certainly deserve their own coffee-table book, and this is the one to buy. Why? Because it is that rare coffee-table book that is also a great read and a legitimate page-turner.

Iowa

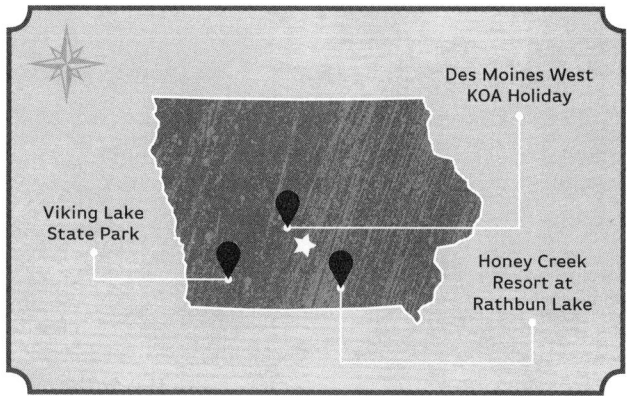

The residents of Iowa seem to be torn between keeping their amazing camping destinations a secret and bragging about their under-appreciated state park gems. One thing is for certain—once you get Iowan campers talking about their favorite campgrounds, the list gets surprisingly long.

Iowa has over 4,700 campsites in its state parks, forests, and recreation areas, many of which are open year-round and even offer electricity hookups in the winter months. About 75 percent of those sites are reservable—and the competition is fierce—so set your calendar reminders for three months in advance of the day you wish to arrive. If your budget is tight, the news gets even better. Full hookup sites top out at $16 per night, with sewer and water hookups adding a mere $3 per night in additional fees. There's also a range of cabins and yurts available if you prefer.

Bottom line? Iowa isn't a drive-through state. If you are passing through on your way to South Dakota, Yellowstone, or Glacier, plan a stop and enjoy some hiking, cave exploring, or kayaking.

BEST IN STATE

Honey Creek Resort at Rathbun Lake

▷   Moravia, Iowa

▷   honeycreekresort.com

▷   Lodge, Cottages, RV Sites

RV owners who love to golf and partake in water sports will be in heaven at Honey Creek Resort. There is an eighteen-hole championship golf course on-site and it is one of the best in the state. Rathbun is Iowa's second largest lake and a perfect place for kayaking and fishing. The resort's variety of accommodations also make this a perfect place for a family reunion or multifamily trip with friends who don't own RVs. The lodge has a wide range of rooms from reasonably priced standard rooms to presidential suites with wet bars and whirlpool tubs. The cottages include full kitchens, wraparound decks, and fireplaces and plenty of room for larger families. The RV park is situated directly on the lake and has gigantic level sites with concrete pads. Campers have access to all of the resort's various facilities—including its Buccaneer Bay indoor water park. Wristbands for the water park are included in the price, no matter which style of accommodation you choose.

Viking Lake State Park

▷   Stanton, Iowa

▷   iowadnr.gov

▷   RV and Tent Sites

Viking Lake State Park is a little slice of camping heaven less than two hours southwest of Des Moines. No wonder it is one of the most popular campgrounds in Iowa. If you live anywhere near the Hawkeye State, this is where you should be camping next. Viking Lake has a wide variety of sites for tents and RVs, and many of them are situated right on the lake. We also love these large sites because they are perfectly angled and easy to back into—making this a top state park for larger rigs. Full hookups are available, and so are a handful of buddy sites that are perfect for group camping. Those who travel with kayaks and SUPs will love vacationing here because the water is calm and clean and there are multiple access points. The lake is also stocked to the brim with bass and a wide variety of other fish. Kids love playing on the sandy beach, and everyone loves taking a refreshing dip on a hot summer day. State park camping doesn't get much better than this.

Cave Explorations

Most folks associate Iowa with corn, but it also has a remarkable number of caves that are worth exploring, especially when trying to stay cool during the dog days of summer. Bring layers, as the average underground temperature is 45–55°F. Here are hikes that will take you to some of Iowa's best caves:

▷ Maquoketa Caves State Park, 1.7 miles

▷ Starr's Cave Park and Preserve, Burlington, .5 mile

▷ Whitewater Canyon Trail, 3.3 miles

▷ Crystal Lake Cave, Guided Tour, 30–45 minutes

▷ Upper Ice Cave Hill Trail, 2 miles

Not into hiking? Take a boat tour into Spook Cave in McGregor, Iowa.

Des Moines West KOA Holiday

▷ Adel, Iowa

▷ koa.com

▷ Glamping Tents, RV Rentals, RV and Tent Sites

This cute and kid-friendly campground serves as a great example of the KOA model. It is close, but not too close, to the highway, so it's easy on, easy off for an overnight, but still peaceful and relatively quiet for those making longer stays. The owners have also given this place a complete facelift over the last six years, so many (if not most) of the amenities are brand new. Their deluxe full hook-up patio sites are dreamy for experienced big-rig owners, and they have new glamping tents and welcoming cabin options for those who might want to take their first camping vacation and see what the fuss is all about. If you pull in late at night and don't feel like cooking, the camp-ground has food delivery options and will bring a hot meal right to your site. Kids love the pool, bounce pillow, ladder golf, playground, and basketball court. Dog owners love the large two-sided dog park with a space for friendly pups who like to play and for less social pups who still need some space to run. The small town of Winterset is John Wayne's birthplace and the home of the historic bridges of Madison County. There is plenty to explore nearby, and this is the perfect base camp for your adventures.

- - - - - - - - - - - - - **Iowa Water Trails Association** - - - - - - - - - - - -

We love that Iowa has a water trails association in order to facilitate the enjoyment of the state's many waterways. The organization provides dozens of waterways maps for canoeing and kayaking free of charge. The maps also include information like boat ramps, restrooms, drinking water access, and more. You can find these resources at iowadnr.gov.

ALSO GREAT

Maquoketa Caves State Park

▷ Maquoketa, Iowa

▷ iowadnr.gov

▷ RV and Tent Sites

A simple and thickly wooded campground with level sites and electric hook-ups that is situated in an incredible state park with thirteen caves to explore, Maquoketa Caves has been a popular destination for day trippers since the

1860s, and it is one of Iowa's most unique outdoor attractions. Dress warm, wear old clothes and hiking boots, and bring a flashlight to explore caves with names like Dancehall Cave and Hernando's Hideaway. Some caves are fully walkable, and others will require getting down on your hands and knees and feeling comfortable in tight spaces.

Luna Valley Farm

▷ Decorah, Iowa

▷ lunavalleyfarm.com

▷ Glamping Tents

Luna Valley Farm is a working organic farm and a community hub that serves up delicious lamb, pork, and beef as well as wood-fired pizzas on Friday nights. And now it is also serving up a unique glamping experience with hardwood floors, luxurious linens, locally roasted coffees, and locally brewed beers. Sit and relax on your private patio or wander onto the farm and mingle with the owners and workers while they make the magic happen. But no matter what you do, make sure you arrive early enough on Friday night to claim a delicious pizza to bring back to your tent.

Honey Creek State Park

▷ Moravia, Iowa

▷ iowadnr.gov

▷ Rustic Pine Log Camper Cabins, Tent and RV Sites

Honey Creek State Park (not to be confused with the Honey Creek Resort listed previously) is another gem in Iowa's excellent state park system. Some sites have full hookups, some have water views, and the pine log cabins are great for first-time campers and folks who have retired their tents. The lake is a perfect summertime retreat for those who love to paddle or fish.

Visit the *Field of Dreams* Movie Site

We don't know why, but camping people are often baseball people. Don't miss a chance to visit the site where the Academy Award–nominated movie was filmed. Take a tour, visit the gift shop, and see if you don't walk away with your own big dream.

Kansas

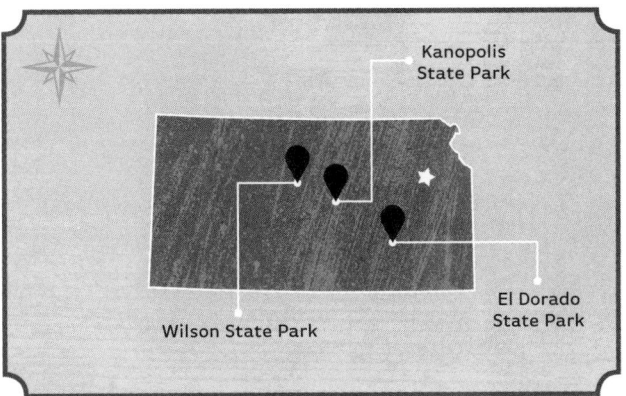

When most of us nonresidents picture Kansas, we imagine endless flat prairie stretching as far as the eye can see. And while there is definitely plenty of prairie grass in Kansas (see page 191 for more info on the Tallgrass Prairie National Preserve), local campers know the state park campgrounds offer a variety of beautiful landscapes. Enjoy hiking through the Smoky Hills, fishing on Wilson Reservoir, and watching the sunset over the Flint Hills. Welcome to the heart of the Heartland.

Photo Op!

The geographic center of the lower forty-eight is just a couple of miles northwest of Lebanon, Kansas. The official center is in the middle of a former hog farm, but you'll be more interested in posing in front of the stone marker and plaque about a half mile away at the end of a paved road.

BEST IN STATE

Kanopolis State Park

- ▷ Marquette, Kansas
- ▷ ksoutdoors.com
- ▷ RV and Tent Sites, Deluxe Cabins

The landscape at Kanopolis State Park is wild and varied and blows up the preconceptions that most people have about Kansas. There are caves and sandstone bluffs and miles of varied hiking trails that wind through the Smoky Hills. This is the Kansas that residents of the state know and love—and it is the Kansas that far too many people never experience. There are almost 450 campsites here in two primary camping areas called Langley Point and Horsethief. There is plenty of primitive camping for those who love to throw a tent in the back of the car and go, and there are full hookups for RV owners who want it all. There are also six deluxe cabins in the Little Bluestem Cabin Area that sleep up to five people and come equipped with full kitchens and bathrooms. These cabins, with names like Buffalo Bill and Bat Masterson, play tribute to the area's rich history, and they let new campers experience the beauty of this park without having to sleep on the cold hard ground.

Wilson State Park

- ▷ Sylvan Grove, Kansas
- ▷ ksoutdoors.com
- ▷ RV and Tent Sites, Cabins

Think Kansas is entirely flat? Think again. About 10 miles North of I-70 in Kansas is a state park campground that will take your breath away. Most folks from out of state drive right by Wilson State Park and never camp there—and that's a crying shame, because this place is beautiful. Many campsites are available right smack on the 9,000-acre Wilson Reservoir, and depending on your site, you might just feel like you have the whole lake to yourself. The

Smoky Hills surround the park, and the edge of the waterfront features rocky cliffs and outcrops, making this a supercool place for kayaking or SUPing if the weather is right. Photographers and bird watchers also love to camp and day trip here. Hiking, swimming, fishing, biking, and hunting are also on the menu at Wilson. Sites are spacious and some have a bit of shade; others are exposed to wind and sun. This may be the most beautiful state park in all of Kansas, and it is an absolute delight for campers of all stripes.

El Dorado State Park

▷   El Dorado, Kansas

▷   ksoutdoors.com

▷   RV and Tent Sites, Cabins

El Dorado State Park is located at the edge of the rolling green Flint Hills, which form one of the prettiest landscapes in all of Kansas. The park is the largest in Kansas, and it has over 1,100 campsites on its 4,000 acres. It is incredible how many of the campsites are directly on the water—so you can fish or kayak directly from your site and watch the sunset with an unobstructed view. There are four campgrounds here that range from rustic to full hookups, and there are also ten cabins for rent. Five of them are camping cabins without water, and the other five are deluxe cabins with bathrooms and kitchens—most of them have lakeside views. El Dorado is filled with hiking, biking, and equestrian trails, and those who fish love to cast a line at a quiet spot along the rocky shoreline. White-tailed deer roam around the campground, and songbirds let loose in the springtime.

---- **Campers Take Note!** ----

Coleman Factory and Museum in Wichita is the perfect road trip stop for those who love collectible camping gear. You can probably find the same gear online, but if you are the sentimental type, this is like walking into the pages of a Coleman catalogue.

ALSO GREAT

Acorns Resort

▷ Milford, Kansas

▷ acornsresortkansas.com

▷ Cabins, Yurts, Lodge Rooms, RV Sites

The Acorns Resort has everything you need to enjoy an epic family vacation without ever leaving its delightful property. Situated on the largest lake in Kansas, Acorns has excellent fishing, boating, hunting, and hiking opportunities. The custom-made cabins are delightful and are perfect for multifamily vacations, weddings, or reunions. The yurts are simple and affordable, and the premium RV sites are large and close to the lake.

Curtis Creek, Farnum Creek, and West Rolling Hills Campgrounds/U.S Army Corps of Engineers

▷ Junction City, Kansas

▷ nwk.usace.army.mil

▷ RV and Tent Sites

Milford Lake is the largest man-made lake in Kansas, and it is home to five U.S. Army Corps of Engineers campgrounds. The three listed above are considered by the Corps to be Class A campgrounds, meaning they have full hook-up sites and bathrooms and they take reservations. All three of these campgrounds have water views and direct access to boating, hunting, swimming, and fishing opportunities that are among the best in all of Kansas.

Tuttle Creek State Park

▷ Manhattan, Kansas

▷ ksoutdoors.com

▷ Cabins, RV and Tent Sites

We love the Rent-A-Camp Program at Tuttle Creek State Park that helps families that are new to camping get set up for a weekend of fun for a small fee. The package includes tents, stoves, lanterns, and other camping supplies for a small fee. Tuttle Creek has five campgrounds with a wide variety of sites and options for hookups and primitive camping. Fishing and boating are excellent at this park, as are mountain biking and horseback riding.

---------- **Tallgrass Prairie National Preserve** ----------

Hundreds of years ago, North America was covered by over 170 million acres of tallgrass prairie. Less than 4 percent of that remains, and you can find a good portion in Kansas. Ranger-guided bus tours run daily from April through October, but make sure to call ahead for reservations since they fill up in advance. There are also guided tours of the 1881 limestone Spring Hill Ranch House. These are less regular, so check the online schedule. If you are traveling with kids, make sure to pick up a Junior Ranger booklet at the visitor's center so they can earn their Tallgrass Prairie badge.

Route 66 Highlights

Many visitors drive through Kansas on their Route 66 pilgrimages. With only 13 miles of the Mother Road, it claims the shortest stretch of this iconic highway. However, those few miles contain a few sweet towns with well-preserved roadside attractions.

Galena

Cars on the Route is a restored Kan-O-Tex service station. The vintage car display here inspired the Mater character in Disney's *Cars*. Stop to enjoy a bite to eat and a host of Route 66 memorabilia.

The Galena Mining and Historical museum is located in an old railroad depot that has been moved from its original location. The website admits that operating hours can be a bit irregular based on volunteer availability, so call ahead before you visit.

The Murals of Galena are perhaps lesser known than other Route 66 attractions. However, they often end up being a favorite photo op for travelers. Park the car and walk down Main Street to truly enjoy the artistic renderings.

Riverton

Old Riverton Store, open since 1925, claims to be the oldest continuously operating store along Route 66. In addition to being a great photo op, it offers snacks and Route 66 souvenirs for sale. The store is credited at the end of Disney's *Cars* as being one of the locations scouted for inspiration during the creation of the animated film.

Baxter Springs

Bush Creek Bridge was constructed in 1923, and it is also referred to as the Rainbow Bridge because of the pair of concrete arches. The bridge is no longer open for traffic, but you can walk across it and take pictures.

Michigan

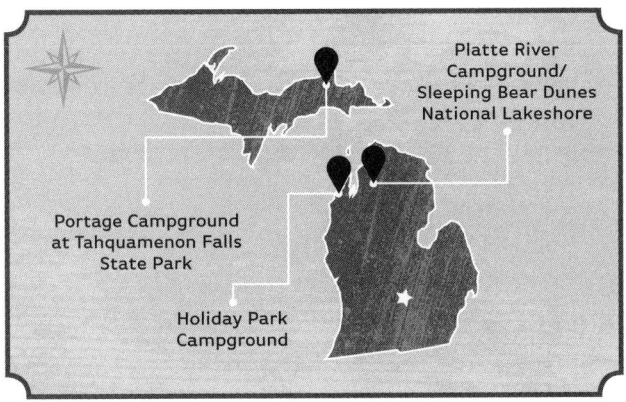

Platte River Campground/ Sleeping Bear Dunes National Lakeshore

Portage Campground at Tahquamenon Falls State Park

Holiday Park Campground

The winters in Michigan can be pretty rough, but the summers are nothing short of magical...as long as you bring your bug spray. Sandy beaches pepper the eastern shores of Lake Michigan and attract visitors to sweet towns like Grand Haven, Holland, and South Haven. The Ottawa County bike path network includes over 30 miles of dedicated trails, and twenty of those miles run right along the coastline. The state park campgrounds in this region are extremely popular, so make those reservations well in advance of your planned visit.

Up the coast, about 150 miles north, you'll find our personal favorite camping destination in Michigan. Sleeping Bear Dunes National Lakeshore is a playground for all ages, with massive dunes to hike up and roll down, plus tubing, hiking, and swimming. Nearby Traverse City is a hip gem of a city, offering a great downtown with coffee shops, bookstores, and craft breweries. Head even farther to the north to explore storied Mackinac Island and the Soo Locks at Sault Ste Marie. End your northern Michigan adventures by stamping your NPS passport at one of the least visited national parks in the country, Isle Royale. Then pack up your camping gear and head back south before the snow rolls in.

BEST IN STATE

Platte River Campground/Sleeping Bear Dunes National Lakeshore

▷ Honor, Michigan

▷ nps.gov

▷ RV and Tent Sites

The Platte River Campground is open year-round, but it is truly a classic summer camping experience. Taking a tubing or kayaking run in the clear, warm waters of the Platte River out to the cooler waters of Lake Michigan is a transcendent national park experience—and there are easy launch points near the campground. Booking a site at Platte River can be difficult, so know your booking window, wake up early with a huge cup of coffee, and pray to the camping gods. We booked six months in advance and recommend you do the same. The stress of booking your site will be a distant memory once you pull into Platte River. The campground is cozy and shaded, and sites are mostly large and private. Some sites even offer electric hookups. But there is no water or sewer at the sites, so plan accordingly. Many of the sites are back-in and have a large area behind them with a picnic table and fire ring. Pull-through (or pull-off) sites are also available, but we liked the back-in sites much better. We liked Loops 2 and 3 best (but take whatever you can get!), and don't forget to catch a ranger program at the amphitheater.

Holiday Park Campground

▷ Traverse City, Michigan

▷ holidayparktc.com

▷ RV and Tent Sites

Traverse City is an absolute gem of a city, with great coffee shops, independent bookstores, breweries, restaurants, and a hip, cool, and outdoorsy
downtown vibe. Holiday Park Campground is fifteen minutes from town
and has a casual hipster charm all its own. The setting is quiet and bucolic,
and the waters of Silver Lake are crystal clear and warm for swimming. This
used to be a seasonal campground for Airstream owners only, with a few
rental sites for transient campers. The restriction was lifted many years ago,
but there are still dozens of sites occupied by classic Airstreams—which
makes for some serious RV eye candy for folks with wandering eyes like us.
The campground actually functions a bit like a co-op—the seasonal campers own their sites. But when they leave to take their RVs elsewhere, they
rent out their sites to the general population. These sites are beautiful, particularly the ones that ring the lake. We lucked out and booked one for a
relaxing lakeside weekend. We could kayak from our site over to the swimming beach, then kayak back for dinner. The fishing here is good. But more
importantly, Moomers ice cream is sold in the camp store.

Portage Campground at Tahquamenon Falls State Park

▷   Paradise, Michigan

▷   www2.dnr.state.mi.us/parksandtrails/Default.aspx

▷   RV and Tent Sites, Cabins and Lodge

Tahquamenon Falls State Park is a nearly 50,000-acre natural wonderland
in Michigan's Upper Peninsula. The sound of the falls is mesmerizing, and
the entire park feels natural and untouched by civilization. This is Pure
Michigan at its finest. There are several options for camping at Tahq falls,
but the Hemlock and Portage Campgrounds are the best options for the
widest variety of campers. Portage is the most beloved by those in the know
because of its proximity to the lower falls, which is only a quarter mile from
the campground. Plan on wading out into the river on a hot summer day
to cool your feet and relax after a rigorous hike. Please make sure to use
bug spray in the summer—mosquitoes can be really bad. Fall might make a

much better time for a trip—and the foliage can be spectacular. The RV and tent sites are almost all spacious, but we recommend exterior sites for more privacy. The interior sites are pretty much out in the open. Plan on disconnecting while you are here—cell service is sketchy at best.

ALSO GREAT

Ludington State Park

 ▷ Ludington, Michigan

 ▷ www2.dnr.state.mi.us/parksandtrails/Default.aspx

 ▷ RV and Tent Sites, Mini Cabin

Michiganders are universally proud of their wide-ranging state park system. Many consider Ludington to be the prettiest park in the system, but the campsites can be difficult to book even though it has three campgrounds. Located between the shores of Hamlin Lake and Lake Michigan, the park has miles of shore to explore. The CCC-built Beach House on Lake Michigan and the Big Sable Point Lighthouse are both charming and historic.

Covert/South Haven KOA Holiday

 ▷ Covert, Michigan

 ▷ koa.com

 ▷ RV and Tent Sites, Rustic and Deluxe Cabins

This KOA is located in the southwest corner of Michigan and is just a few miles from the beautiful shores of Lake Michigan. The campground features an array of fun recreational activities for the kids including a ga-ga ball pit and trampoline basketball court. Another unique highlight? The u-pick blueberry field that greets visitors as they pull into the campground.

Sunset Bay RV Resort & Campground

▷ Allouez, Michigan

▷ sunset-bay.com

▷ RV and Tent Sites, Cabin Rentals

This remote campground is one of the oldest on the entire Upper Peninsula, and it can serve as a base camp for the even more remote Isle Royale National Park. The campground is small and quirky (it actually charges by length of your RV), but the views of Lake Superior from the rocky beach are epic.

------------------ **A Day in Traverse City** ------------------

Traverse City is one of our favorite American cities. We love walking the streets of downtown, hopping from one brewery to another, and paddling around the lake. The fifteen-minute drive to Moomers Ice Cream is worth every mile. Don't miss out on tasting what some folks claim is America's best ice cream.

✧ Higher Grounds for a cup of coffee

✧ Brilliant Books for the perfect independent bookstore experience

✧ The River Traverse City for kayak and SUP rentals

✧ The Filling Station Microbrewery for pizza and a pint

✧ Mission Point Lighthouse for a tour and splashing in the lake

✧ Jolly Pumpkin Brewery for dinner and a brew

✧ Moomers Ice Cream for a sweet treat

A Quick Guide to Sleeping Bear Dunes National Lakeshore

Sleeping Bear Dunes is the perfect place for a family national park adventure. There is something for every age and ability level, including swimming, hiking, tubing, and sightseeing. Visit in July or August to find out what a magical Michigan summer is all about.

Where to Camp
▷ Platte River Campground
▷ Holiday Park Campground
▷ Traverse City State Park Campground

Where to Stock Up
Empire is considered the gateway town to Sleeping Bear Dunes, and that's where you'll find the main visitor's center. You'll also find a small grocery and some dining options. Glen Arbor is another small town near the dunes with more dining and shopping options, including the famous Cherry Republic. Then there's Traverse City, a forty-minute drive, which has all of the big box stores plus plenty of local mom-and-pop options as well.

Your First Day in Sleeping Bear Dunes
Visit the Philip A. Hart Visitor Center in Empire. There are daily ranger programs here along with an interpretative exhibit. Make sure to pick up your Junior Ranger book at the beginning of your visit if you plan on completing the program; because many of the activities are location specific and things are very spread out in Sleeping Bear Dunes, you'll want to have a plan of attack.

Drive the Pierce Stocking Scenic Drive. This 7.4-mile loop is a fantastic introduction to the park. There are twelve official stops on the national park map, and some of the best dune and lake overlooks are on this loop. Plan on returning to many of these locations for more extensive hiking or exploration later on your trip.

Head to the Dune Climb. These dunes top out at more than 400 feet above the Lake Michigan Shoreline. Although physically strenuous, it's a blast to climb the dune and then race back down to the bottom. Our kids enjoyed doing this over and over again, begging to return later during our trip. Make sure to visit in the morning or late afternoon when the sand is not so hot. Also avoid going during windy weather.

Hikes in Sleeping Bear Dunes

▷ *Empire Bluff Trail*. This 1.5-mile out-and-back trail runs through a beech and maple forest, then emerges along a dune ridge with stunning views of Lake Michigan and an observation deck that sits 450 feet above the shoreline. Bring the camera.

▷ *Alligator Hill Trail*. This 4.7-mile loop trail has great shade for much of the hike, then emerges to offer beautiful views of Glen Lake.

▷ *Pyramid Point Loop*. This 2.8-mile loop trail has a steep elevation gain, but the lookout point hundreds of feet above Lake Michigan is worth the effort. You can shorten the hike to just over a mile by going to the lookout and then heading back to the trailhead.

Swimming in Sleeping Bear Dunes

▷ *Platte River Point*. This is where Platte River meets Lake Michigan, and you could happily spend your entire vacation at this spot. Folks bring their tubes to float down the river into the lake, then walk back up and do it all over again. There are ever-changing sandbars created by the tides and plenty of fun tidal pools to play in.

▷ *Glen Haven Beach*. This dog-friendly beach is located right next to the Cannery Boat Museum and offers beautiful views of the Manitou Islands.

▷ *North Bar Lake*. This is a very popular beach in the park on account of the warm, shallow water. At times the tides connect this lake with Lake Michigan, and visitors have a blast floating along with the current. We rented paddleboards from a nearby shop and spent the whole day at this beach, swimming and paddling our hearts out.

Pets in the Park

Some national parks are pet-friendly and some are not. Sleeping Bear Dunes is a bit of a hybrid, restricting dogs in a range of places mostly on account of the endangered bird population. Luckily, the park offers very clear guidance on where you can bring your furry friend: www.nps.gov /slbe/planyourvisit/pets.

Minnesota

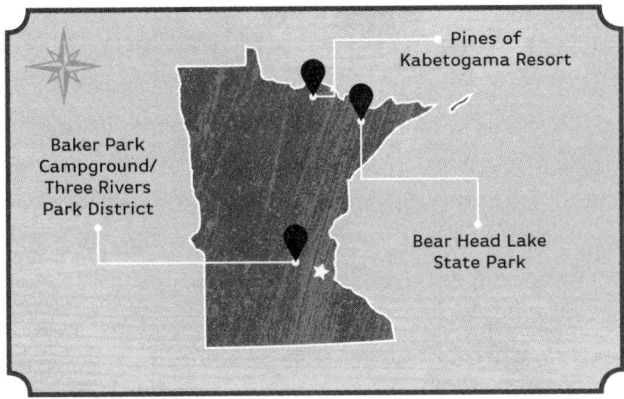

It's no surprise that the Land of 10,000 Lakes offers plenty of opportunities for waterfront camping opportunities. Minnesota camping is all about the boat launches and rentals—bring your own kayaks and paddleboards to get the most out of your getaways, or rent them from a nearby marina. The walleye, bass, and trout are another big attraction for outdoor enthusiasts in this state.

The state park system is well run and well-funded, so those campgrounds might be the perfect way for you to camp affordably in some of the most scenic places in our country. However, there are also private campground options that offer additional amenities like playgrounds and private sand beaches.

BEST IN STATE

Pines of Kabetogama Resort

▷ Kabetogama, Minnesota

▷ thepineskab.com

▷ RV Sites, Luxury RV Rental, Luxury Cabins, Paul Bunyan Home

If your journey takes you to Voyageurs National Park in the rugged Northwoods of Minnesota, but you want to camp in the lap of luxury and not in the rustic and remote options inside the park, then you simply must consider camping at the Pines of Kabetogama Resort. The cliffside and lakeview cabins are well-appointed and furnished with regional decor. Traveling with multiple families or taking a guys' or girls' trip to get back to nature and spend time fishing on the lake? Then consider renting the spacious five-bedroom, two-bath Paul Bunyan Home. Big-rig owners and RVers who like a resort camping experience will also fall in love with the premium RV campsites—these sites have views of the lake and come with an electric golf cart and a dock space for one boat. The rest of the RV sites are good, but these are truly great. Figure out how you are going to stay, then it's time to play. The marina offers motorboat rentals, and the sandy beach has kayak and paddleboard rentals. Though this might make the perfect place for a romantic couple's getaway, it is also a perfect place to bring the kids. They will love the alligator water trampoline, the playground, and fishing from the docks at the end of another perfect summer day.

Bear Head Lake State Park

▷ Ely, Minnesota

▷ dnr.state.mn.us

▷ RV and Tent Sites, Canoe Sites, Camper Cabins, Guest House

If natural beauty, seclusion, and lake life are your thing, then Bear Head Lake State Park in the Northwoods of Minnesota will be your new happy place. The entire Minnesota State Park system is beautiful and much loved by Minnesotans, but this might be the prettiest park in the state. Fishing, hiking, and boating are all excellent here. Bass and trout are abundant in the lakes, and the hikes are easy but fun. If you travel with a kayak or SUP, you will also find yourself a very happy camper. There is also a nice swimming beach that is sandy and shallow, making it perfect for the littles. The campground here is a wee bit challenging for big rigs to navigate, but most campers will do just fine. Most sites are wooded and spacious. Simple but comfortable cabins are also available for rent here, and so is a three-bedroom guest house—neither option comes anything close to glamping. But this is the rugged Northwoods of Minnesota—if you want to get fancy, you might be in the wrong place.

Mall of America

We never thought we would be talking about a mall in a camping book, but this one in Bloomington, Minnesota, deserves a name check. There's plenty of shopping, but there are also attractions like Nickelodeon Universe with a roller coaster, Ferris wheel, and hot air balloon rides. Also make time for the Lego Store, Crayola Experience, and Sea Life Aquarium.

Baker Park Campground/Three Rivers Park District

- ▷ Maple Plain, Minnesota
- ▷ threeriversparks.org
- ▷ RV and Tent Sites, Camper Cabins

Baker Park Campground would be great even if it was in the middle of nowhere. You could spend a long weekend or short vacation here and never leave. But considering it is less than thirty minutes from downtown Minneapolis, we think this place is excellent. The campground has over 200 sites for RV and tent camping, and most of them are level and spacious.

They are not private and deeply wooded—but there are plenty of that kind of site in Minnesota if you want it. Cabin campers love the rentals here— they are set against a wooded backdrop and have screened-in porches and electricity. A clean and modern restroom and showering facility is located nearby. All sites are a short walk from Lake Independence, where there is good fishing and swimming as well as SUP, kayak, and canoe rentals. The lake gets really busy on summer weekends, so you might decide to head into the city on Saturday or Sunday to catch a baseball game or do some sight- seeing. This is a social campground that is often filled with families, and while the sound of kids playing will certainly fill the air during the daytime, the park settles down nicely at night as kids drift off to sleep and adults relax around the campfire.

Legendary SPAM

The best free entertainment in the state of Minnesota might just be the SPAM Museum, located in downtown Austin. Spambassadors roam the museum eager to answer any one of your burning SPAM questions. Some of them may be pass- ing out free samples of SPAM. Try your hand at canning along a mock assembly line, then leave with a list of all the surrounding restaurants serving SPAM.

ALSO GREAT

Lamb's Resort & Campground

▷   Schroeder, Minnesota

▷   lambsresort.com

▷   RV and Tent Sites, Cabins

Lamb's Resort is a family-owned mom-and-pop campground with a half mile of private beach and stunning views of Lake Superior. Some campsites are right on the lake and some are tucked away in the woods—but all of them are lovely and spacious. The log cabins here are Instagram-worthy and several of them have commanding water views. Make sure to get coffee and pastries at the Schroeder Baking Company, which is walking distance from your site.

Itasca State Park

▷ Park Rapids, Minnesota

▷ dnr.state.mn.us

▷ Douglas Lodge Rooms, Wide Variety of Cabins, RV and Tent Sites

The mighty Mississippi River starts here! Itasca State Park was established in 1891 and is Minnesota's oldest state park. It is also gigantic. It encompasses 32,000 acres and has over 100 lakes. Park-run lodging options here are top notch. The Douglas Lodge has been hosting lovers of the great outdoors for over one hundred years, and a variety of other classic CCC-built cabins are also available for rent. There are two campgrounds here, Bear Paw and Pine Ridge, and both offer excellent sites that are large and wooded.

Lebanon Hills Regional Park Campground

▷ St. Paul, Minnesota

▷ co.dakota.mn.us

▷ RV and Tent Sites

This campground is a quiet and shady oasis located right smack in the suburbs of the Twin Cities. Downtown Minneapolis is only thirty-five minutes away, and the Mall of America is less than twenty minutes away. Lebanon Hills Regional Park Campground is the perfect base camp for those destinations, but it is also a destination in its own right. This spotless park is filled with trails and lakes for hiking, biking, and boating—and the swimming at Schulze Lake Beach is also good, so don't forget your bathing suit.

Voyageurs National Park

With under a quarter million visitors per year, this national park is one of the least visited NPS sites in the country along with its Michigan neighbor, Isle Royale National Park. In the Land of 10,000 Lakes, it makes sense that 40 percent of Voyageurs is covered by water. That means this national park experience will be unique, but you should plan in advance to make the most out of a visit.

- ✧ Think about your watercraft plans. You can bring your own boat or kayak, take guided boat tours with rangers, or rent boats and reserve tours through a list of approved local vendors.

- ✧ Pack layers of clothing, even in the summer months. A jacket and even a hat will probably be welcome at night. Also pack your bug spray (because water = mosquitoes!). Binoculars will help you enjoy the wildlife sightings more.

- ✧ Check out the winter activities and programs if you are a hearty adventurer. Ride on a snowmobile, cross-country ski, drive the ice road, or rent an ice fishing house. This park does not close down in the snow.

- ✧ Borrow a Discovery Pack from one of the visitor centers. Voyageurs has seven themed discovery packs that will help bring the history and geology of the park alive. Learn about the fur trade, regional plants and animals, and—of course—water.

- ✧ Use the park maps and moon phase calendar to plan your stargazing. This is an amazing place to see the night sky. The Voyageurs Forest Overlook, Beaver Pond Overlook, and Kettle Falls Dam are particularly good locations. A clear, moonless night is akin to winning the lottery at Voyageurs.

· *Missouri* ·

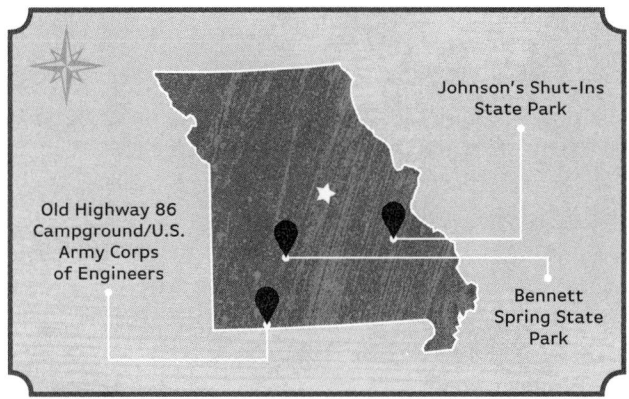

Johnson's Shut-Ins
State Park

Old Highway 86
Campground/U.S.
Army Corps
of Engineers

Bennett
Spring State
Park

Missouri doesn't appear on a lot of destination bucket lists, but the people who live there know it is full of beautiful camping destinations. In fact, the state park campgrounds are enough of a well-kept secret that residents may not be thrilled with us spilling the beans about them. The northern part of the state contains the wide-open plains that come to mind when we picture the quintessential Midwest. The southern region, however, hosts a beautiful slice of the Ozarks, with lakes, rivers, and cave systems popular for boating, fishing, and hiking enthusiasts.

Of course, Missouri also contains a solid 300 miles of Route 66, which slices across the state from St. Louis to Joplin. If you are interested in jour-neying along the Mother Road, Missouri has great campgrounds located directly on historic Route 66, including the St. Louis West/Historic Route 66 KOA. The state is also known as the home of Bass Pro Shops, established in Springfield, where the headquarters is still located. Founder John Morris also created Big Cedar Lodge on Table Rock Lake as a family vacation des-tination committed to natural conservation. Camp Long Creek, located on the same property, is a great place to camp and simultaneously enjoy the resort lodge amenities and stunning lakefront property.

---------- **What to Eat in Springfield, Missouri** ----------

We learned from our Missourian friends that they are all about the cashew chicken—fried bites of chicken tossed in a brown gravy and topped with cashews and green onions. This dish, invented by David Leong in the 1960s, has now made its way to menus across the country...but it got its start in Springfield.

BEST IN STATE

Bennett Spring State Park

▷ Lebanon, Missouri

▷ mostateparks.com

▷ RV and Tent Sites, Cabins and Motel Rooms

Known for its excellent hiking and trout fishing, Bennett Spring State Park is an idyllic campground in the southwest corner of Missouri, just an hour from Springfield and three hours from St. Louis. Bennett Spring offers a wide variety of lodging options, including cabins and motel rooms, for families and couples that want a back-to-nature experience at an affordable price. Tent campers and RV owners also love it here and return year after year, and generation after generation. There are actually five campgrounds at this park. Campground #1, which is close to the Niangua River, has full hookups, but it feels a bit like a parking lot. If you can do without the full hookups, then Campgrounds #2–5, which are up a steep hill, are all lovely and deeply wooded. The trees are beautiful here, and the sites are large and private. Many of those sites in Campgrounds #2–5 do have electric, so you

• can run the all-important air conditioner if you are RVing in the heat of the summer. The rustic and cozy on-site dining lodge, which was built by the CCC in the 1930s, is not to be missed. Locals also love the park store, which has everything you need to gear up for a great weekend of camping and fishing in the Show Me State.

------------ **Great Missouri State Park Hikes** ------------

Castle Trail, Ha Ha Tonka State Park

A short 0.7-mile hike along an ADA accessible trail, leading to an abandoned castle and beautiful lake views.

Johnson's Shut-Ins State Park Trail, Johnson's Shut-Ins State Park

A 2.5-mile loop trail with some rock scrambles and steep stair climbs, offering views of the shut-ins—large rocks with water flowing over and around them, creating a sort of natural water park for visitors to enjoy.

Hidden Springs Trail, Lake of the Ozarks State Park

A 2.5-mile family-friendly and pet-friendly loop trail, with some views of the lake and an old family cemetery.

River Scene Trail Loop, Castlewood State Park

A 3.1-mile loop trail with sweeping views of the Meramec River and a long, wooden staircase that descends to the water.

Wanna rest your legs? Lost Canyon Cave & Nature Trail at Big Cedar Lodge

If you want to take a break from hiking, hop on an electric cart at the Top of the Rock Welcome Center and enjoy the 2.5-mile ride through the scenic Ozarks.

Old Highway 86 Campground/U.S. Army Corps of Engineers

> ▷ Blue Eye, Missouri

> ▷ recreation.gov

> ▷ RV and Tent Sites

Old Highway 86 Campground is a gem in the often-overlooked U.S. Army Corps of Engineers network of campgrounds. It is situated on a peninsula that juts out into Table Rock Lake, so every site has views of the water—and many of the sites (about 75 percent of them) back right up to the water. If you travel with kayaks or SUPs, there may be no better place to camp in the entire Midwest. If you don't have a site with direct water access, there is a sandy swimming beach with picnic tables and a public dock for launching. When you book a site at recreation.gov, you can see a picture of each site—it is well worth it to do a bit of research and nab a waterfront site. There isn't much immediately around this campground, but Branson is only about thirty minutes away and has entertainment galore. Think theme parks, mini golf, go-kart tracks, and tons of shopping and dining. But at the end of the day, we think you should be back at your campsite at Old Highway 86 relaxing around the campfire watching the sunset melt into the lake. Camping just doesn't get much better than this.

Johnson's Shut-Ins State Park

> ▷ Middle Brook, Missouri

> ▷ mostateparks.com

> ▷ RV and Tent Sites, Camper Cabins

What the heck is a shut-in? It's kind of like a natural water park in a river created by rock that is resistant to erosion. The shut-ins at this state park are filled with all kinds of neat little swimming holes and spots for rock jumping and exploring. The Ozark Trail also runs through the park and forms one of several popular hikes in the park. Johnson's Shut-Ins State

Park was rebuilt in recent years after a nearby mountain reservoir failed and flooded the park, destroying many of its facilities. The new facilities and rebuilt campground are real favorites among Missouri campers for good reason. The sites are large, paved, and mostly private, and many even have full hookups. The tent sites and camper cabins are also a real treat here. Cabins feature electricity, heat, and air conditioning, but they don't have running water or bathrooms. The Shut-Ins area gets mighty crowded in the summertime, but there is a separate reserved parking area for those staying in the campground, which is a nice touch if you ask us!

ALSO GREAT

Camp Long Creek at Big Cedar Lodge

▷   Ridgedale, Missouri

▷   bigcedar.com

▷   Shepherd's Huts, Camp Cabins, Glamping Tents

The glamping tents at Camp Long Creek have stunning water views and charming (and very private) stone patios that feature firepits and outdoor tubs. Leave the kids at home for an unforgettable romantic weekend. Traveling with kids? Choose the one-bedroom camp cabin and play a game of cards at night on the screened-in porch and watch the fireflies dance outside on a long summer night.

Lake of the Ozarks State Park

▷   Kaiser, Missouri

▷   mostateparks.com

▷   Cabins and Yurts, RV and Tent Sites

The RV and tent sites are great at Missouri's most visited state park, but the real star of the show is the aptly named Outpost area in the heart of the park. Here you will find eight picture-perfect, Instagram-worthy cabins sur-rounded by an oak-hickory forest. You need to bring all of the gear and bed-ding for these cabins, but the price is such a bargain you won't mind at all. Adorable yurts are also available in a separate section of the park.

St. Louis West/Historic Route 66 KOA Holiday

▷ Eureka, Missouri

▷ koa.com

▷ RV and Tent Sites, Caboose Camping Cabin, Deluxe Cabins

This KOA serves as a great base camp for exploring St. Louis, which is about thirty minutes away. Six Flags St. Louis is only a mile away. But the real cherry on top is that this campground is located directly on historic Route 66 and makes for a more than comfortable overnight stop for those exploring the Mother Road. The Kozy Caboose rental is cute, and you can fall asleep inside of a piece of Route 66 history.

Top Missouri Route 66 Attractions

Ted Drewes Frozen Custard

6726 Chippewa Street, St. Louis, MO 63109

This place is always hopping, but it's worth the wait for a delicious hot fudge sundae or a Concrete—a shake so thick, it's served upside down.

Missouri Route 66 State Park

97 N Outer Road E, Suite 1, Eureka, MO 63025

Picnic areas, trails, fishing, and of course, a visitor center that features the history of Route 66 in Missouri.

Wagon Wheel Motel

901 E Washington Boulevard, Cuba, MO 65453

Even if you choose camping over iconic roadside motels, make sure you stop for a picture of the classic, neon-trimmed wagon wheel sign.

The World's Largest Rocking Chair

5957 Highway ZZ, Cuba, MO 65453

Even though the official name hasn't changed, this is now actually the world's second largest rocking chair. It still makes a great Route 66 photo op.

Gary's Gay Parita

21498 MO-266, Everton, MO 65646

An out-of-service gas station packed with Route 66 memorabilia, this is one of the most popular stops along the Mother Road.

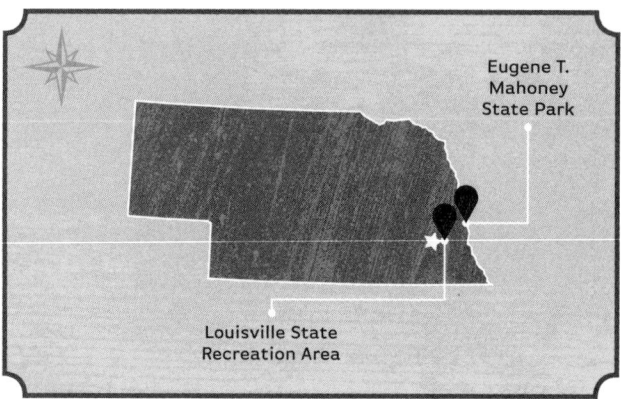

Nebraska

Eugene T. Mahoney State Park

Louisville State Recreation Area

Nicknames like the Cornhusker State may lead folks to think Nebraska has a whole lot of fields and not much else. Nebraskans seem to understand and embrace this reputation with a sly sense of humor. The state tourism bureau uses the tagline, "Honestly, it's not for everyone," and we can't stop laughing at that one. However, Nebraska has more miles of river than any other state in the lower forty-eight, and a strong outdoor culture of fishing and hunting is evident here—this is where Cabela's was founded back in 1961.

BEST IN STATE

Eugene T. Mahoney State Park

▷ Ashland, Nebraska

▷ outdoornebraska.gov

▷ RV and Tent Sites, Cabins, Peter Kiewit Lodge

Mahoney State Park, located midway between Lincoln and Omaha, is the pride and joy of Nebraska's excellent state park system. Designated as one of the state's four "outdoor venture parks," Mahoney has benefited from recent public and private funding and had its activities and amenities bolstered and modernized. The Go Ape ropes course will please adventurous campers of many different ages and ability levels. Families will also love the full-featured aquatic center (with two giant waterslides!) and the arts and crafts center. The park also offers indoor rock climbing when the weather gets cold and an indoor playground on steroids—and this is just the beginning of Mahoney's adventurous offerings. The Peter Kiewit Lodge offers forty comfortable guestrooms and also has an excellent on-site restaurant in Caddy's Parkside Grill. Over fifty secluded ridgetop cabins are available to rent, and the park has two campgrounds for RV owners and tent campers. The campgrounds are simple and straightforward here (and there is road noise from the interstate), but the amazing amenities and activities at this park will keep you busy from dawn to dusk if that's your thing. If you simply want peace and quiet, you might pick another one of Nebraska's beautiful state parks instead.

Louisville State Recreation Area

▷ Louisville, Nebraska

▷ outdoornebraska.gov

▷ RV and Tent Sites

The wild and wacky Wibit floating playground at Louisville State Recreation Area is not something you usually see at a state park campground. It does cost an additional fee here, but the price of camping is so low that we are still calling it a bargain. If huge inflatable slides are not your speed, then you will be happy to know that there are four other lakes at this lovely state park that offer excellent fishing, swimming, canoeing, and kayaking. Non-motorized boat rentals are also available. Most of the camping facilities here were recently upgraded, and the showers and restrooms are practically brand new. The parklike campground has nice open lawns and plenty of trees, but some sites lack privacy. A train goes by across the lake from the campground, so fully enclosed RV owners will have a better time sleeping than those in pop-up campers and tents. This campground is also close to Platte River State Park, which is well worth a visit.

---- **Four Reservoirs in Nebraska with Campgrounds** ----

Lewis and Clark Lake

Open year-round for camping and has a full-service marina.

Lake McConaughy

Nebraska's largest reservoir, this one offers developed and primitive camping options.

Branched Oak Lake

There are nine total campgrounds at Branched Oak. Two have hookups and seven are primitive.

Johnson Lake

Here you'll find a campground with electricity and one without. Reservations can be made up to a year in advance.

ALSO GREAT

Platte River State Park

▷   Louisville, Nebraska

▷   outdoornebraska.gov

▷   Camper Cabins, Modern Cabins, Glamping Cabins, RV Campground under Construction at Time of Writing

The brand-new glamping cabins at Platte River State Park are on point and gorgeous. Private campground owners should take note. The bright and airy space is designed so that you can sleep inside or outside by simply rolling the bed out onto the private deck. Fully equipped "modern" cabins are also available, as are rustic, and affordable, camper cabins. At the time of this writing a modern RV park was under construction—which will make this action-packed state park one of the best places to camp in all of Nebraska.

West Omaha/NE Lincoln KOA Holiday

▷ Gretna, Nebraska

▷ koa.com

▷ RV and Tent Sites, Camping Cabins, Deluxe Cabins

If you are passing through Nebraska on your way to all points west, then this is a great stopover for a good night's sleep. But it is also much more. This KOA serves as a great base camp for travelers who want to explore nearby Omaha and Lincoln, and it is also a fun campground for regional campers looking for a weekend of fun. Kids love the bounce pillow and tractor rides, and who doesn't love getting pizza delivered right to their site?

------------------- **Ready to Go Tanking?** -------------------

We're not sure if tanking was invented in Nebraska, but we've certainly never seen it anywhere else. "What is it?" you non-Nebraskans may ask. Well, you simply repurpose an extra-large stock tank as a giant flotation device, hop in with a few of your closest friends, and float down a river. It's what tubing looks like when you put farmers in charge. There are plenty of outfitters who will help you enjoy this experience, dropping you off upstream with your tank and coolers, then picking you up downstream a few hours later.

Fisher's Cove RV Park

▷   Silver Creek, Nebraska

▷   fisherscovervpark.com

▷   **RV Sites**

Fisher's Cove RV Park is a relaxing place for a simple, back-to-nature camping experience. Campers come here to recreate on the calm and tranquil waters of its 21-acre stocked lake, which is excellent for fishing and paddling. Spacious RV sites back right up to the sandy beach, which is also quite welcoming for a summer swim. There are good eats to be had in downtown Silver Creek if you don't want to grill at your site. Check out Great Plains Cafe—it offers affordable downhome Nebraska cooking at its best.

· North Dakota ·

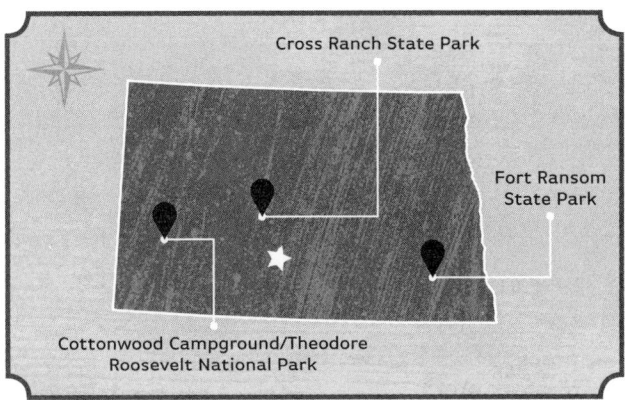

North Dakota might be one of the most under-the-radar camping destinations in America, but the folks who do visit will tell you that it was worth the detour. Many visitors are drawn to the state by a desire to visit one of the more remote NPS sites in the United States, Theodore Roosevelt National Park. Roosevelt came to North Dakota to hunt bison and to grieve the death of both his mother and wife. As it turns out, his time spent in this state impacted decades of conservation policy in our country, and North Dakota is dotted with historical sites that speak to this legacy.

Of course, the Peace Garden is known for endless blue skies, wheat fields, and wildlife, but there is also plenty of fun to be had in Fargo, the state's largest city, and Bismarck, the state capital. The craft breweries, farmers markets, and a growing food scene are worth checking out. You might want to put the Fargo Film Festival on your travel agenda if visiting during the spring. And don't miss out on a photo op of Fargo's infamous wood chipper on permanent display at the visitor's center.

BEST IN STATE

Fort Ransom State Park

▷   Fort Ransom, North Dakota

▷   parkrec.nd.gov

▷   Yurts, Covered Wagons, Cabins, Home Rental, RV and Tent Sites

The modest folks at Fort Ransom State Park don't like to call their yurt and covered wagon rentals "glamping," but they look pretty darn glampy to us—especially the yurts. They are called the Pederson & Redetzke Yurts and they each have a full kitchen, a bathroom, two bedrooms, a loft, and a pull-out couch. Most of the RV sites have electric and water, and over thirty sites are designed for horse owners and have corral access at the sites. This park is secluded, and outdoor activities abound. The Sheyenne River Valley offers canoeing, birdwatching, horseback riding, fishing, and cross-country skiing in the winter. There are also over 20 miles of lovely hiking trails in this park, so bring comfortable shoes, bug spray, and lots of water. Fort Ransom State Park is remote but well worth putting on your ever-expanding bucket list of great American campgrounds.

Cottonwood Campground/Theodore Roosevelt National Park

▷   Medora, North Dakota

▷   nps.gov

▷   RV and Tent Sites

Theodore Roosevelt National Park is an underrated gem. Roosevelt's time spent here as a young man in the 1880s shaped his life and the life of our nation. World-class wildlife viewing and hiking opportunities can be found in this park without the crowds that are often associated with Yellowstone, Badlands, and Glacier. For those who are willing to dry camp, there are also excellent options. Cottonwood Campground, which is partially situated along the banks of the Little Missouri River, is probably the best. Half of the sites here are reservable, and half are first-come, first-served—but all of them are simple, quiet, and beautiful. Book as early as possible because the campground does fill up despite the generally uncrowded nature of the park—and bring your own soap to the bathhouse because the park often runs out. If you are just a little bit lucky, you will see bison wandering through the campground and maybe even onto your campsite. Keep your distance and get ready to be in awe of these mighty and magnificent creatures.

Cross Ranch State Park

  ▷   Center, North Dakota

  ▷   parkrec.nd.gov

  ▷   Cabins, Yurts, Tepees, RV and Tent Sites

North Dakota's state park system is excellent through and through. It offers unique outdoor lodging in several of its best parks, making them exciting places for those who love to camp but don't own RVs and have no interest in sleeping in a tent. Cross Ranch State Park is located along a wild and peaceful stretch of the Missouri River and offers outdoor recreation of just about every type, but it is particularly excellent for hiking, mountain biking, and cross-country skiing. RV and tent sites are spacious, private, and primitive, but some of the lodging options, like the cabins and yurts, offer full kitchens and bathrooms. The York Cabin and Pretty Point Yurt are particularly impressive as both offer comfortable digs and stunning views of the Missouri River. There are actually three distinct campgrounds within Cross Ranch. Sanger is probably the prettiest, but big rigs need not apply. It is designed for tent campers and smaller RVs. Bringing a pop-up camper here on a cool summer night would be near wild heaven.

- **Before you go...** -

  ▷   **Read:** *The Rise of Theodore Roosevelt* by Edmund Morris

ALSO GREAT

Bismarck KOA Journey

▷ Bismarck, North Dakota

▷ koa.com

▷ RV and Tent Sites, Camping Cabins and Deluxe Cabins

This KOA wins high marks for extraordinary customer service and close proximity to downtown Bismarck, which is about twelve minutes away. The park-like setting is pretty, and the RV sites are more than adequate. Many of the tent sites are out in the open, but the cabins are nice. This KOA is also open year-round—which is quite unusual for a private campground in this part of the world. It shut down water to the sites but will deliver it to your RV if needed.

Lake Metigoshe State Park

▷ Bottineau, North Dakota

▷ parkrec.nd.gov

▷ Lodges, Cabins, Yurts, RV and Tent Sites

Lake Metigoshe State Park is situated in North Dakota's Turtle Mountains near the Canadian border and is far, far away for most people. But it is well worth getting to for world-class fishing, boating, and swimming. Its unique outdoor accommodations also make this an all-star pick for campers seeking comfort. The Slemmen Lodge is perfect for a larger group and is surrounded by gorgeous hiking trails.

---------- **Drive It: The Enchanted Highway** ----------

This 32-mile drive stretches from Gladstone, North Dakota, to Regent, North Dakota, and features large metal sculptures along the road. The art installations include *Geese in Flight*, *Deer Crossing*, and *Grasshoppers*. You can purchase a souvenir of your favorite sculpture at the small gift shop in Regent.

What to Do in Theodore Roosevelt National Park

▷ Soak in the North Dakota Badlands at Painted Canyon Visitor's Center.
▷ Drive the 36-mile scenic loop drive in the morning or evening for best wildlife viewing.
▷ Visit the Maltese Ranch Cabin, built from 1883–1884 at the request of Theodore Roosevelt.
▷ Track down the isolated Elkhorn Ranch Site deep in the North Dakota Badlands.
▷ Drive the 14-mile Theodore Roosevelt North Unit Scenic Byway.
▷ Stop at the Oxbow Overlook for a sweeping view of the Little Missouri River.
▷ Watch (but don't feed!) the prairie dogs.

Popular Hikes in Theodore Roosevelt National Park

South Unit
▷ Ridgeline Nature Trail (0.6)
▷ Coal Vein Trail (0.8)
▷ Wind Canyon Trail (0.4)

North Unit
▷ Little Mo Trail (0.7)
▷ Caprock Coulee Nature Trail (1.5)
▷ Sperati Point via the Achenbach Trail (1.5)

Don't Miss It: The Medora Musical

The Medora Musical is a live musical attraction that has been performed in Medora for over fifty years. Get the dinner and a show package to enjoy an outdoor buffet before the musical extravaganza. This is the perfect way to end a day at Theodore Roosevelt National Park.

· Ohio ·

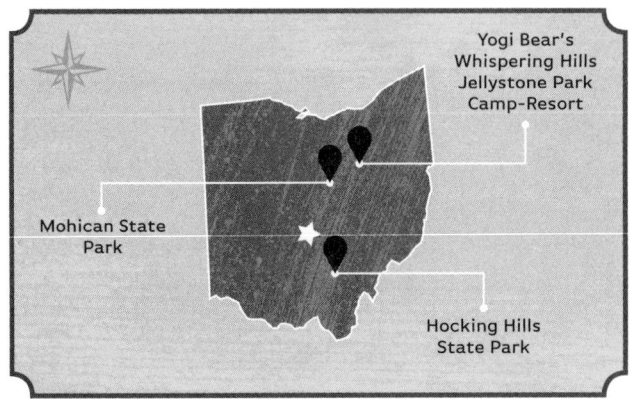

If you've only driven across the northern stretch of Ohio along I-80 and I-90, you might think the whole state is potholes, construction, and corn fields. However, the people who live and camp in this state know better. There are some gems to be discovered, whether you are looking for a quiet state park or a rollicking resort.

In 2014, a state panel allotted $88 million dollars to the Ohio Department of Natural Resources specifically to improve and upgrade the state park facilities. Campers and RVers are now reaping the benefits years later. Hocking Hills State Park might be the best kept secret among all of America's most beautiful state parks, and Ohio residents might not be too happy with us for spreading the word. It's filled with beautiful hikes, waterfalls, and caves. Don't worry if you can't book a campsite at the last minute—there are many other beloved state park campgrounds to visit, including Caesar Creek, Findley, Maumee Bay, and Mohican.

Looking for some more resort-like amenities for your camping trips? You may already know that the Roller Coaster Capital of the World is in the

Buckeye State. But did you know you can camp within walking distance of Cedar Point at Lighthouse Point? There are also plenty of well-reviewed Jellystones and KOAs with pools, jump pillows, and organized activities. There is an abundance of choices for quick weekend getaways or weeklong lazy family vacations in the beautiful state of Ohio.

BEST IN STATE

Hocking Hills State Park

- ▷ Logan, Ohio
- ▷ thehockinghills.org/
- ▷ RV and Tent Sites, Cabin Rentals

Hocking Hills State Park is one of the most beautiful state parks in the country. The park is a hiker's delight and features cliffs, gorges, and waterfalls that will surprise and delight nature lovers of all ages. The campground is not quite as spectacular as the park itself, but its location within walking distance of Old Man's Cave and a variety of excellent hiking trails can't be beat. The campground has a wide variety of site offerings, and some even offer full hookups. Many of the sites are not level, so come prepared with blocks to straighten out your rig. If you are in a tent, resourcefulness may be required to get comfortable. This campground is incredibly popular and is full almost all summer long. It can be noisy on weekends, but most folks settle down at a reasonable hour. RV owners with self-contained rigs will have an advantage here because the public restrooms can get messy at peak season. If you aren't picky about every little detail you will love it here. Plan on bringing comfortable hiking shoes and spending hours exploring this magnificent park.

Yogi Bear's Whispering Hills Jellystone Park Camp-Resort

▷   Big Prairie, Ohio

▷   whisperinghillsjellystone.com

▷   Cabins, Lodges, Yurts, RV and Tent Sites

This well-managed Jellystone strikes a perfect balance. You can unwind here surrounded by the lush and lovely rolling hills of Amish country, or you can go full tilt and have nonstop fun with your family and friends. RV sites and cabins are peaceful, while the common areas (the pool, playground, sporting fields, indoor recreation center, and more) are filled with options for organized activities and free play. Our boys navigated a corn maze, competed in a cannonball contest, and played tons of basketball, baseball, and ga-ga ball. We also spent time fishing at the lake and tooling around the campground on our rented golf cart. We also loved the fairly vigorous hiking trail that rings the campground. The RV and tent sites here are more than adequate, but the real star of the show may be the wide variety of cabin, chateau, and manor rentals. They are charming and some of them can easily accommodate multiple families. This would be a perfect place for a family reunion or group camping trip with folks who are not RV owners. But it was also a perfect place for our family of five to enjoy a handful of long, lazy summer days. We loved it here and you will too.

Mohican State Park

▷   Loudonville, Ohio

▷   ohiodnr.gov/wps/portal/gov/odnr

▷   RV and Tent Sites, Cabins, Mohican Lodge

Mohican State Park is one of the prettiest state parks in the entire Midwest, and it also has excellent accommodations for RV owners, tent campers, cabin renters, and those who prefer the comfort of an excellent lodge. This 1,110-acre state park has lovely hiking through hemlock forests and regionally renowned fishing in the Clear Fork River, which is stocked with brown trout every year. The campground here looks a bit more like a lovely private campground than the typical state park setup. Most sites are out in the open and a bit smaller than a typical state park site. This is not a complaint. The wide open parklike feel of the campground makes it a friendly and social place, and it is easy to watch your kids ride bikes or play catch from the comfort of your site. Those who prefer a deeply wooded private site may want to look elsewhere. The cabins here are clean and modern with woods behind them and lots of room in between sites. Very few private campgrounds have better options than the ones offered here. The lodge comes close to having the comfort and classic charm of one of our great national park lodges, and in some ways it is better. There are indoor and outdoor pools and a sauna for lodge guests. Bromfield's Dining Room, right inside the lodge, offers up breakfast, lunch, and dinner with a view of Pleasant Hill Lake. Grab a seat near the grand fireplace on a chilly fall night after a long hike to experience the best that this great state park has to offer.

--- **An Urban Treasure: Cuyahoga Valley National Park** ---

This NPS site flies under the radar for many folks, but Cleveland and Akron locals treasure the national park that borders their urban neighborhoods. There are lots of opportunities for hiking, biking, paddling, and nature photography.

- ✧ Hike to Brandywine Falls via the 1.4-mile Brandywine Gorge Trail.
- ✧ Take a ranger-led hike around the Ledges and learn about the geology of the sandstone cliffs.
- ✧ Visit Beaver Marsh early in the morning for wildlife viewing and bird photography.
- ✧ Bike the Ohio and Erie Canal Towpath Trails. From May through October, you can ride in one direction and then return by train via the Cuyahoga Valley Scenic Railroad's Bike Aboard! Program.
- ✧ Bring your own kayaks and paddle the Cuyahoga River.

ALSO GREAT

Dayton KOA Resort

▷   Brookville, Ohio

▷   koa.com

▷   Glamping Tents, RV and Tent Sites, Rustic and Deluxe Cabins

This campground pretty much has it all and serves as a great example of the KOA brand at its best. Themed weekends during the summer (think Galactic Takeover and Western Weekend) are a huge hit with families and campers of all ages. Activities and amenities are also on point and appealing for all ages. Teenagers love basketball, volleyball, and soccer, and the youngsters love free train rides and gem mining. At night, just about everyone can be found relaxing around the campfire and laughing with family and friends.

Streetsboro/Cleveland SE KOA Holiday

▷   Streetsboro, Ohio

▷   koa.com

▷   Glamping Tent, Camping Cabins, Deluxe Cabins, RV and Tent Sites

One of my best camping memories of all time happened in the pool at this pretty and well-managed KOA. I looked around and realized that there were about six sets of twins relaxing in and around the pool with us (we have twin boys). At first I thought I was hallucinating, but then I saw the sign welcoming all of the twins into town for Twins Days in nearby Twinsburg. We weren't camping here for that event, but we quickly changed plans and went. Turns out this campground is a great base camp for exploring Cleveland and checking out the world's largest annual gathering of twins. Make sure you buy some homemade fudge from the general store while you are here—and bring your fishing poles. Its lake is well stocked!

Best Trails in Hocking Hills State Park

Buckeye Trail and Gorge Overlook Loop

This is a 6.1-mile loop trail with waterfalls and a lake view that passes by popular park attractions like Cedar Falls and Old Man's Cave.

Cedar Falls Trail

This short mile out-and-back hike offers an easy way to view Cedar Falls. The waterfall is more impressive in the spring and fall.

Cantwell Cliffs Loop

This is a 1.9-mile loop trail that offers more of a challenge than most other hikes in the park, with steep, well-worn steps and some narrow passageways.

Old Man's Cave

This short 0.6-mile out-and-back hike brings you to one of the most popular (and most photographed) places in the park, Old Man's Cave. Hit the trailhead in the early morning to avoid crowds.

Rock House

A short 0.9-mile loop trail with lots of payoff for little work. There are great views and a cave to explore.

• South Dakota •

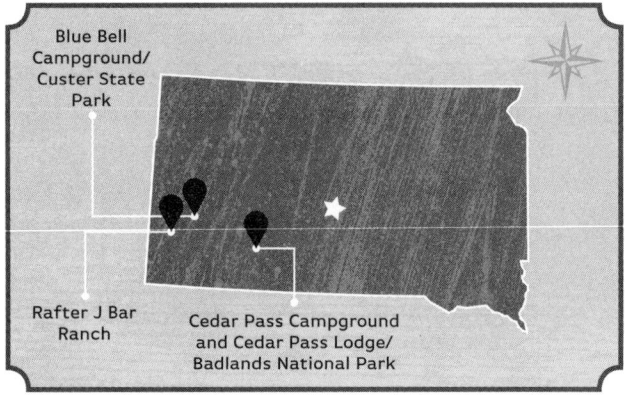

Blue Bell Campground/ Custer State Park

Rafter J Bar Ranch

Cedar Pass Campground and Cedar Pass Lodge/ Badlands National Park

Many people only visit South Dakota on the way to or from more popular destinations like Yellowstone National Park and Grand Teton National Park. But we believe with all our hearts that South Dakota has so much more to offer than many folks realize. Yes, there is Mount Rushmore, and no, you should not listen to anyone who says this national monument is "overrated." There is so much more to do than take a couple of pictures at this iconic destination. The evening program, ranger walks, and interpretive exhibits made lasting impressions on our children...and ourselves.

Mount Rushmore also happens to be located in the beautiful Black Hills, which rivals so many other national parks in terms of wildlife spotting and natural beauty. With many, many amazing campgrounds to choose from, we truly believe you should settle in and enjoy this unique region of our country for more than just a few nights. Other underrated (in our humble opinions) NPS sites in South Dakota include the Badlands, Wind Cave, Jewel Cave, and Minuteman Missile National Historic Site. You'll also want to visit the Mammoth Site in Hot Springs, South Dakota, an active fossil dig site featuring the world's largest concentration of Columbian mammoths. If you live close enough to South Dakota for regular camping adventures, consider yourself very, very lucky.

---------------------- **Quick Cave Tips** ----------------------

Both Wind Cave National Park and Jewel Cave National Monument are in South Dakota, just a short drive from Custer State Park. There are some quirks to visiting these caves, though.

Wind Cave National Park

All the Wind Cave National Park caves can be seen only by guided ranger-led tours, and there are no reservations for any of the tours except for Candlelight and Wild Cave tours. The rest are first-come, first-served. Arrive nice and early to get tickets for the Natural Entrance Tour, perfect for all ages.

Jewel Cave National Monument

This cave site does allow for advance ticket sales for a limited number of guided tours. There are quite a few rules about the reservations, so make sure to check out the NPS site for details.

Lastly, the temperature in these caves is in the mid-50s no matter the season, so dress in layers!

BEST IN STATE

Rafter J Bar Ranch

- ▷ Hill City, South Dakota
- ▷ rafterj.com
- ▷ RV and Tent Sites, Cabin Rentals

We think that Rafter J Bar Ranch is one of the best campgrounds in the country. The sites are incredibly spacious for a private campground, and the views of the Black Hills that rim the campground are close to spectacular. This private campground combines the natural beauty of a state park with the amenities of a real RV resort. And did we mention that Rafter J is located about fifteen minutes away from Mount Rushmore and serves as a near-perfect base camp for exploring the entire region? The large heated pool and hot tub are absolutely perfect after a long day of exploring Crazy Horse and Mount Rushmore, and we really loved the on-demand outdoor fireplace for warming up right after a swim. We spent hours relaxing around the camp-fire with a book or magazine in hand while the kids splashed in the pool or played nearby. But our individual site was the highlight of our trip. We had a large grassy field right in front of our RV, and we played soccer and catch in the parklike setting surrounded by the beauty and stoic grandeur of South Dakota—one of our favorite states in the union that is often overshadowed by points further west.

Blue Bell Campground/Custer State Park

- ▷ East Custer, South Dakota
- ▷ gfp.sd.gov/csp-campgrounds/
- ▷ RV and Tent Sites, Cabins

Custer State Park is one of the best state parks in the entire country. Its incred-ible hiking, wildlife viewing, and natural beauty put it on par with our finest national parks. Custer is also blessed with an abundance of excellent camp-grounds. Among those, Blue Bell Campground, which is filled with delightful-smelling ponderosa pine trees, is our favorite. As we set up camp there, a family passed along the trail at the back of our site on horseback. It was a per-fect start to a perfect stay. We were impressed by everything here—the ranger-led talks at the amphitheater were excellent and took place just steps from our site, the bathrooms were immaculately clean, and the camp hosts were kind and helpful. We also loved that the Blue Bell Lodge was a short walk from our site. The resort has a full-service restaurant and bar, and you can depart on an epic chuck-wagon dinner right from its front door. For those of you who have never experienced a chuck-wagon dinner, think cowboy songs on a scenic hayride (hopefully with bison on either side of the road) followed by the most delicious steaks you've ever had in your life.

Get Your Souvenirs!

The Black Hills are filled with natural wonders but also small towns overflowing with tourist attractions and kitschy delights. Here are three of your options.

▷ *Deadwood:* This town is known for its daily Wild West reenactments and Main Street shootouts during the summer months. In the evening you can catch *The Trail of Jack McCall*, a stage show about the trial of Wild Bill's murderer. Note that there are plenty of casinos and bars in this town.

▷ *Keystone:* Located only 3 miles from Mount Rushmore, Keystone offers a calmer downtown experience with plenty of restaurant and shopping opportunities in a former gold-mining town. You can also board the 1880 Train in Keystone and enjoy a two-hour, narrated ride through the Black Hills.

▷ *Custer:* Our favorite small town in the Black Hills, Custer has great shopping and dining options along with plenty of Wild West charm and grit. You can visit the 1881 Courthouse Museum, which details the history of gold prospecting in the late 1800s.

Cedar Pass Campground and Cedar Pass Lodge/Badlands National Park

▷ Interior, South Dakota

▷ nps.gov

▷ RV and Tent Sites, Cabin Rentals

Sometimes location really does trump everything else. There is absolutely nothing spectacular about the Cedar Pass Campground. The RV sites are unlevel, the bathrooms are funky, and the amenities are spartan at best. But the campground is in a sweet spot in Badlands National Park and is surrounded by an astonishing and unearthly beauty that is unique to this great NPS site. Camping at Cedar Pass is a visually spectacular experience, particularly when a blood-red sunset colors the mountains that are just steps away. The best hikes in the park are nearby, and when you come back to your site, just sitting in a camp chair and having a cold drink is a magical and profoundly relaxing experience. The lodge is a short walk from the campground and has an excellent camp store and a surprisingly good, but somewhat expensive, restaurant. The cabins at the lodge, which were built by local craftsmen, are climate controlled, cozy, and comfortable. The open-air amphitheater is located between the campground and the lodge, and we highly recommend that you attend a ranger talk or night sky program.

ALSO GREAT

Yogi Bear's Jellystone Park of Sioux Falls

▷   **Brandon, South Dakota**

▷   **jellystonesiouxfalls.com**

▷   **RV and Tent Sites, Cabin Rentals**

Heading in or out of South Dakota on the eastern side of the state? Then we recommend the Sioux Falls Jellystone for a fun overnight stop and a quick trip into Sioux Falls. The Jellystone is located right next to Route 90, but road noise is fairly minimal. The pull-through sites here are spacious and easy to navigate, and the cabins are cute. Our boys loved stretching their legs on the bounce pillow and cooling off in the pool. We all enjoyed visiting the falls and having a delicious western steakhouse dinner at Minerva's in downtown Sioux Falls.

America's State Park: Things to Do in Custer

- ✧ Stop in the visitor center to check out the interactive and engaging displays.
- ✧ Drive the Custer State Park Wildlife Loop Road in the early morning or evening for best wildlife spotting.
- ✧ Drive the Needles Highway, which is only 8 feet wide and 11 feet tall.
- ✧ Hike and swim at Sylvan Lake. The Sunday Gulch Trail is a challenging 3-mile loop hike, but you can cool off in the chilly lake afterwards.
- ✧ Drive the Iron Mountain Road. The driving is one of the best parts about Custer State Park. On this road there are multiple tunnels about 13-feet wide.
- ✧ Take the Buffalo Safari Jeep Tour. These Jeeps are allowed to go places that cars are not, plus the drivers are dialed into the local wildlife scene.
- ✧ Get tickets for the Hayride & Chuckwagon Cookout. This is an amazing experience with a cowboy singalong, fantastic food, and dancing under the big, open sky.
- ✧ Go horseback riding at Blue Bell Stables. These stables are right next to the Blue Bell Campground and offer one- or two-hour rides, half-day, or full-day excursions.

Mount Rushmore KOA at Palmer Gulch Resort

- ▷ Hill City, South Dakota
- ▷ koa.com
- ▷ RV and Tent Sites, Camping Cabins and Deluxe Cabins

Folks almost come to blows over which campground is better for a trip to Mount Rushmore, Rafter J or Palmer Gulch. They are both awesome—so take your pick and enjoy it. This KOA offers a real resort camping experience. The pools and amenities (like a rock climbing wall) are delightful, and the campground even has its own on-site restaurant and chuck-wagon dinner! The RV sites are not as big as Rafter J's, but there are definitely more on-site activities for those who like to camp close to the action.

Elk Mountain Campground/Wind Cave National Park

▷   Hot Springs, South Dakota

▷   nps.gov

▷   RV and Tent Sites

Elk Mountain does not accept reservations, so have a backup plan if you decide to go and try to nab a first-come, first-served site. The campground has only sixty-one sites, and RV sites have a max length of 40 feet. Even with these limitations, we can't help but recommend this beautiful campground for an immersive Black Hills camping experience. Make sure to catch a ranger program at the amphitheater. Programs run every night in the summer.

Tips for Visiting Mount Rushmore

Tip #1: Mount Rushmore is not just a pass-through destination.
Many folks treat Mount Rushmore as a quick stopover on their way out to visit the "more exciting" destinations of Yellowstone, Grand Teton, or Glacier National Parks. We have heard from so many listeners over the years that they wished they had spent more time in the Black Hills region. Take your time and enjoy the Black Hills. It's truly a national treasure.

Tip #2: Visit early or later in the summer to avoid the crowds.
Another common complaint from people is how crowded the Mount Rushmore memorial and surrounding area can get during the peak summer season. Crowds and heat can conquer even the most intrepid travelers. Consider visiting toward the end of August, when many kids in the South are back to school. Or you might try visiting in early June, when most East Coast schools are still in session. Avoid the 4th of July and Sturgis Bike Rally if you want a more peaceful experience.

Tip #3: Attend the Evening Lighting Ceremony first.
Attend the Evening Lighting Ceremony on the very first day you arrive in the Mount Rushmore area, then return the following day for all the ranger talks and tours. The Evening Lighting Ceremony is grand and inspiring, and you will be pumped up and ready to return for more the next day.

Tip #4: Attend a park ranger talk or walk.
There are a wide variety of ranger walks and talks every day at this national park. The tricky part is that the schedule is not advertised online, but rather displayed at the ranger stations on-site. Try talking to the rangers when you arrive for the Evening Lighting Ceremony and plan out the following day. The junior ranger program is excellent, offering separate booklets for kids up to five years old and kids over five years old.

Tip #5: Avoid the gift shops if rampant consumerism is not your thing.

Some visitors say that Mount Rushmore felt overly consumeristic. The main gift shop is gigantic with an almost Disney-esque vibe. However, you don't have to go to the gift shop. Stick to the visitor's center, memorial, and walking paths for a non-commercial experience.

Tip #6: Try the TJ's Ice Cream.

It seems pretty gimmicky, but TJ's Ice Cream is off-the-hook yummy. Apparently, President Jefferson is credited for bringing the first written ice cream recipe to the United States back in 1780. The vanilla ice cream really is rich, sweet, and super vanilla-y. Try not to cringe at the price when you make your purchase.

Wisconsin

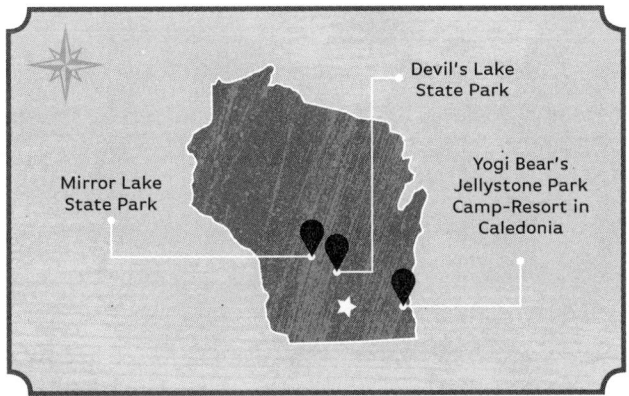

The camping season is a bit limited in this state, but the locals take full advantage of the warm summer months and head out to the lakes in droves to enjoy swimming, boating, fishing, and every other water sport imaginable. Whether you want to explore the city of Milwaukee or the famous Wisconsin Dells, there are fantastic resort camping or state park camping options, depending on your own personal preferences.

The state park campgrounds in Wisconsin are popular with seasoned campers, offering access to some of the region's most beautiful lakes for under $40 a night, even during the peak summer season. Reservations can be made up to eleven months in advance, so make sure to set a reminder in your phone and book as early as possible. You'll pay significantly more (upwards of $80 per night) for a spot at a resort campground. However, many of these have on-site waterparks, resort amenities, and organized activities. Families like ours often save money staying at these campgrounds, since all of our vacation entertainment is wrapped into the cost of a campsite.

BEST IN STATE

Mirror Lake State Park

▷ Baraboo, Wisconsin

▷ dnr.wi.gov

▷ Cabin and Cottage Rentals, RV and Tent Sites

Wisconsinites (who are among the friendliest campers in the world) absolutely love their state park system and often debate about which park is best. The aptly named Mirror Lake State Park is certainly a top contender—especially for campers and glampers. For goodness sake, it has a stunning Frank Lloyd Wright cottage for rent. The Seth Peterson Cottage has one bedroom and may be Wisconsin's most romantic accommodation. For the price of many of the glamping tent rentals in this book, you can cozy up next to a blazing fire in the living area surrounded by views of pine trees and slivers of the lake—or if you are feeling outdoorsy, head out for a paddle on the lake. A canoe and firewood are included in the rental. The rest of this state park is also stunning and romantic. The Ishnala Supper Club is located in the heart of the park and also has excellent water views and fine dining. Over 150 beautiful sites are available for tent campers and RV owners at three different campgrounds within the park. The Sandstone and Cliffwood campgrounds have electric sites, and Bluewater Bay is all non-electric. This is classic American camping at its best.

---------------- Cheese Curds? Yes, Please! ----------------

It sounded less than appetizing, but the first time these East Coasters tried a plate of cheese curds, we were immediately hooked. Don't miss the chance to taste this regional treat when visiting Wisconsin.

Yogi Bear's Jellystone Park Camp-Resort in Caledonia

- Caledonia, Wisconsin
- jellystone-caledonia.com
- RV and Tent Sites, Cabins

With a reputation as one of the best RV parks in Wisconsin, Jellystone Park Camp-Resort in Caledonia brings a big dose of family fun to the Milwaukee region—and catching a Brewers game and grabbing some good eats in Cream City should be on your list when visiting. This award-winning campground (a former Jellystone Park of the Year) recently underwent a major transformation, almost doubling its size. It added almost 150 campsites and many modern cabins after purchasing land beside the existing park. This Jellystone offers pools, a "sprayground," and waterslides as part of Yogi's Water Zone. Campers love cooling off here and at the lake in the summer. If you want your water with a side of competition, join in the Water Wars, where water balloons zoom through the air. Laser tag is also popular here, as is the outdoor theatre where kids congregate and watch both modern and vintage Yogi Bear cartoons and movies. The Bear Paw Swimming Beach is located adjacent to the campground, and campers are granted free access to the beach and discounted tickets to the ridiculously fun Adventure Island area that is packed with blow-up slides and obstacles. The word "bored" was banned at this campground a long time ago—so be ready for loads of family fun from dawn to dusk.

Devil's Lake State Park

- Baraboo, Wisconsin
- dnr.wi.gov
- RV and Tent Sites

Devil's Lake is only creepy on cool, foggy mornings during the off-season. In the summer, it is a magical place for swimming, hiking, picnicking, and camping. Five-hundred-foot quartzite bluffs provide stunning views of the 360-acre lake, and there are over two dozen miles of stellar hiking trails, making this a virtual wonderland for those who love the great outdoors. Wisconsin's most visited state park has three campgrounds with over 420 sites, and each one has different strengths with few drawbacks. The Quartzite Campground, which is largely open and parklike, is best for larger RVs, and many of the sites have electric hookups. Quartzite is also closest to the lakeshore. The Northern Lights Campground has a mixture of shady, wooded sites and sites out in the open and also offers electric hookups. It is 0.5 miles from the lakeshore. The Ice Age Campground is most popular with tent campers and those with pop-up campers and other small RVs. It is about 1 mile from the lakeshore. Unfortunately, there are no cabin options at Devil's Lake. Rock climbing is allowed here—but the park warns that you do so at your own risk. Boating, canoeing, and kayaking are great options, and the park has rentals and two no-fee boat landings. Mirror Lake State Park is only twenty minutes away and well worth a visit if you are camping at Devil's Lake—and vice versa.

ALSO GREAT

Edenwood Ranch & Reserve

▷   Wautoma, Wisconsin

▷   edenwoodranch.com

▷   Glamping Tents, Safari Suites, Lodge Rooms, Cabins

Glamping isn't just for hipsters living on the coasts. Edenwood Ranch & Reserve gives its guests a distinctly midwestern glamping experience that includes luxurious and spacious accommodations and the option to cook your own food or have your own personal chef. You can also kick back and read a book or choose to live the strenuous life and go hunting, fishing, ATV riding, zip-lining, or mountain biking. This is an excellent spot for a romantic getaway, but families are also welcome.

Wisconsin Dells KOA Holiday

▷ Wisconsin Dells, Wisconsin

▷ koa.com

▷ RV and Tent Sites, Camping Cabins and Deluxe Cabins

Wisconsin Dells is known as the "waterpark capital of the world," and this campground is only 1 mile away from downtown and serves as a great base camp for exploring the region. The deluxe patio sites are popular with RV owners, as are the spacious pull-through sites on the upper level. The cabins are also clean and comfortable. A train does go by at night, so ask for a quieter spot if you are a sensitive sleeper.

Peninsula State Park

▷ Fish Creek, Wisconsin

▷ dnr.wi.gov

▷ RV and Tent Sites

Peninsula State Park is located on the beautiful Door County Peninsula in northeastern Wisconsin, and it has 8 miles of pristine Lake Michigan shoreline. This is probably the single most popular place to camp in Wisconsin, and even though the park has five campgrounds with over 450 sites, it can be tough to book one on busy summer weekends. When it comes to outdoor recreation, this park pretty much has it all including hiking, biking, kayaking, fishing, and even golfing. Is it any wonder that Wisconsinites love their state parks?

Best Waterparks in the Waterpark Capital of the World

Noah's Ark Water Park
This is the largest outdoor water park in the United States, with over fifty waterslides and two giant wave pools.

Wilderness Resort
This self-proclaimed "largest waterpark resort in America" does sell single-day passes. You can get fancy and rent luxury poolside cabanas with dedicated waitstaff, fans, and a television.

Chula Vista
Located a few miles off the "strip," this waterpark has a more natural feel to it, with waterfalls and a man-made beach.

Mt. Olympus
There is a waterpark and theme park here, making it perfect for families that enjoy wave pools and roller coasters.

Kalahari Waterpark
Yes, it's a chain waterpark with locations around the United States, but it's still a favorite, according to water park experts in the Dells.

Hiking in Wisconsin State Parks

Ishnala and Echo Rock Trail Loop, Mirror Lake State Park

An easy and scenic, 3.2-mile loop trail with very little elevation gain.

Northwest Trail Loop, Mirror Lake State Park

This mostly shaded 2.8-mile loop trail runs along the edge of the water for a good portion of the hike. Wear your bug repellent during the summer months.

Devil's Lake via West Bluff Trail

A 4.7-mile loop trail with fantastic views. Hit the trailhead early in the day to beat the crowds at this popular location.

Ice Age Trail, Devil's Lake State Park

Up for a challenge? The Ice Age Trail, 1,200 miles total in length, is one of eight National Scenic Trails, with 11 miles running through Devil's Lake State Park. The trail is rated as difficult.

Eagle Trail, Peninsula State Park

This short, 2-mile loop trail can be challenging on account of the rock scrambles. However, the cliffs and water views are a great payoff for the effort.

The
WEST

• Alaska •

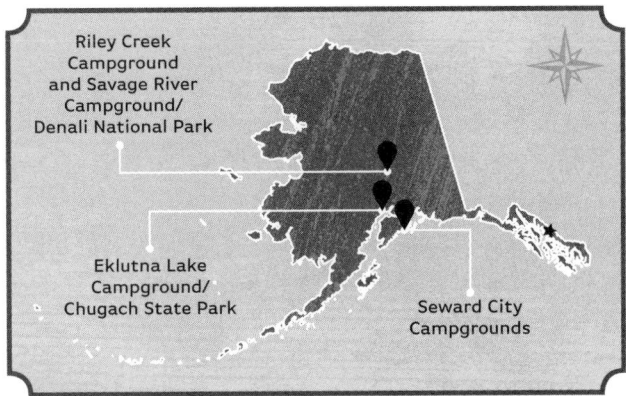

Riley Creek Campground and Savage River Campground/ Denali National Park

Eklutna Lake Campground/ Chugach State Park

Seward City Campgrounds

One of the most common questions in the RVing community is, "Have you done Alaska yet?" It's practically assumed that Alaska is the ultimate destination for any self-respecting RVer. Perhaps it is because the sheer scale of planning and executing an RV trip to Alaska is unlike any other RVing adventure. There is an entire mythology about the roads alone, spawning content on windshield damage, flat tires, frost heaves, and construction. Then there is the culture of dispersed camping, lending to an underground network of boondocking GPS coordinates. And the size. Alaska is bigger than Texas, California, and Montana combined, so it is virtually impossible to see all the highlights in one trip. The good news is that all these factors have led to there being a ton of great online content about RVing in Alaska, and we have shared some of our favorite resources in this chapter. Of course, many of us have no interest in making the long drive up to the forty-ninth state. Lucky for us, there are plenty of RV rental options available throughout Alaska.

If there is one thing we hear most from our camping friends in Alaska, it's that visitors should not expect the same sort of campground amenities that are often found in the lower forty-eight. The camping season is short for all but the hardiest of souls, and campgrounds are often just places to park a rig or pitch a tent. The great outdoors is Alaska's greatest amenity. Enjoy it responsibly.

BEST IN STATE

Riley Creek Campground and Savage River Campground/ Denali National Park

  ▷   Preserve, Alaska

  ▷   nps.gov

  ▷   RV and Tent Sites

With six million acres of wild land, the size of Denali National Park is almost hard to comprehend. Ninety-two mile Denali Park Road is the only road in the park—and during the summer months (late May to early September) private vehicles are only allowed to traverse the first 15 miles of road to a spot called Savage River. For further exploration in the park, you have to take a tour bus for a fee or a complimentary park transit bus. Mount Denali can be seen as early as mile 9 (on clear days) and wildlife can certainly be seen on this stretch of road—but delving further into the park on a bus will guarantee more wildlife and more magnificent mountain views. There are two campgrounds on the paved stretch of road. Riley Creek is the biggest campground in the park, offering the best services and the most convenient location. The campground is right inside of the park's entrance and offers almost 150 sites for tents and RVs up to 40 feet. Sites are semi-private and situated near fragrant spruce trees near Riley Creek. This campground is a good choice for most people because it is close to the visitor center (which is a hub for hiking trails) and the Riley Creek Mercantile, which offers basic camping supplies, groceries, and fresh coffee. Savage River Campground is located at mile marker 14 and offers RV and tent sites with fewer amenities than Riley Creek Campground. But on clear days you can take a short walk from your site and see Denali in all its magnificent splendor.

Seward City Campgrounds

▷ Seward, Alaska

▷ cityofseward.us

▷ RV and Tent Sites

Seward, Alaska, is a welcoming seaside village just 2 miles from Anchorage that is filled with good bars and restaurants and is surrounded by opportunities for epic outdoor adventures. This postcard-worthy town is located directly on Resurrection Bay and also serves as the gateway to Kenai Fjords National Park—home to nearly forty glaciers and the world-famous Harding Icefield. Seward manages a series of ten campgrounds that sprawl across the waterfront and provide a wide variety of sites for tent campers and RV owners. The sites are not much to speak of, but the location is spectacular. Mountains surround you, and the bay is a short walk from your site no matter which campground you choose. You can also walk right into town for a night out and not worry about having to drive back to your site. A lovely walking and biking trail runs across the waterfront, and there are several playgrounds. If you are camping with kids, you might want to choose the Otter Beach Campground, which is right next door to a nice playground and skate park. Obihiro Campground and Marathon Campground are also located near Obihiro Park, which is a nice place to enjoy a morning cup of coffee and soak in some of Alaska's most stunning views.

Eklutna Lake Campground/Chugach State Park

▷ Anchorage, Alaska

▷ dnr.alaska.gov

▷ RV and Tent Sites, Cabins

Eklutna Lake Campground offers up a great escape less than an hour from downtown Anchorage. The campground is part of Chugach State Park, which encompasses an enormous 495,000 acres, making it one of the four largest state parks in America. Though the park may be huge, this campground is small and intimate. Only fifty sites are available, and many are large, wooded, and private. Kayaking and fishing are excellent here, and so are the hiking trails along the lake. More adventurous souls ride ATVs in the park, and the Eklutna Trail is open for them Sunday to Wednesday. The park is also packed with wildlife. Black bears can be seen in the spring and fall, so please pack away your food in the bear-safe storage containers. Rangers do occasionally give tickets to careless campers who leave food out around their sites. Four of Alaska's excellent public use cabins are also available—they are super cute on the outside and clean on the inside, but you will need to bring some of the comforts of home, such as cozy pillows and blankets, to "glamp" things up.

ALSO GREAT

Ocean Shores RV Park

▷ Homer, Alaska
▷ homeralaskarvpark.com
▷ RV and Tent Sites

Ocean Shores shut down a few years back and has since reopened under new management that is making moves to improve the facilities, especially the showers and restrooms. But if you are in a fully self-contained RV, then the status of those amenities won't matter much to you. Views of Kachemak Bay are stunning here, and you can walk into town from the campground. The area known as the Homer Spit is about 7 miles away—make sure you venture out there and take a stroll on its windswept, rocky beaches.

---------------- **Public Use Cabins in Alaska** ----------------

If you aren't interested in RVing and tent camping is off the table, Alaska's public use cabins may be the perfect way for you and your family to enjoy the wilderness. Alaska's state park system has more than eighty of these cabins reservable through Reserve America. The cabins are located in remote locations, and some are not even accessible by vehicle. There is a cabin access page online that will give details about each location. Bird Creek Campground is a great place to try out a public use cabin. The cabins are situated near the Seward Highway, an easy drive from Anchorage.

Diamond M. Ranch Resort

▷ Kenai, Alaska

▷ diamondmranchresort.com

▷ Lodge Room, Suites, Rustic Cabins, RV and Tent Sites

Diamond M. Ranch Resort offers a wide variety of accommodations and heartfelt Alaskan hospitality on the beautiful Kenai Peninsula. The resort is located on a bluff overlooking the Kenai River and the Cook Inlet, and you can access the water directly from the campground. Sites for large RVs are a bit tight and out in the open, but the area for smaller RVs is wooded and a bit more private. The tenting area is located on a grassy knoll and is surprisingly comfortable.

K'esugi Ken RV and Tent Campground/Denali State Park

▷ Trapper Creek, Alaska

▷ dnr.alaska.gov

▷ RV and Tent Sites, Cabin Rentals

The grand opening ceremony for this modern state park campground was in 2017, so in "campground years" it is a brand-new baby. RV sites have electric hookups and accommodate big rigs. Tent sites are large and private, and some of them border a peaceful stream. The cabins are adorable but sparse, and they have woodstoves for heat. A few of the campsites have stunning views of Denali.

> ---- **Alaskan Adventures from a Local's Perspective** ----
>
> Plenty of folks visit Alaska and write about their experiences, but if you want some great recommendations from a local's perspective, check out Erin Kirkland's blog *AK on the Go*. Erin is a travel expert that has lots of camping content on her blog. She even provides some RV rental recommendations.

The RV Pilgrimage: Alaska Files

It seems to be a rule: If you are a popular RV YouTube personality, you must film the journey to Alaska. This means there is a lot of quality and helpful content out there to help you plan your own Alaskan pilgrimage. Here are our favorite series of videos for your binging pleasure.

▷ *The Long, Long Honeymoon*: This Alaskan YouTube playlist has eight videos on planning, budgeting, and various destinations.

▷ *Gone with the Wynns*: This Alaskan playlist has eighteen videos and some of the best cinematography of any videos on YouTube. The Wynns specialize in dispersed camping—camping on public land without designated campsites—if that is your jam.

▷ *Less Junk, More Journey*: This channel has thirty-eight videos on the Alaska playlist. You'll get lots of good campground insight, but the videos focus fairly heavily on family situations.

▷ *Keep Your Daydream*: This fifteen-video Alaska playlist also tends to focus more on personal stories than straight-up travel intel, but there are videos on the Alaskan Highway and other specific destinations like Seward and Homer.

▷ *Mortons on the Move*: This couple teamed up with Lance Campers to make a twenty-episode series called *Go North*. They took a truck camper on an epic 15,000-mile journey to Alaska and the Arctic Ocean. Their goal was to camp in some of the most remote locations possible.

Arizona

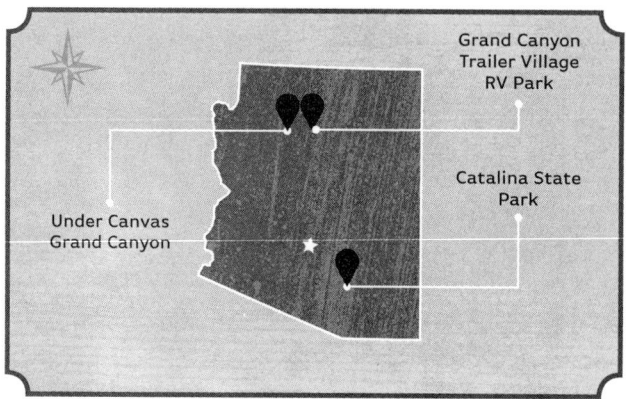

Grand Canyon
Trailer Village
RV Park

Catalina State
Park

Under Canvas
Grand Canyon

It's no secret that Arizona is a pretty amazing camping destination. Over two million snowbirds flock to the state each winter, and many of them arrive in RVs. Plan on making campground reservations far in advance, especially if visiting during peak season—November through April. Also plan on double-checking restrictions at some of the RV resorts, as more than you may suspect have a "fifty-five and older" policy. There are so many reasons to go camping in Arizona: the legendary Grand Canyon, the Red Rocks of Sedona, the Seven Wonders of Flagstaff, and one of the most famous photo ops along all of Route 66 in Winslow. The best news is that you can explore all of these famous destinations and stay in either a well-appointed RV resort or a rustic camping retreat—your choice.

BEST IN STATE

Under Canvas Grand Canyon

▷   Valle, Arizona

▷   undercanvas.com

▷   Glamping Tents

This glamper's delight is only twenty-five minutes away from the South Rim entrance to the Grand Canyon. This is an excellent location, and options for getting closer to the majesty of this treasured NPS site are few and far between. Under Canvas offers three types of glamping tents on 160 peaceful acres of Juniper Forest. The Suite Tent is suitable for adventurous families and has its own shower, sink, and toilet so you don't have to wander out of the tent at night for potty breaks. But we like the Stargazer Tent the best—it has a viewing window above the king bed so you can fall asleep while gazing at the stars. Under Canvas Grand Canyon has its own "adventures" concierge who will help you choose each day's outing. When you get back to base camp, you can take a few minutes to relax in the Zen Garden before enjoying delicious pan roasted trout or mushroom ravioli for dinner. When you return to your tent you will find that housekeeping has cleaned your room and refreshed your selection of organic soaps. If you feel like socializing, head out to the campfire for s'mores.

Catalina State Park

▷   Tucson, Arizona

▷   azstateparks.com

▷   RV and Tent Sites

The Arizona State Park system is pretty amazing, and many people—especially RV owners and tent campers—think Catalina State Park is the crown jewel. The campground has 120 water/electric sites, and big rigs are welcome. The sites at this state park are large, paved, and lovely. Shade and privacy vary from site to site, but everyone has plenty of elbow room and many sites have stunning views of the Santa Catalina Mountains. The bathhouses are pleasant and clean, and the showers have free hot water. Giant saguaros and cacti are everywhere, and so are wildflowers in the springtime. There are eight delightful hiking trails in the park that range from under a mile to over 9 miles. The trails are filled with mountain views, and many of them cross over water from mountain runoff, so plan on cooling off your feet and stopping for a drink and a snack on a hot day. This campground is almost perfect and feels like a great escape from everyday life—but if you need supplies there is a Walmart conveniently located right across the street.

Grand Canyon Trailer Village RV Park

▷   Grand Canyon Village, Arizona

▷   visitgrandcanyon.com

▷   RV Sites

Full hook-up RV Sites inside Grand Canyon National Park? And less than a mile from the South Rim? Yes, thank you very much! It may not be the most scenic national park campground, but the proximity is literally unbeatable if you are looking to take your RV or RV rental to the Grand Canyon. The sites are basically all the same. Some have more shade than others, but most are a bit tightly packed. Few complain about the simplicity of the sites because they get to run their AC during the heat of the summer. If the heat isn't unbearable, you can walk to the visitor center, but a wide-ranging shuttle is available as well. This shuttle is clutch for those renting RVs who don't have cars with them. Nothing about this simple campground is magnificent, but everything about the Grand Canyon is. The Grand Canyon Trailer Village RV Park is a place to sleep and eat and take breaks from the heat during your visit to one of the most breathtaking places on earth.

ALSO GREAT

Grand Canyon Railway RV Park (and Hotel)

- ▷ Williams, Arizona
- ▷ thetrain.com
- ▷ RV Sites and Hotel Rooms

The Grand Canyon Railway RV Park is part of the newly refurbished and old-school luxurious Grand Canyon Railway and Hotel, and guests at the RV park have access to all the hotel amenities. Guests also have access to the Grand Canyon train, which has been transporting visitors into the National Park since 1901. This neat and tidy RV park is located only two blocks from downtown Williams and historic Route 66, and there is pretty much nothing to dislike about it. Williams has long been called the Gateway to the Grand Canyon, but it is a fantastic stop on its own with great food and drink and lots of funky "out west" shopping.

Rancho Sedona RV Park

- ▷ Sedona, Arizona
- ▷ ranchosedona.com
- ▷ RV Sites

A river doesn't run through it—but a pretty little creek does. So try to get a creekside site if you can. But don't worry if you can't; the whole campground is lovely and well kept. The sites are fairly spacious and many are semi-private. Bathhouses are also Disney World–level clean and borderline luxurious. Amenities are pretty basic—tetherball, volleyball, and a very basic playground. This RV park is the perfect base camp for exploring the stunning red rock landscapes and pine forests of this gorgeous section of the Grand Canyon State.

Tucson/Lazydays KOA Resort

▷ Tucson, Arizona

▷ koa.com

▷ RV and Tent Sites, Deluxe Cabins

We want to retire here. Seriously. Fruit trees fill the park, and the RV sites are nicely manicured—some even have patios and fireplaces. The new activity court has pickleball, and there is a nine-hole chip and putt course on-site. We also love the RV sites that are covered by a solar panel structure—making this look like a campground for the future. A Lazydays RV dealership is right next door. Go take a look at the Airstreams—they look mighty pretty shining in the Tucson sun.

------------ What's the Deal with Quartzite? ------------

The small town of Quartzite has only a few thousand year-round residents, but every winter around two million RVers descend and stake out a boondocking spot in the desert. Millions of acres of public land that surround downtown Quartzite are free (or very, very inexpensive) to camp on, and folks take advantage of that perk to enjoy the warm, dry weather. It basically looks like a dusty parking lot with a sea of RVs, but people return year after year to meet up with friends and attend the variety of rallies and an annual RV show, known as The Big Tent Show, which has been held every year since 1983.

BLM Locations near Quartzite

✦ La Posa Long Term Visitor Area

✦ Plomosa Road BLM Camping Area

✦ Hi Jolly BLM Camping Area

✦ Road Runner BLM Camping Area

Learn more at blm.gov

What about other National Park Sites in Arizona?

The Grand Canyon gets all the press, but there are many other NPS sites in Arizona that are worth a visit. In particular, Arizona is home to remarkably well-preserved cliff dwellings and other artifacts of indigenous populations in North America. Explore the history of this continent at these locations:

Petrified Forest National Park
Petrified Forest, Arizona

Explore petroglyphs, sandstone ruins from the 1200s, and the Painted Desert Inn National Historic Landmark.

Montezuma Castle National Monument
Camp Verde, Arizona

Here you'll find one of the best-preserved cliff dwellings on the continent, which were home to the Sinagua people for over 400 years.

Saguaro National Park
Tucson, Arizona

The Tucson region is home to this country's largest cacti, and these giant plants are protected at this NPS site.

Walnut Canyon National Monument
Flagstaff, Arizona

The 1-mile Island Trail and 0.75-mile Rim Trail provide visitors with access to more than twenty-five cliff dwellings from the 1100s.

Sunset Crater Volcano National Monument
Flagstaff, Arizona

Formed by a series of eruptions around 1085, this volcano is the youngest cinder cone in the San Francisco Volcanic Field.

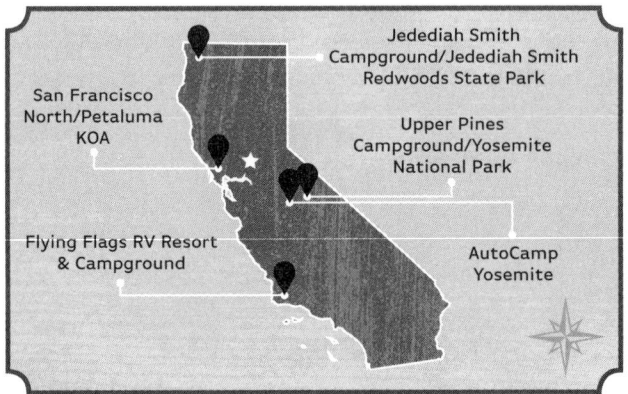

California

Jedediah Smith Campground/Jedediah Smith Redwoods State Park

San Francisco North/Petaluma KOA

Upper Pines Campground/Yosemite National Park

Flying Flags RV Resort & Campground

AutoCamp Yosemite

There is no doubt that California has some of the most enviable camping destinations in the entire country. It's also true, however, that they are some of the most difficult to book. Folks in every state will complain about how quickly the best state parks are snapped up, but campers in California really do have it a bit worse than the rest of us. Let's face it—who doesn't want to camp on the beach as the sun sets over the Pacific? For those of you who can't plan ahead far enough in advance to get those sites, it is perfectly possible to find a few amazing private campgrounds in the most popular places, from the northern Redwoods down to San Diego.

California is truly the camping version of choose-your-own-adventure. Head to the far north to the Redwoods and wander through some of the oldest forests in the world. Visit Lake Tahoe for extraordinary hiking and boating. Park the RV right outside of San Francisco and explore the Golden City. Watch the big-wave surfers in Santa Cruz. Wander around wine country, snap a pic at the end of Route 66, or soak in the sun in San Diego. If there is a dreamy California destination that you've been dying to visit, we promise there is a great camping option nearby. You just have to plan ahead to snag a spot.

-------------------- **Before you go...** --------------------
▷   **Read:** *Disney's Land: Walt Disney and the Invention of the Amusement Park That Changed the World* by Richard Snow

BEST IN STATE

AutoCamp Yosemite

▷   Midpines, California

▷   autocamp.com

▷   Airstream Suites, Luxury Tents, Classic Cabins, Studio Suites

Ever dreamed of owning an Airstream and touring our iconic national parks? You aren't the only one, that's for sure. AutoCamp's Yosemite property can give you a taste of that dream at a fraction of the price. Its custom Airstream rentals will make you swoon, and so will its mid-century modern club-house and lounge areas where food, wine, and beer are served for hungry and thirsty hikers returning from the park. If Frank Lloyd Wright and Wally Byam had a love child, this property would be it. Everything here feels del-icately carved into the landscape, including the private patios and outdoor fireplaces at each site. Luxurious glamping tents and comfortable and styl-ish tents and suites are also available if you don't want to live riveted. There are no sites for transient RVs and tent campers—we suspect that would risk the stylish and curated feel of just about every inch of this unique property. Yosemite National Park is about forty minutes away, and a shuttle is avail-able if you don't want to drive in and search for parking. The hip little town of Mariposa is nearby and offers quirky shopping and a handful of excellent places for food and drink. AutoCamp Yosemite offers a unique combination of comfort and connection to the great outdoors. Modern glamping doesn't get much better than this.

---------------- **Camping Near Disneyland?** ----------------

Unlike Fort Wilderness Resort in Orlando, Florida, there is no amazing camping option in or around Disneyland. However, Anaheim RV Park will offer you a clean, comfortable place to park your RV while you party with the mouse. This is the definition of an urban campground, nestled smack dab in the middle of a bustling neighborhood. Amenities include a pool and hot tub on-site, plus a complimentary continental breakfast. Shuttle service to the park is available.

Jedediah Smith Campground/Jedediah Smith Redwoods State Park

▷   Crescent City, California

▷   parks.ca.gov

▷   RV and Tent Sites, Cabins

The location of the Jedediah Smith Campground is storybook stunning. Camping among the old growth redwood trees along the Smith River is peaceful and restorative to the soul. Kids can spend the entire day swimming and splashing in the river while you relax on the shoreline and dive in for a dip if you get hot. More adventurous souls should swim across the river like we did and do some very mellow cliff jumping on the other side. Just watch your step and take caution if you do. This is also a great spot for kayaks, so bring 'em if you got 'em. Also plan on attending the evening ranger programs, which provide an excellent introduction to the almost mystical qualities of the redwood trees. Sites are perfect for tent campers, and cabin rentals are simple and charming, but RV sites only accommodate trailers up to 21 feet and motor homes up to 25 feet. The Hiouchi Trail runs along the Smith River and takes you to Stout Grove—an incredible spot for viewing the redwoods up close and personal. It is one of our favorite family hikes of all time. Going for a swim in the river after getting hot and sweaty on the hike was a classic summertime in California experience that we will never forget.

San Francisco North/Petaluma KOA

▹ Petaluma, California

▹ koa.com

▹ RV and Tent Sites, Camping Cabins and Deluxe Cabins

Located just 34 miles north of the Golden Gate Bridge, this KOA serves as a reasonable base camp for day tripping into the Golden City. It's located right in the heart of Sonoma County's wine country, with redwood trees and beaches nearby, and it makes a great vacation destination even if you don't want to visit the city. The campground is large and packed with activities and amenities, and kids love the jumping pillow, farm-themed playground, pool, and rock climbing wall. Your kids will flip when they find the Slurpee machine in the camp store. Younger kids will also love the small petting zoo. It can get super busy on the weekends, especially holiday weekends, so those seeking peace and quiet might choose to book a site far away from the action or visit during the week. Full hook-up and RV sites and cabins are not cheap here—but nothing is in this part of California. If you are an Alfred Hitchcock fan, make sure you visit Bodega Bay, where *The Birds* was filmed. Just take caution if they start to gather.

Upper Pines Campground/Yosemite National Park

▹ Yosemite National Park, California

▹ nps.gov

▹ RV and Tent Sites

Wake up surrounded by the delicious smell of ponderosa pines, the gentle sounds of the Merced River, and views of Yosemite's granite cliffs at this iconic national park's largest campground. Upper Pines has 238 sites that can handle trailers up to 25 feet and motorhomes up to 35 feet; it is also a tent camper's paradise. There are three other campgrounds inside of Yosemite National Park, but this is our top pick because of the wide variety of sites for small- and medium-sized RVs. The back-in sites on the exterior side of each loop are preferable because there will be no one behind you. Interior sites are still great if that's all you can get, but you will have less privacy and more neighbors. You can walk directly from your site to several of the park's most famous hiking trails—some of which are easy, like the hike to Mirror Lake, and some of which are incredibly difficult, like the hike to Half Dome. Getting reservations can be tricky, so try to make your reservations right when the booking window opens. Cancellations do happen occasionally, so be sure to keep checking if you are initially unsuccessful.

Santa Ynez Valley

Staying at the Flying Flags RV Resort? Here are our favorite area attractions.

- Solvang Trolley
- Ostrich Land
- Quicksilver Miniature Horse Ranch
- Hans Christian Andersen Museum
- Madonna Inn

Flying Flags RV Resort & Campground

- Buellton, California
- highwaywestvacations.com
- Cottages, Cabins, Airstream and Vintage RV Rentals, Safari Tents

Flying Flags offers a California glamping experience that may be unrivaled in the entire Golden State. The resort's list of "unique outdoor accommodations" ranges from surfing-themed cabins, to swanky safari tents, to vintage Airstream rentals. Its "ultra-premium" RV sites with covered patios and outdoor kitchens are also pretty darn swanky for those who like to roll in style. The resort-style amenities at this campground serve as a model for other campgrounds in the high-end outdoor hospitality biz. Sample local wines or a craft cocktail at the Sideways Lounge located right next door at the Sideways Inn—a sister property. The food at the Campfire Cafe is also excellent and significantly better than traditional campground fare without being significantly more expensive. The pool and hot tub areas also look like they were ripped out of the pages of *Travel + Leisure* magazine. But if Flying Flags looks like a place that is just for romantic getaways, think again. This campground, and all of Highway West's campgrounds, is incredibly family-friendly. It also specializes in group events like family reunions and weddings. Getting married at a campground like Flying Flags sounds dreamy to us.

---------- **Drive It: Death Valley Scenic Byway** ----------
Drive 81.5 miles along this scenic byway to enjoy the lowest point and hottest place in North America.

ALSO GREAT

Crescent City/Redwoods KOA Holiday
▷ Crescent City, California
▷ koa.com
▷ RV and Tent Sites, Camping Cabins and Deluxe Cabins

This KOA feels like two separate campgrounds on one property. The "first" campground offers pretty standard fare—it has a recreation room for rainy days and pancake breakfasts, and playgrounds and bike rentals for the kids. The RV sites are nice but not spectacular, and the cabins are comfortable and well equipped. The "second" campground is actually inside a 10-acre Redwood Forest, and it is absolutely magical. Tent sites, rustic cabins, and sites for small RVs are surrounded by towering Redwoods and the deep shade that they provide. Proximity to Crescent City and the national and state parks is also excellent.

Inn Town Campground

- ▷ Nevada City, California
- ▷ inntowncampground.com
- ▷ Glamping Tents, Retro RV Rental, RV and Tent Sites

Inspired by the Holiday Parks in New Zealand where owners Dan and Erin Thiem lived and road-tripped for five years before returning to settle in Nevada City, the Inn Town Campground offers RV sites, tent sites, and glamping tents surrounded by towering pine trees. It is located just 2 miles from downtown Nevada City. The Commons area is a great place to meet other campers and cook a delicious meal in its well-equipped community kitchen.

Thornhill Broome Beach Campground/Point Mugu State Park

- ▷ Malibu, California
- ▷ parks.ca.gov
- ▷ RV and Tent Sites

Some will complain and say that Thornhill Broome's campsites are nothing more than parking spots on the side of the road. But, oh what a glorious road it is! You can step out of your trailer and walk directly onto the sandy beaches of Point Mugu State Park. Tent campers can pitch their tents directly on the shoulder. When you are settled around the campfire under a bed of California stars, that parking spot will become one of the most magical places to camp in all of America.

Wine (and Beer Country): Family Style

Lagunitas Brewery and Tap Room

Lagunitas is a mecca for craft beer lovers. Not only can you tour its brewery, it also has a great taproom, which has live music nightly. It serves food and is totally kid-friendly with a ton of space for them to run around. There is also a store. It's only 1.5 miles away from the San Francisco/North Petaluma KOA.

Brewsters Beer Garden

Downtown Petaluma is small and quaint with a lot of shops and restaurants. Brewsters is a great family-friendly place to eat and drink. If you're not a beer lover you can easily find a glass of pinot or chardonnay. There is often a wait for the covered eating area, and the outdoor area is first-come, first-served.

V. Sattui Winery

If you want to get a little of the Napa experience but are traveling with kids, V. Sattui Winery is a great option. It has a deli, fantastic wines, and a large grassy area where you can picnic with the family. It does get crowded on the weekends (as does all of Napa). October and November is crush season, so it's packed with visitors, but the colors throughout Napa's vineyards are spectacular.

Redwoods National and State Parks

Before you go...

▷ **Read:** *The Wild Trees* by Richard Preston

▷ **Watch:** *National Geographic Explorer: Climbing Redwood Giants*

▷ **Bring:** *Best Easy Day Hikes: Redwoods National and State Parks* by Daniel Brett

Our favorite hikes...

▷ Hiouchi Trail to Stout Grove

▷ Ladybird Johnson Grove Trail

▷ Yurok Trail to Hidden Beach

▷ Fern Canyon

Other places to explore...

▷ Eat out in Crescent City.

▷ Swim or fish in the Smith River.

▷ Complete a Redwoods EdVentures Quest (redwood-edventures.org).

• Colorado •

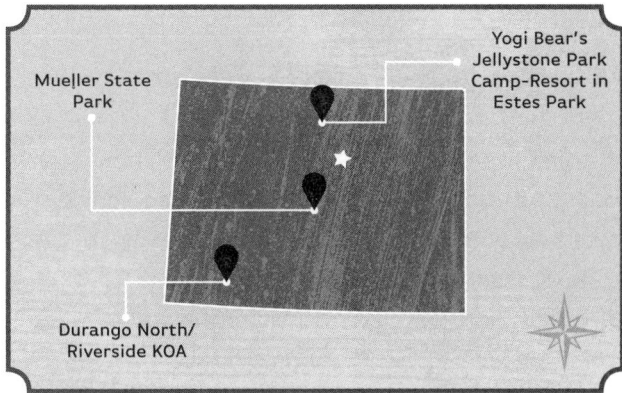

Colorado is definitely one of the most popular camping destinations in the country, and as a result you might experience difficulty getting a spot at some of the most beautiful campgrounds in the state. It's worth the effort, though. Reservations at all state parks can be made up to six months in advance, either online or by phone. The reservable campsites at Rocky Mountain National Park can also be booked up to six months in advance, or you can take your chances at the first-come, first-served campgrounds, which often fill up by early afternoon during the summer months.

If you find yourself frustrated by the crowded campgrounds outside the Denver/Colorado Springs region, don't lose hope. Just head to one of the other NPS treasures a bit farther afield. Mesa Verde National Park protects almost 5,000 active archaeological sites, including 600 well-preserved ancient cliff dwellings. The Great Sand Dunes are the tallest in North America and offer sand sledding and tubing in the Medano Creek. Dinosaur National Monument has amazing reptile remains embedded in rock in addition to well-preserved petroglyphs. It's no wonder Colorado is considered a mecca for outdoor and camping enthusiasts.

Yogi Bear's Jellystone Park Camp-Resort in Estes Park

▷   Estes Park, Colorado

▷   jellystoneofestes.com

▷   RV and Tent Sites, Cabins and RV Rentals

If you want to experience a Rocky Mountains National Park adventure with full hookups and plenty of fun amenities and activities for the kids back at the campground, then Jellystone of Estes is an obvious choice. This Jellystone is nestled among the Colorado Rockies and the Roosevelt National Forest and has panoramic views of the surrounding mountains. Proximity to the gateway town of Estes Park is also good—you can be there in about ten minutes. The cabins here are excellent, and many of the sites are too, but big rigs should call and make sure they get a site that they can settle into easily as the campground roads are steep and some sites are difficult to access. After spending the morning hiking and exploring in the national park, the kids will love coming back here and going for a swim or playing a round of mini golf. Organized activities like craft time, karaoke, and dance parties are also abundant here, particularly during the high summer months and weekends.

---------------- **Drive It: Trail Ridge Road** ----------------

Trail Ridge Road is the highest continuous paved road in the United States. It runs 48 miles between Estes Park on the east side of Rocky Mountain National Park to Grand Lake on the west side. No park shuttles navigate this road, so you will have to drive yourself. Plan at least a half day for the adventure, stopping for lunch and the restrooms at the Alpine Visitors Center.

Mueller State Park

▷ Divide, Colorado

▷ cpw.state.co.us

▷ RV and Tent Sites, Cabins

Located just east of the Continental Divide and about forty-five minutes west of Colorado Springs, this state park campground is packed with wildlife and natural beauty. Elk and black bear sightings are not unusual here, and wildflowers and stacks of pine and spruce trees are everywhere. Views of Pikes Peak lie right across a valley, and some sites have unobstructed views, so do your homework when booking. Avoid the campsites on the main road, especially if you are camping with young kids. The campground also has national park–level ranger talks about topics like raptors, and in the summer there are activities like archery lessons that are fun for kids and adults alike. Hiking and mountain biking options are excellent here, and the campground is open year round for those who love winter sports like sledding and cross-country skiing. Those traveling with pets should know that dogs are not allowed on the trails in this park because of the native wildlife. The Colorado Wolf and Wildlife Center is only fifteen minutes away from Mueller, and it is an absolutely awesome experience.

Durango North/Riverside KOA

▷ Durango, Colorado

▷ koa.com

▷ RV and Tent Sites, Deluxe Cabins and Camping Cabins

The sites along the Animas River are the real stars of the show at this charming and laid-back KOA, which is located less than twenty minutes north of Durango. But if you can't reserve one, don't despair; the rest of the campground, which is set among fragrant ponderosa pines, is also lovely. After a day exploring Durango and the many natural wonders nearby, come back to the campground for dinner in the pizza lodge and an outdoor movie. If the weather isn't good, stretch your legs and play a game of pool in the spacious game room. But hopefully you have bright, sunshiny days for exploring this region, where outdoor activities abound. The Durango Silverton Narrow Gauge Railroad is nearby, and so are opportunities for whitewater rafting and Jeep tours. But we think you really shouldn't miss the Bar D Chuckwagon Supper Show, because we have never met a chuck-wagon dinner that we didn't love! Expect great steaks and even better live music and comedy. You'll sleep like a champ back at this KOA, and the sounds of the river will soothe you whether you are staying in a tent, RV, or cabin.

--- **Tips for Visiting Great Sand Dunes National Park** ---

✦ Hike the dunes in the morning before the sand gets too hot during the summer months.

✦ Rent the right equipment for sandboarding and sand sledding. Don't bother trying your snow gear. The ones made for sand have an extra slick base and special wax. Splurge on the fee.

✦ Cool off in Medano Creek during the warmest parts of the day. If you are lucky, you'll experience the mysterious "surge flow," a phenomenon of shallow water where underwater dunes create waves as water flows over them.

✦ This is a designated International Dark Sky Park, so make sure to catch one of the many night sky programs.

✦ Pick up a Junior Ranger program booklet when you first arrive. This is an amazing national park for kids!

ALSO GREAT

Collective Vail

▷ Wolcott, Colorado

▷ collectiveretreats.com

▷ Glamping Tents

Do you want to glamp under the Colorado stars and sleep under 1,000 thread-count linens while a wood burning stove keeps you cozy and warm? Then Collective Vail has got you covered—if not totally pampered. Choose either a Summit Tent (with en suite bathroom) or a Journey Tent (with shared bathroom), and download your Collective Vail Field Guide to start planning an epic vacation that combines outdoor adventure with exquisite and Instagrammable accommodations.

Piñon Flats Campground/Grand Sand Dunes National Park & Preserve

- ▷ Mosca, Colorado
- ▷ nps.gov
- ▷ RV and Tent Sites

Grand Sand Dunes National Park & Preserve is an absolute gem for families with young kids. Flying down the dunes on rented sandboards is a once-in-a-lifetime experience that your camping crew will talk about for decades to come. Piñon Flats is inside the park and close to the action and has over eighty sites for tents and RVs 35 feet and under. There are mountain views from most sites, and the campground is filled with piñon pines.

Moraine Park Campground/Rocky Mountain National Park

- ▷ Estes Park, Colorado
- ▷ nps.gov
- ▷ RV and Tent Sites

Many sites at Moraine Park Campground (which sits at an elevation of 8,160 feet) have excellent mountain views. Sites in Loop C overlook the valley below and may be the best in the campground. Access to the park's shuttle system is close to the campground, and you should plan on using it if you want to do a popular hike like Bear Lake, where the trailhead parking lot fills up very early.

Visiting Rocky Mountain National Park

Rocky Mountain National Park is the third most visited national park in the country, so that means you will have to plan ahead and navigate crowds during your visit. Here are some tips that will help.

▷ The following NPS campgrounds can be reserved up to six months in advance in the summer: Aspenglen Campground, Glacier Basin Campground, and Moraine Park Campground. These campgrounds are first-come, first-served in the winter.

▷ The following NPS campgrounds are first-come, first-served year-round: Longs Peak and Timber Creek. They usually fill up by early afternoon during the peak summer months.

▷ Campers are only allowed to stay seven nights total parkwide from May through October. Check out private campground options if you're looking for a longer stay.

▷ If hiking one of the many popular trails in the Bear Lake Area, arrive before 8:00 a.m. during the summer season to snag a parking spot.

▷ Plan on using the free shuttle service to get around the park. The Bear Lake Shuttle and Moraine Park Shuttle access most of the popular park destinations.

RV length limits in Rocky Mountain National Park Campgrounds

▷ Aspenglen: 30 feet
▷ Glacier Basin: 35 feet
▷ Moraine Park: 40 feet
▷ Timber Creek: 30 feet
▷ Longs Peak: Tents only

Hawaii

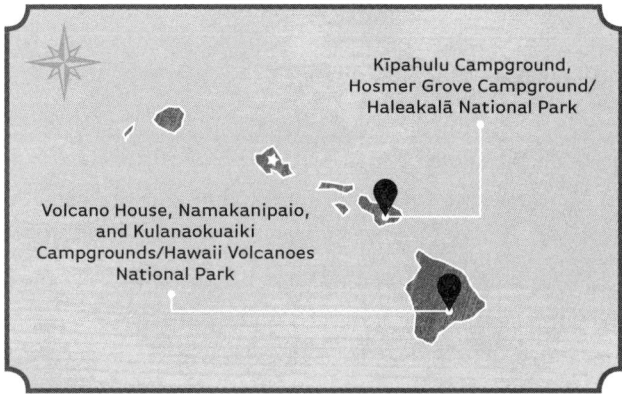

Kīpahulu Campground, Hosmer Grove Campground/ Haleakalā National Park

Volcano House, Namakanipaio, and Kulanaokuaiki Campgrounds/Hawaii Volcanoes National Park

Camping culture is so much different in Hawaii than in the continental United States. RVing and RV parks are just not part of outdoor life like they are in the other forty-nine states. Rather, locals and tourists are much more likely to use tents and campervans when enjoying the national and state parks.

If camping in all fifty states is on your bucket list, you might want to consider a campervan rental in Hawaii. Stay as small as possible: The winding country roads can be difficult to navigate with big rigs, and gas prices are often shocking to tourists. Also be aware that there are strict rules about overnight camping in nondesignated areas. Boondocking is basically against the law, and permits are required for all camping.

BEST IN STATE

Volcano House, Namakanipaio, and Kulanaokuaiki Campgrounds/Hawaii Volcanoes National Park

- ▷ Hawaii Volcanoes National Park, Hawaii
- ▷ nps.gov
- ▷ Lodge Rooms, Cabins, Tent Sites

Hawaii Volcanoes National Park is home to two of the world's most active volcanoes. It is also home to an excellent lodge and two small but charming campgrounds—one of which has adorable cabins. Volcano House offers thirty-three comfortable rooms that are, in our humble opinion, almost glamping. Like many national park lodges, they are lovely but not luxurious. The lodge sits at the edge of the Kilauea Caldera, providing guests with views of the volcano from the dining room and many of the guest rooms. If the price for a volcano view is a bit too rich for your blood, then try one of the cute A-frame cabins in Namakanipaio Campground just 3 miles up the road. These cute-as-a-button cabins sleep four and are bright and cheery inside— but a bit sparsely decorated, so plan on bringing your own cozy blankets and pillows to glamp it up a little. The two campgrounds at Volcanoes National Park are very small and do not accommodate RVs—which are rarely seen in Hawaii—but you can rent a tent from the concessionaire (who will set it up and break it down for you) or bring your own and do it the old-fashioned way.

Kīpahulu Campground, Hosmer Grove Campground/ Haleakalā National Park

- ▷ Makawao, Hawaii
- ▷ nps.gov
- ▷ Tent Sites and Campervan Sites

Haleakalā National Park is a stunning national park for those with adventurous spirits. The park has two districts that both have distinct features—and thankfully, each of them has a campground. The Kīpahulu District is accessed by driving 12 miles on the beautiful, but occasionally dangerous, Hana Highway. But once you arrive (hopefully in one piece) you will be treated to once-in-a-lifetime ocean views, waterfalls, and incredible options for swimming and hiking. You can hear the sound of waves crashing onto ocean cliffs just a short walk away from your basic site at the Kīpahulu Campground. No water is available here, so bring your own, or plan on getting it nearby at the visitor center. The Summit District of Haleakalā is like no other place on earth. At an elevation of over 10,000 feet, this place gets cold and you may want to think twice about going if you have health issues or suffer from altitude sickness. The Hosmer Grove Campground is tiny and intimate and puts you pretty close to the summit—and there is drinking water. But even campers at Hosmer Grove need reservations to see the sunrise at the top. You can get them at recreation.gov.

ALSO GREAT

Bellows Field Beach Park

- ▷ Waimanalo, Hawaii
- ▷ camping.honolulu.gov/campsites/search
- ▷ Tent Sites, Campervan Sites

Bellows Field Beach Park has fifty basic sites for tents and campervans at the edge of a gorgeous sandy white beach. The campground is part of an active military base, but a portion is open to the public for camping. Sites are only available Friday to Monday. This is basically a small, friendly campground located in paradise. The waves are fun for bodyboarding and bodysurfing, so plan on getting wet!

------------ **Looking to Rent a Campervan?** ------------

Outdoorsy and RVShare are peer-to-peer RV rental companies, and many small rental companies in Hawaii also list their rigs on these sites. The search features, reviews, and clear cancellation policies make these websites our favorites for RV rentals. We've used them both in the past and had only good experiences. Campervan Hawaii is a well-reviewed rental company that showcases its nine RVs on the Outdoorsy platform.

A few tips for renting an RV:

✦ Make sure basics like linens and cooking equipment are included. You do not want to fly into Hawaii and shop for sheets.

✦ Read the reviews carefully and pick an owner with a lot of positive feedback.

✦ If you are new to RVing, pick an owner that is happy to provide a lot of education and support.

✦ If it's your first time visiting Hawaii, pick an owner that offers local camping and travel expertise. Renting from a great RV owner can also mean getting the best insider destination tips.

✦ Check cancellation policies carefully. They vary from platform to platform and owner to owner. Consider purchasing your own travel insurance if necessary.

Camp Olowalu

▷   Lahaina, Hawaii

▷   campolowalu.com

▷   Tent Sites, Car Camping Sites, Tentalows, Cabins

The beachfront tentalows (aka glamping tents) and cabins at Camp Olowalu look like they were staged for a Visit Hawaii tourism shoot or a magazine spread—but they are real and they are rentable. The campsites and car camping sites are a bit less romantic because they are situated in a dirt/sand area—but they are also steps from the beach and a fraction of the price. Rent a SUP or kayak right on-site, or go snorkeling or scuba diving and see what lies beneath the surface of these magical waters.

---------------- **More Beachfront Camping** ----------------

Salt Pond Beach Park

Eleele, Hawaii

Hāpuna Beach State Park

Waimea, Hawaii

Kea'au Beach Park

Waianae, Hawaii

Malaekahana Beach Campground

Kahuku, Hawaii

Polihale State Park

Waimea, Hawaii

· *Idaho* ·

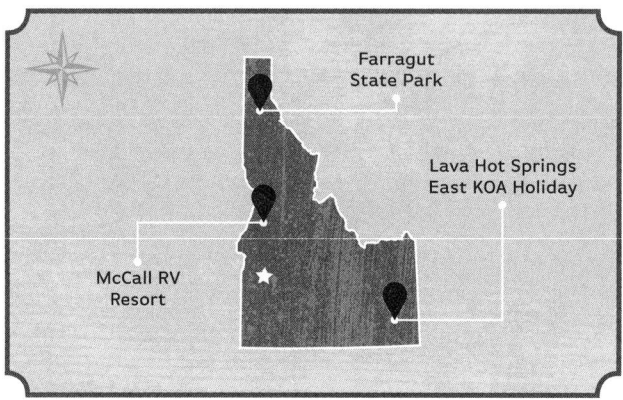

Nestled in between states like Montana, Washington, and Utah, Idaho is often overlooked as a premier outdoor vacation destination—but it shouldn't be. Many campers don't realize that Idaho provides a perfect base camp for access to the West Gate of Yellowstone. Places like Buffalo Campground are nestled near Island Park, known as the quiet gateway to one of America's most popular national parks. Idaho is also home to more than 130 soakable hot springs, more than any other state in the country, and while many of these are rustic, wild, and free to the public, others are privately maintained with entrance fees and additional spa amenities. And then there is the fishing. Visitors flock to the state to catch trout in the streams, and for the opportunity to reel in a king salmon in one of the rushing rivers during spring, summer, and fall. So while Idaho is extremely proud of its potato, it also has much, much more to offer the adventurous camper.

BEST IN STATE

McCall RV Resort

▷ McCall, Idaho

▷ g7rvresorts.com

▷ RV Sites and Cabins, No Tents

Real resort camping is far more popular in the American East, which makes places like McCall, which is situated along the rugged North Fork Payette River, stand out even more. This is one of the best resort campgrounds in the American West. The warm and welcoming Center Lodge sets the scene, and the indoor pool, spa, and steam room look like they were ripped straight out of the pages of *Sunset* magazine. The RV sites range from good to excellent, and we are particular fans of the back-in sites that back up to stacks of towering and shady trees, and of the buddy sites that allow up to four campers to share a central green. The cabins are not glampy or luxurious, but they are clean and comfortable, and the price is right for such a beautiful location with high-end amenities. Deer wander through the campground every day, and there really is no better campground for a morning or evening stroll with a cup of coffee in your hand. The staff here is also excellent—providing exceptional western hospitality that discerning travelers will realize is a cut above and beyond the typical campground experience.

---------- **Drive It: Hells Canyon Scenic Byway** ----------

Drive 22 miles along the Snake River to Hells Canyon Dam on a narrow, winding road with steep grades and beautiful views. Stop and spend some time in Hells Canyon National Recreation Area, which features the deepest gorge in North America.

Popular Hot Springs Near Our Recommended Campgrounds

Gold Fork Hot Springs near McCall RV Resort and Ponderosa State Park

A family-friendly hot springs destination with six mineral pools, a kiddie pool, lockers, and a snack bar.

Lava Hot Springs near Lava Hot Spring East KOA

There's no sulfur in the water here and therefore no odor, making this a popular destination. Check out the on-site Olympic Swimming Complex, indoor aquatic center, and waterslides with a 60-foot vertical drop.

Goldbug Hot Springs near Wagonhammer Campground

Visiting these public hot springs will require a 4-mile round trip strenuous hike, but the payoff will be worth the effort. Multiple pools of varying warmth are nestled into the side of the mountain. Be forewarned that this is often treated as a clothing-optional bathing area.

Farragut State Park

▷ Athol, Idaho

▷ parksandrecreation.idaho.gov

▷ RV and Tent Sites, Cabins

Located at the southern tip of Lake Pend Oreille, Farragut State Park has a fascinating history that is worth learning. This 4,000-acre park was once the site of the Farragut Naval Training Station during World War II. Views of the lake were stunning for naval officers back then, and they are stunning for campers and day-trippers now. There are several campgrounds here and each one has its devotees, but all of them are great for different reasons. Waldron is the largest and the best suited for bigger rigs, Gilmore is shadier and feels a bit more remote, and Whitetail is more deeply wooded, has no hookups, and is better suited for tent campers. All campers will struggle with cell service, no matter which campground they choose. There are vast recreational opportunities at this park, including birdwatching, boating, fishing, and hiking. The campground is packed during summer weekends, so plan accordingly. If you get bored of this park's beauty and tranquility, take a day trip to Silverwood Theme Park. It's the Pacific Northwest's largest theme park, and it's less than fifteen minutes away from Farragut.

-------------- Other Popular Hot Springs --------------

Kirkham Hot Springs, Lowman, Idaho

One of more popular public hot springs in Idaho, these pools are dotted along the scenic Payette River. Kirkham Campground, a National Forest Service property, is right next door and offers vault toilets, potable water, and not much else in the way of amenities. But at $15 a night for a campsite, it's a great place to park your rig while you soak.

Burgdorf Hot Springs, McCall, Idaho

These springs are open to day guests, but cabins are also available for those who want to stay awhile. The cabins are truly rustic, offering no plumbing or electricity. Visitors must bring their own food, water, and sleeping bags. Want to get even more adventurous? Go during the winter when you have to rent a snowmobile to access the hot springs.

Lava Hot Springs East KOA Holiday

▷ Lava Hot Springs, Idaho

▷ koa.com

▷ RV and Tent Sites, Deluxe Cabins and Camping Cabins

The Portneuf River winds its way along the edge of this adorable KOA, making it possible to fly fish, swim, or even go tubing directly from its riverfront RV sites. Campers love to park their rigs right along the edge of the river so they can hear it roll by while they fall asleep at night. The rest of this campground is filled with nice pull-through sites and cute cabins that have views of surrounding hills and ample shade. An activities center serves as the social hub of the campground and features tetherball, volleyball, and horse-shoes. This KOA is located on the historic Old Oregon Trail (aka U.S. Highway 30), and the hot springs are only a short walk away from the campground. Water temperatures range from 102–112°F, and the springs are sulfur free and open year-round, as is this KOA. Light sleepers and tent campers might choose to stay elsewhere, as there is road noise from the highway.

ALSO GREAT

Ponderosa State Park

▷ McCall, Idaho

▷ parksandrecreation.idaho.gov

▷ Lakeview Deluxe Cabins, RV and Tent Sites

This popular campground borders Lake Payette and is sold out on most weekends in the summer. RV sites and tent sites are large and private, but the Lakeview Deluxe Cabins may be the star of the show here. The park has nine of them with names like Moose, Bear, Eagle, and Elf—and they are all lovely and perfectly situated. Osprey Point and North Beach have panoramic views, and downtown McCall is charming and filled with good eats and artsy, down-to-earth shopping.

The Wagonhammer Campground

▷ North Fork, Idaho

▷ wagonhammercampground.com

▷ RV and Tent Sites, Tepees

The Wagonhammer Campground has an idyllic location, right on the banks of the Salmon River and surrounded by the rugged beauty of the Central Idaho Rocky Mountains. Many of the sites are right on the water, so you can fall asleep to the sound of rushing water. Keep your eyes open for elk and bighorn sheep in the hills surrounding this delightful campground.

---- **National Monuments and Historic Sites in Idaho** ----

▷ Craters of the Moon National Monument and Preserve: International Dark Sky Park has a loop drive and hikes to caves and craters.

▷ City of Rocks National Reserve: Climbers from around the world come to test their skills on these towering granite pinnacles. There's also plenty of mountain biking and bird watching.

▷ Hagerman Fossil Beds National Monument: This site contains parts of the Oregon Trail and fossil remnants of the saber-toothed cat, mastodon, camel, and ground sloth.

▷ Minidoka National Historic Site: This site preserves the Minidoka War Relocation Center, which detained 13,000 Japanese Americans from 1942–1945. Visitors can walk a 1.6-mile trail and learn about life in the camp from twenty-seven outdoor exhibits.

Buffalo Campground

▷ Island Park, Idaho

▷ audicampgrounds.com/idaho-islandpark-dubois

▷ RV and Tent Sites

Located thirty-five minutes southwest of the West Gate of Yellowstone, this hidden gem serves as a perfect base camp for exploring America's first national park. The Buffalo River runs through the park, and the fishing and tubing are very good. Enjoy the smell of Lodgepole Pines as you cast your line or float through the campground. Smokey Bear often appears on weekends.

Montana

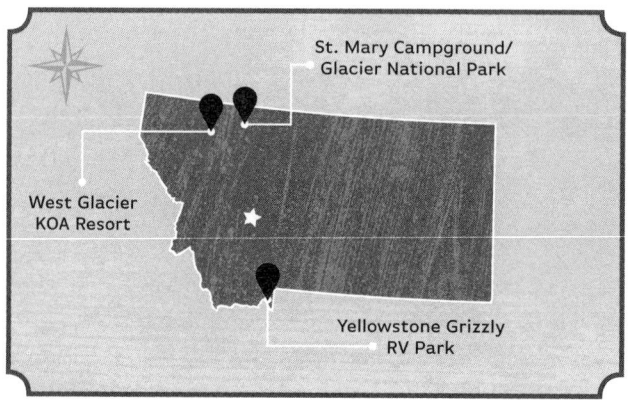

Our friends from Montana know that the entire state is filled with jaw dropping natural beauty and plenty of places to set up camp and enjoy the views. However, most visitors flock from far and wide to visit the "crown jewel of the continent," Glacier National Park. We are ridiculously jealous of the folks who can reach this magical destination in under a day, since for us it requires a cross-country pilgrimage. There are thirteen campgrounds within the national park, but only three offer advance reservations: St. Mary, Fish Creek, and Many Glacier. If you are not brave enough to risk first-come, first-served or lucky enough to snag a coveted reservation, you still have plenty of amazing private campground options on both the west and east sides of the park.

The rest of Montana is teeming with national forests and state parks. Out of the fifty-five state parks, twenty offer reservable campsites, and a handful have other fun accommodations to enjoy like tepees, yurts, and cabins. Situate yourself at one of the many great campgrounds near Bozeman to enjoy outdoor adventures like fly fishing and river rafting, followed by a craft beer downtown.

BEST IN STATE

West Glacier KOA Resort

▷   West Glacier, Montana

▷   koa.com

▷   Camping Cabins, Deluxe Cabins, Multifamily Lodge Rental, RV
     and Tent Sites

This West Glacier KOA is one of the most beautiful campgrounds in the country. Period. The smell of pine trees and the mountain views are ravishing—and so is the hand-dipped ice cream at Scoops. Breakfast at the Lazy Bear Cafe is also excellent. We ate there just about every morning before heading out for another epic hike in Glacier National Park. We stayed in a charming deluxe cabin (with a loft for the boys) with an outdoor firepit and seating area that looked like it had been ripped from the pages of a landscape design magazine. Our boys loved the large basketball and ga-ga ball courts, and they spent hours there each night making fast friends with the rest of the campground kids. We appreciated the adults-only pool and hot tub area. The RV sites at this campground, particularly those at the bottom of the mountain, are among the most beautifully manicured sites we have ever seen. The West Glacier KOA Resort charges top dollar, and it deserves to do so. Proximity to the west side of the park is also excellent.

Yellowstone Grizzly RV Park

▷   West Yellowstone, Montana

▷   grizzlyrv.com

▷   RV Sites, Cabins

The west entrance to Yellowstone National Park is only four blocks away from Yellowstone Grizzly RV Park, and a wide variety of shopping and dining options are also located nearby. So this is a perfect base camp for RV owners and cabin renters who want to explore the park from its western side. The entire park is clean and nicely landscaped—but the stars of the show here are the back-in sites along the edge of the campground with national forest land directly behind them. Non-RV owners should take note—the cabins are cute, but tent camping is no longer allowed. Activities and amenities are somewhat limited at Yellowstone Grizzly, but the camp store offers free coffee in the morning, and the camp workers are kind and knowledgeable about the area. When you are this close to Yellowstone, do you really need a pool or bounce pillow anyway? Make sure that you grab breakfast at Ernie's Bakery and Deli before heading into the park. After a long day of hiking and exploring, get a cone of huckleberry ice cream at The City Creamery. You won't regret it. There is also a tasty Taco Bus in town.

St. Mary Campground/Glacier National Park

▷   Browning, Montana

▷   nps.gov

▷   RV and Tent Sites

St. Mary Campground has otherworldly views of Singleshot, East Flat Top, and Red Eagle Mountains that will take your breath away. The interior roads and the campsites themselves did not look super friendly for larger RVs, so take a look at the nearby KOA if you are in a big rig. But those in smaller RVs with dry camping capabilities will be delighted. The campground is close to the St. Mary visitor center and some of the best hiking and wildlife viewing in the park. We saw more moose and black bear on the east side of Glacier in one day than we saw in four days on the west side. The restrooms are clean and potable water is available, but other amenities are sparse. Tent campers and those with soft-sided RVs beware. When there is bear activity in the campground you may be reassigned to the Two Medicine Campground—or end up with no place to sleep in a somewhat remote section of the park. The town of St. Mary is nearby, but hotel rooms are expensive and availability is limited.

--- **What to Bring: Packing for Glacier National Park** ---

We've been to a lot of national parks, but the remote location of Glacier National Park did require us to pack a bit differently. Be aware that there is little to no cell reception or Wi-Fi in most of the park, so plan accordingly.

- ✦ Bear spray
- ✦ Bear bells
- ✦ Prepaid phone cards
- ✦ Printed confirmations and reservations

- ✦ Good-quality binoculars
- ✦ AllTrails App, Pro Version
- ✦ Layers of clothing
- ✦ Quality hiking gear

ALSO GREAT

Under Canvas Glacier

▷ Coram, Montana

▷ undercanvas.com

▷ Glamping Tents

After spending a long day hiking in one of America's most spectacular national parks, you will be thrilled to kick up your heels in one of Under Canvas's luxurious safari glamping tents. Tents have sinks, showers, and bathrooms, and some have wood-burning stoves. Wrap a blanket around your shoulders and head out onto your own private deck to gaze at the night stars.

Under Canvas Yellowstone

▷ West Yellowstone, Montana

▷ undercanvas.com

▷ Glamping Tents

There are plenty of options for roughing it in and around America's first national park, but when it comes to real high-end glamping, Under Canvas Yellowstone is the best option that offers real proximity to the park. Located just ten minutes from the west gate, this spacious location gives you land and a starry sky above. Under Canvas's locations also do a great job of offering accommodations for families with multiple kids and couples who are trying to get away from it all. If you want to end a long day of adventuring in the park tucked in under luxurious linens with a wood burning stove nearby keeping your tent toasty and warm, then this is where you should camp next.

The Resort at Paws Up

▷ Greenough, Montana

▷ pawsup.com

▷ Safari Tents

This luxurious resort is situated on a working 37,000-acre cattle ranch. Paws Up serves up six different "glamping camps," including the stunning Cliffside Camp perched on the edge of a river, and the Moonlight Camp tucked away in a private corner of this massive property. No matter which camp you choose, your glamping tent will be comfortable if not downright decadent. Think fine linens, rustic western furniture, organic soaps, and your own camping butler to make sure that every little detail is just right.

St. Mary/East Glacier KOA Holiday

▷ Babb, Montana

▷ koa.com

▷ RV and Tent Sites, Camping Cabins, Deluxe Cabins, Four-Bedroom Home

The location of this campground is just about perfect—and so are the views. The amenities, like the large pool, hot tub, and bocce ball courts, are also excellent. We *loved* it here, and we would go back in a Montana minute, but some folks leave a bit less than impressed. Why? Because this KOA is expensive and the landscaping is a little shaggy and rough around the edges. None of those things really bothered us though. Ice cream and coffee in the camp stores were excellent—and so was the almost concierge-level service.

Five Favorite Hikes in Glacier National Park

Sunrift Gorge to St. Mary Falls Trail

The St. Mary Falls Trail is a popular and easy 3-mile hike, but by a happy accident we did a longer version that started at the Sunrift Gorge parking lot. We are so glad we ended up experiencing this 5.5-mile round-trip hike instead. The first mile runs along a ridge that gives hikers stunning views of St. Mary Lake. We enjoyed watching three moose through our binoculars. Some people do swim at the base of St. Mary Falls, so bring a suit if you'd like to take a dip.

Grinnell Glacier

There are only twenty-five active glaciers left in Glacier National Park, and this is one of the easiest to get to—but it's still a 12-mile round-trip hike over very difficult terrain. We did it. We were exhausted. And it was worth every step for that amazing payoff experience. You will need to be at the Many Glacier Hotel before 8:00 a.m. to snag a parking spot to reach the trailhead.

Hidden Lake Trail at Logan Pass

Logan Pass is definitely one of the most crowded places in the park, and this is probably the most crowded trail. Hike it anyway. You won't care about all the people when you see the mountain streams bordered by brilliant wildflowers. The wildlife viewing is phenomenal. We watched families of mountain goats wander alongside the trail and a half a dozen hoary marmots play in a field. This is the single most difficult place to park in all of Glacier. Get there early or take the shuttle.

Iceberg Lake

If you aren't up for the Grinnell Glacier hike, this might be a great alternative. It's a bit shorter, at just 9 miles, and the hike is not as strenuous. The payoff is just as good, though. Many people swear this is their favorite hike in the entire park.

Avalanche Lake via the Trail of Cedars

This is one of the easier hikes in all of Glacier, yet the payoff views at Avalanche Lake are as stunning as anything in the park. It's a 5-mile round-trip hike without a lot of elevation gain. The first part of the hike is the Trail of Cedars, an accessible boardwalk hike. Get there early to park at the crowded trailhead, or take a shuttle from any of the visitor centers.

Other Great Activities at Glacier National Park

Take the Red Bus Tour
Our favorite is the half-day Eastern Alpine tour. These tours allow you to take in the beauty of the landscape without the stress of navigating Going to the Sun Road. The guides are also brilliant at bringing to life the history and geology of the park.

Enjoy a Ranger Program at the St. Mary Campground
The topics vary greatly from bear safety to glaciers, but the beautiful setting is breathtaking no matter the subject.

Have Dinner and Drinks at the Many Glacier Hotel
Even if you aren't staying at the hotel, make time to enjoy the epic views in this iconic national park lodge.

Go Horseback Riding with Swan Mountain Outfitters
Swan Mountain Outfitters is the concessionaire that runs all the stables in Glacier National Park. It has a wide variety of hour-long, half-day, and full-day rides. If you need a break from hiking, this is a great way to see the park.

Take a Boat Ride on Lake McDonald or St. Mary Lake
The Glacier Park Boat Company has been operating Glacier National Park since 1938. The classic boats are a wonderful part of this national park's history. A few boat rides a day include an onboard park ranger talk. The other tours host an onboard naturalist who interprets the land around the lakes.

· *Nevada* ·

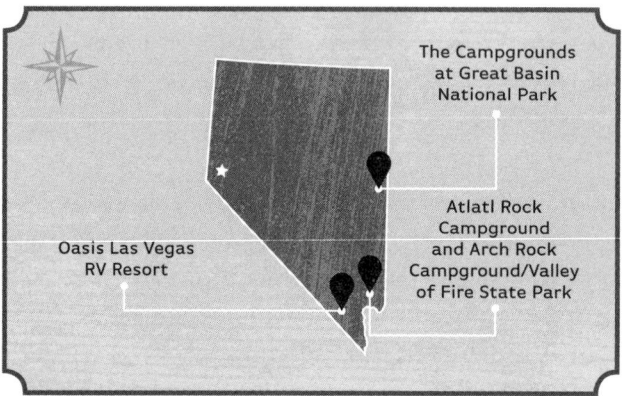

The Campgrounds at Great Basin National Park

Atlatl Rock Campground and Arch Rock Campground/Valley of Fire State Park

Oasis Las Vegas RV Resort

Nevada is most known for two things that couldn't be more different: the bright lights of the Las Vegas Strip and the stunning natural beauty of places like Lake Tahoe and Red Rock Canyon. The good news for folks like us is that Nevada offers great camping options no matter what type of excursion you are planning. From RV resorts in Las Vegas that mirror the amenities of their hotel competitors to state parks that showcase some of the most stunning scenery in this country, Nevada may surprise the first-time visitor.

Of course, the key to enjoying a camping trip here is understanding the wide variations of climate. The southern desert will be almost too hot to bear in the summer months, while the northern mountains see plenty of single-digit temperatures and snowfall in the winter. Camp accordingly.

Before you go...

▷ **Watch:** *Las Vegas: An Unconventional History*, part of the American Experience collection from PBS

BEST IN STATE

Oasis Las Vegas RV Resort

▷ Las Vegas, Nevada

▷ oasislasvegasrvresort.com

▷ RV Sites

A clean and comfortable RV resort with a *Casablanca* theme close to all the action in Las Vegas? With great amenities and friendly customer service? You can count us in every time we head to Vegas, that's for sure. The club-house here is excellent and packed with amenities. It serves breakfast and lunch, has a convenience store with groceries and souvenirs, and features a nice exercise room and a theatre that is used for movie nights on Mondays. There is also a bocce ball court and horseshoes for unwinding after a long day of exploring the city. Concierge service is available if you need help with show tickets or restaurant reservations. Pull-through sites are long and easy to navigate, but they are not wide, so you will be close to your neighbor. The property is gated and has excellent security, and there are palm trees at almost every site for shade. Visiting Las Vegas in an RV can be daunting and a bit difficult to navigate. That is why we love the Oasis Las Vegas RV Resort so much—its excellent customer service takes the guesswork out of the equation.

Atlatl Rock Campground and Arch Rock Campground/Valley of Fire State Park

▷ Overton, Nevada

▷ parks.nv.gov

▷ RV and Tent Sites

Campers in the know are well aware that many of our country's best state parks can stand side by side with our national parks. They don't get the same attention, and they don't benefit from mutual marketing or the same shared mythology—but their excellence is unquestioned. Valley of Fire State Park is one of the most beautiful state parks in the country. The red Aztec sandstone outcrops are visually stunning, and hikes through shaded slot canyons beckon adventurous campers and day-trippers of all ages. Valley of Fire has two campgrounds that are perfectly positioned to enjoy the best that this park has to offer. The RV and tent sites at Atlatl Rock Campground are absolutely epic. Many back right up to the bright red rock formations and form the perfect backdrops for Instagram photos that will wow your friends.

About twenty of these sites have water and electric, so you don't have to rough it in the heat of the summer. Arch Rock campground is also beautiful, but there are no hookups there. Neither of these campgrounds accept reservations, so getting a site is first-come, first-served. Godspeed camper! We wish you luck! Tag us in your photos!

The Campgrounds at Great Basin National Park

▷   Baker, Nevada

▷   nps.gov

▷   RV and Tent Sites

Great Basin National Park is one of the least visited units in the National Park System with well under 200,000 visitors a year. When Zion National Park and the Grand Canyon are in your *general* vicinity, I guess it is easy to see how you could get overshadowed. But we think that Great Basin National Park is pretty grand in its own right. This park has mountains (Wheeler Peak at 13,000 feet) and underground caves (Lehman Caves, to be visited by guided tour only) for above and below ground exploration. It also has groves of bristlecone pines and some of the darkest night skies in the country. Thankfully there are also five developed campgrounds to choose from, and all of them are beautiful. Almost all reservations are on a first-come, first-served basis with limited reservation opportunities for tent camping available only at recreation.gov. All RV sites are first-come, first-served. These five campgrounds are each very small—if you come without a reservation on a weekend or during peak season, make sure you have a back-up plan in case you can't get a site.

ALSO GREAT

Las Vegas KOA at Sam's Town Journey

▷ Las Vegas, Nevada

▷ koa.com

▷ RV Sites

This KOA, like many urban campgrounds, could be looked at as a glorified parking lot—or it could be looked at as the perfect base camp for exploring Sin City. If you park your rig here, you are officially a guest at Sam's Town Gambling Hall (a popular spot not on the main strip) and have access to its various facilities including pools and hot tubs. Don't leave without getting the sampler plate at Big Mess BBQ—the ribs are oh-so-tender.

Cathedral Gorge State Park

▷ Panaca, Nevada

▷ parks.nv.gov

▷ RV and Tent Sites

Camping at Cathedral Gorge State Park is like camping on another planet. The campground is small, but this state park is mighty. It is located in a narrow valley where erosion has created a stunning landscape of cathedral-like spires that change color when the sun rises and sets. The hiking is amazing here, and some trails feature slot canyons with dramatic walls. There are only twenty-two sites, but they are spacious and private. Some even offer picnic tables under shelters that provide much-needed shade.

Welcome Station RV Park

▷ Wells, Nevada

▷ wsrvpark.com

▷ RV and Tent Sites

This may be the prettiest little RV park in all of Nevada—and the friendliest too. The owners were full time RVers for sixteen years, so it's no wonder that they know how to do this right. The park is grassy and filled with shady trees, and a river runs through it. Campers here often refer to this place as an oasis, and it's easy to see why. Tent campers are also welcome and report sleeping very nicely on the soft grass that fills the park. This is a classic mom-and-pop owned campground that is doing it right. Make sure you stop by for a night if you are passing through—but be forewarned, you might not want to leave.

------------ **Drive It: Lake Tahoe Scenic Drive** ------------

This 72-mile loop is often referred to as the "most beautiful drive in America." Enjoy a day of scenic overlooks, historic sites, and regional museums. The Lake Tahoe Visitor Bureau has an excellent brochure available online that details twenty-four suggested stops along the loop.

Away from the Strip: Outdoor Excursions near Las Vegas

Red Rock Canyon

The 13-mile scenic drive through Red Rock Canyon has plenty of places to stop, soak in the view, and take photographs that can be hash-tagged "nofilter." There are also dozens of hikes that will take you down into the canyon or up to the peaks, according to your fancy. This is a famous rock climbing spot, and staff and climbing guides are available with maps and permit information.

Valley of Fire State Park

There's a scenic loop road to drive, and also a ton of short—1 mile or less— hikes that showcase some of the most stunning features in this park. Favorites include The Beehives and White Dome Hike. It's only about fifty minutes from Las Vegas, so you can stay at a campground resort like Oasis or stay in the state park campground.

Lake Mead Recreational Area

America's first recreational area is located only forty minutes from Las Vegas. It encompasses 1.5 million acres and has countless opportunities for boating, fishing, hiking, biking, and swimming. The Black Canyon Area has a concentration of water excursion options. The Lake Mead Visitors Center is in the Boulder Basin area and is a good place to plan out your adventure with help from park rangers.

Hoover Dam

The Hoover Dam formed Lake Mead and is a must-visit destination when exploring this part of Nevada. There are three different tour options; some tickets are available in advance and some are only available on a first-come, first-served basis. Decide in advance if you would like to do a self-guided tour or dive a bit deeper with a guided tour of the historic tunnels.

New Mexico

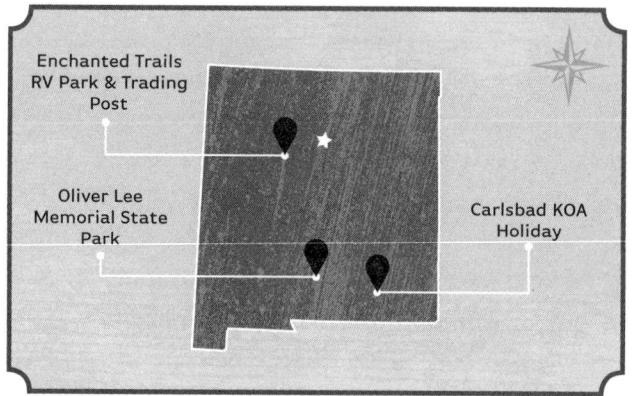

It didn't take us long to figure out why New Mexico is nicknamed the Land of Enchantment. In fact, we were so mesmerized by the landscape during our first visit that we were plotting a return camping trip while we were still there. The mountain views and fiery sunsets are awe-inspiring, even when urban camping in downtown Albuquerque. We particularly love the fact that we could explore ancient petroglyphs, hike to volcanoes, and eat lunch at a famous Route 66 diner all in one day.

Many folks lucky enough to live in this beautiful state love the mix of wonderfully wild state parks, well-situated KOAs, and beautiful RV resorts. The temperatures can get high in the summer, so September and October tend to be popular camping months. Note that the popular Albuquerque Balloon Festival takes place in early October, bringing hundreds of thousands of visitors into the state. Make those reservations far in advance if visiting the region during that time of year.

BEST IN STATE

Oliver Lee Memorial State Park

▷ Alamogordo, New Mexico

▷ emnrd.state.nm.us

▷ RV and Tent Sites

The rugged landscape and ravishing views of the Sacramento Mountains on one side and a sweeping desert landscape on the other will make you fall in love with Oliver Lee Memorial State Park the second you back into your spacious and private site. New Mexico natives love this park and often use it as a base camp when visiting White Sands National Park, which is about thirty minutes away—though plenty of folks also like to just kick back here and enjoy all that Oliver Lee has to offer. Enjoy a leisurely stroll on the Riparian Nature Trail or challenge yourself with a strenuous hike up the Dog Canyon Trail for stunning views on all sides. Sunrise and sunset are typically beautiful here, so plan on bringing an extra SD card for your camera! Jackrabbits run through the park, and a wide variety of birds, such as owls, hummingbirds, and mockingbirds, also pass through depending on the season. The exhibits at the visitor center are also worth checking out, and the rangers and camp hosts are friendly and helpful.

Enchanted Trails RV Park & Trading Post

▷ Albuquerque, New Mexico

▷ enchantedtrails.com

▷ RV and Tent Sites

Enchanted Trails is located on historic Route 66, and everything about it matches the dusty grandeur and mojo of the Mother Road. We were wowed by the vintage trailer village at the front of the park. At the time of our visit the trailers were for rent, but the owner has since converted them into a charming little vintage trailer museum in order to preserve them as historical artifacts. You can't spend the night in them anymore, but if you ask the owner she will graciously let you take a leisurely peek inside. These units are all named, and we developed a particular fondness for Dot, the 1963 Winnebago, and Geneva, the 56 Yellowstone. Vintage Airstream fans will also want to say hello to Josephine! The rest of the park has a quirky and timeless charm though it is filled with modern RVs. Desert views surround the park, as do views of three extinct volcanoes. We also loved the vintage curiosities in the clubhouse and the southwestern foods and gifts in the trading post. If you love vintage anything like we do, then get hip to this timely tip and book a site at Enchanted Trails.

------------ It's All about the Hatch Chilies... ------------

The locals will fight all day long about where to get the best hatch green chili dishes, but we recommend just eating your way through Albuquerque to find your own personal favorites. Or you can attend the Hatch Chile Festival, which takes place every year in September.

Carlsbad KOA Holiday

▷ Carlsbad, New Mexico

▷ koa.com

▷ RV and Tent Sites, Camping Cabins and Deluxe Cabins

This KOA is about forty-five minutes away from Carlsbad Caverns National Park, which has no campground options within its borders. This is our base camp pick if you want to explore the caverns while enjoying a campground with rock solid amenities. This KOA has an on-site smoker and owners who love to cook and deliver BBQ right to their guests' sites. You might have a tough time choosing between the Pecan & Mesquite Wood Smoked Combo Brisket with Pork & Sausage and the BBQ Baby Back Pork Ribs—but it is all good. Bobby Flay even featured the camp's grub on his show *BBQ With*

Bobby Flay. The BBQ may be the star of the show, but other amenities also shine. The laundry facilities and bathrooms are immaculate, and so are the pool and playground areas. Tent campers also love the hexagonal tent village that offers shade, privacy, a storage locker, and water and electric hookups at each site. Many KOAs have invested in their tent camping sites over the last ten years, and this is a great example of that trend.

ALSO GREAT

Albuquerque North/Bernalillo KOA Journey

- ▷ Bernalillo, New Mexico
- ▷ koa.com
- ▷ RV and Tent Sites, Camping Cabins

This KOA, which is located north of downtown Albuquerque, is loved by kids and adults for very different reasons. There are lots of activities and fun amenities for the kids, like basketball, horseshoes, an outdoor movie theatre, and a decent pool. But adults traveling sans kids also adore it. Why, might you ask? Because of the secret path that leads directly to the Kaktus Brewery, where live music, great food, and homemade beer are always on tap.

Elephant Butte Lake RV Resort

- ▷ Elephant Butte, New Mexico
- ▷ elephantbuttelakervresort.com
- ▷ RV Sites

Less than a mile away from New Mexico's largest lake, this friendly and beautifully landscaped resort treats its guests like family. Too many RV parks throw the word "resort" into their names even though they offer few luxurious amenities. But this is a real resort camping experience. The resort has an indoor pool and hot tub and an on-site spa for massage and aromatherapy.

Recreational options like pickleball, basketball, and horseshoes are also robust. The huge dog park and dog wash also make this a premier spot for those traveling with their pups.

Lea Lake Campground at Bottomless Lake State Park

▷   Roswell, New Mexico

▷   emnrd.state.nm.us

▷   RV and Tent Sites

Campers who come to the Roswell area seeking UFOs and alien life forms often leave disappointed, but those seeking outdoor recreation with a backdrop of red rocks, wide open skies, gorgeous sunsets, and bottomless lakes will find those things in spades. The campground at this state park is small but has great sites for tents and RVs. Camp here in the off-season if you want to avoid the flies and overcrowding at the swimming lake.

------- **Exploring Petroglyph National Monument** -------

One of the largest petroglyph sites in North America is located just minutes from downtown Albuquerque. This fascinating place is worth a visit.

✧   Watch the movie at the visitors center and get a trail map from the rangers.

✧   Visit Boca Negra Canyon and hike the Mesa Point Trail, Macaw Trail, and Cliff Base Trail featuring more than one hundred petroglyphs.

✧   Enjoy a picnic lunch at the picnic area in Boca Negra Canyon.

✧   Drive to the Volcanoes Day Use Area. Hike the undeveloped trail system enjoying views of the Rio Grande Valley and the Sandia Mountains.

A Nearly New National Park!

White Sands was a national monument from 1933 to 2019, when it was redesignated as a national park. You'll want to do a bit of planning before you visit this otherworldly destination, which hosts the largest gypsum dune field in the world. Here's what you need to know:

▷ Pay attention to the weather. Wind storms, dust storms, and thunderstorms are common at various times throughout the year. Plus, temperatures can exceed 100°F in the summer months.

▷ Check for closings due to testing at the White Sands Missile Range. These closures usually last a few hours, so make sure you plan ahead.

▷ Make sure you have the right sled for the dunes. Bring your own or buy one from the visitors center. Just make sure it has a waxed bottom for the best sledding experience.

▷ Bring your furry family members. White Sand Dunes is one of the most pet-friendly national parks in the country, allowing dogs on every one of the trails. Make sure that you explore the sand before it gets too hot for their paws in the summer months.

▷ Be prepared for strenuous hiking. People who haven't hiked on sandy trails before are often surprised by how much more difficult it is. Be prepared with plenty of water and appropriate clothing.

▷ Look into the ranger-led walks. From sunset strolls to full moon hikes, these ranger programs are a great way to learn more about a remarkable ecosystem.

· *Oregon* ·

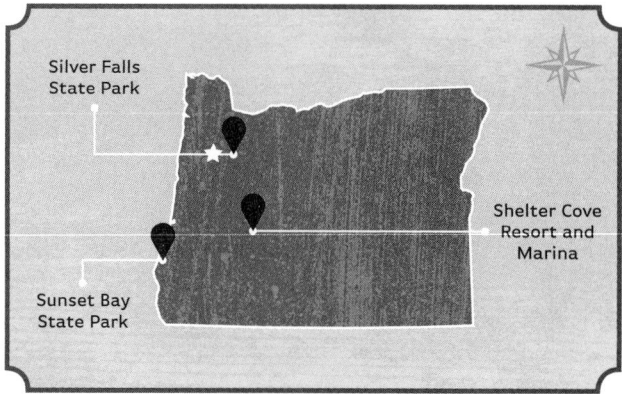

Camping enthusiasts in Oregon are truly blessed with a diversity of natural beauty combined with a vibrant and well-funded state park system. Oregon is one of our very favorite places to vacation as a family, and it pains us that we live too far away to camp there on a regular basis.

This large state is divided into distinct regions that offer very unique camping experiences. There's the magical coastal area, with rocky out-croppings, oyster farms, and enormous dunes perfect for adventurous ATV riders. Crater Lake in the south offers stunning natural views and hiking opportunities. Wallowa Lake in eastern Oregon is a favorite camping destination for locals in the know. And Portland, of course, is an urban treasure offering hip downtown shopping and dining just 30 miles east of the Columbia River Gorge.

The state parks are extremely popular for camping, and reservations open up nine months in advance. If you are looking to stay at places like Sunset Bay State Park or Silver Falls State Park, put a booking reminder in your phone and log onto their reservations system at midnight to snag a site.

BEST IN STATE

Sunset Bay State Park

▷   Coos Bay, Oregon

▷   oregonstateparks.org

▷   RV and Tent Sites, Yurts

We think that every inch of the Oregon coast is spectacular, but the stretch of coast occupied by Sunset Bay State Park (and its adjacent sister state parks Shore Acres and Cape Arago) cranks it up another windswept notch. The campground is cozy and just steps away from a magical spot where sunsets melt into the ocean. It also offers full hook-up sites for RVs, along with yurts and tent sites near the water. RV sites are not huge but offer shade and privacy. A series of hiking trails connects Sunset Bay with nearby Shore Acres and Cape Arago. Our family did an 8–9-mile round-trip hike that hugged the coastline and took in all three of these state parks on a gorgeous July day a few years back. We also spent another afternoon exploring the home and gardens that once formed the estate of Timber Baron Louis Simpson at Shore Acres State Park. The Pacific Northwest is so beautiful that it almost seems unfair to these East Coasters. Three stunning state parks all within walking distance of each other? Seriously!

Shelter Cove Resort and Marina

▷   Crescent, Oregon

▷   highwaywestvacations.com

▷   Cabins, Lodge, Tent and RV Sites

The lakefront cabins at Shelter Cove are the most beautiful and comfortable cabins we have ever seen at a campground. I still dream about the Willamette two-bedroom cabin with loft and private boat launch on cold winter nights. Our family spent long summer days on rented kayaks and SUPs splashing and paddling around in front of our private front yard with a firepit. We also rented a pontoon boat from the campground's on-site marina and headed out onto the lake for swimming and a picnic lunch. The RV sites at Shelter Cove are top notch. They are quiet, shady, and spacious. The Hook and Talon Cafe up at the camp store had the best burgers and breakfast sandwiches we have ever had at a campground. Shelter Cove felt like a dream from a storybook for these East Coasters. Glamping here was truly a great escape. Odell Lake is a legendary fishing spot for West Coast aficionados—and for those who love to fish and camp, I can think of no better place in America.

Silver Falls State Park

▹ Sublimity, Oregon

▹ **oregonstateparks.org**

▹ **Tent and RV Sites, Cabins**

The Oregon state park system is a national treasure. It's no surprise that two of its campgrounds made our top picks list. Silver Falls State Park would be a great campground even if it was not located adjacent to the breathtaking Trail of Ten Falls hiking trail. But this magical 7.2-mile round-trip hike turns this campground into an obvious bucket list destination for just about any kind of camper. Where else can you hike from your site and end up behind a 177-foot waterfall like South Falls? Hikers and photographers will take particular joy in nabbing a spot at Silver Falls—and those who love both will find themselves in a lush Pacific Northwestern paradise. The campground offers a wide variety of good sites, and many are wooded and private. Rustic cabins are also available along with group RV and tent sites. Bring a comfortable set of shoes and a sense of adventure and plan on booking your site when the window first opens. Silver Falls is beloved by Oregonians and campers across the country.

ALSO GREAT

The Vintages Trailer Resort

▷ Dayton, Oregon

▷ the-vintages.com

▷ Vintage RV Rentals

Located in the heart of Oregon's wine country, the Vintages Trailer Resort operates as a campground within a campground. The owners bill the resort as a "neighborhood" within the Willamette Wine Country RV Park—and stepping into it feels like stepping out of a time machine. Choose from over twenty vintage RVs including several Airstreams from the '50s, '60s, and '70s.

---------------------- **Before you go...** ----------------------

▷ **Watch:** *The Goonies*, filmed in Astoria. Many of the scenes take place right on Cannon Beach.

Out'n'About Treehouse Treesort

▷ Cave Junction, Oregon

▷ treehouses.com

▷ Treehouse Rentals

The history of the Out'n'About Treehouse Treesort is almost as charming as the property itself. Check its website to learn how it survived multiple zoning related shutdowns by selling limited edition T-shirts with its treehouses on them—then book yourself a stay. We love the Majestree and Peacock Perch, but all of its rentals are charming beyond belief.

Astoria/Warrenton/Seaside KOA Resort

▷ Hammond, Oregon

▷ koa.com

▷ Tent and RV Sites, Deluxe Cabins and Camping Cabins

This KOA resort has all of the trimmings. The Big Foot Activities Center and heated indoor pool and hot tub are particularly popular. No excuses for being bored during a rainy Pacific Northwest day here. Shared communal spaces like the camp store and bathrooms are immaculately clean, as are the cabins. This is a jewel in the KOA system, and the location near some of Oregon's most charming coastal towns couldn't be much better.

---------------- **Ten Oregon Coast Highlights** ----------------

From Oregon Dunes National Recreation Area down to the tiny town of Bandon, here are some of our favorite things to do along the southern coast:

1. Hiking at Shore Acres State Park
2. Watching the sunset at aptly named Sunset Bay State Park
3. Taking the guided tour at the Umpqua Lighthouse State Park
4. Eating oysters at Umpqua Aquaculture
5. Learning about Coos Bay at the Charleston Marine Life Center
6. Watching the four-wheelers fly down the dunes at Sand Lake Recreational Area
7. Driving the Charleston to Bandon Tour Route
8. Crabbing off the docks at the Charleston Marina
9. Getting our morning brew at Bayside Coffee
10. Eating a big bowl of chowder at the Bandon Fish Market

A Quick Guide to Crater Lake National Park

This is Oregon's only national park and home to the country's deepest lake. Crater Lake was formed over 7,000 years ago when the volcano Mount Mazama collapsed, creating the basin of pure and visually spectacular water.

Where to Camp

There are two campgrounds in the park: Mazama Campground and Lost Creek Campground. Lost Creek is self-serve tent camping only, and you can't make reservations. Mazama Campground has RV and tent camping sites, available to reserve thirteen months in advance for July, August, and September. There are only a handful of sites with electric hookups.

You might want to consider a National Park Lodge for this visit. Crater Lake Lodge and the Cabins at Mazama Village offer stunning views of the lake and easy access to park activities.

We visited Crater Lake National Park while camping at Shelter Cove Resort and Marina. It was only a little over an hour's drive and made for an easy day trip.

What to Do

▷ Watch the educational film at the Steel Visitor Center. We are rarely impressed by the NPS movies, but this one was the perfect introduction to the geological history of Crater Lake.

▷ The breathtaking Rim Drive is a 33-mile loop with thirty overlooks. You can take a ranger-guided trolley tour, which we always recommend, from the Rim Village if you prefer not to drive yourself.

▷ Hike the Garfield Peak Trail, which brings you to stunning lake views. The 3.4 miles are made more difficult by more than 1,000 feet of elevation gain. Take your time and enjoy the spectacular sites.

▷ Take the Wizard Island Boat Tour. You'll have to hike over a mile to the boat dock and then hike back up when the tour is over. But the effort will earn you three hours for hiking on Wizard Island and swimming in the cold, cold waters.

▷ End at least one day in the park with cocktails on the Crater Lake Lodge terrace. Try your best *not* to talk about the color of the water the entire time.

We only had one full day at Crater Lake, but we still managed to pack in a lot of the sites. So even if you only have time for a quick stop, this national park is worth it. However, we think two full days (three camping nights) would be the perfect amount of time to enjoy the wonders of Crater Lake.

Utah

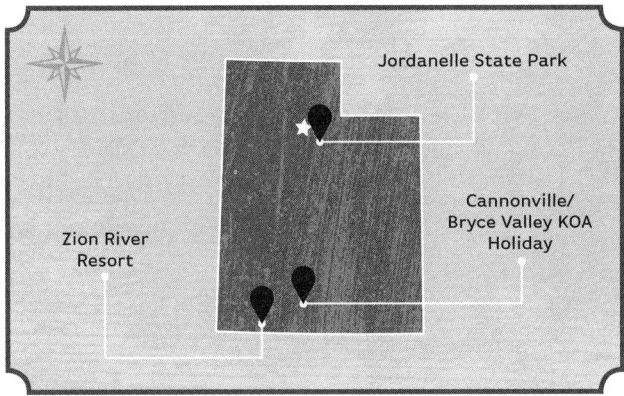

Let's be honest—Utah is not an underrated camping state. One of the reasons there are so many amazing campground options is because of the large amount of designated public lands. Utah hosts thirteen National Park Service sites, including five national parks, often referred to as the Big Five: Arches, Bryce Canyon, Canyonlands, Capitol Reef, and Zion. All of the national parks include well-maintained campgrounds, and then there is always a cluster of great campground options outside of the parks for those in search of more amenities. With over fifteen million visitors a year, you'll want to plan in advance when visiting the more popular national parks. Check for transportation restrictions, as some require the use of the park shuttles in certain high-traffic locations. Also be prepared for a wide range of temperatures depending on when you camp.

The state park system also offers a dizzying array of campgrounds at some of the lowest prices you will find anywhere in this country. Many have fees as low as $17, which also includes park entry. Local favorites include Antelope Island, Jordanelle State Park, and Dead Horse Point State Park.

BEST IN STATE

Jordanelle State Park

▷   Heber City, Utah

▷   stateparks.utah.gov/parks/jordanelle/

▷   RV and Tent Sites, Cabin Rentals

Jordanelle State Park, which is situated on the pristine shores of the Jordanelle Reservoir, is about forty to sixty minutes away from downtown Salt Lake City and is incredibly popular with denizens of that great city— particularly with those who love water sports. So if you are looking to camp here, get on it early! Jordanelle actually has four different campgrounds. Hailstone has over one hundred RV sites with water and electric, and all of them have water views. McHenry Campground is designed specifically for tent campers and has clean bathrooms and showers and a modern play-ground. There is also a hike-in campground and a group campground. Jordanelle also offers five spacious and relatively new cabins with heat and air conditioning that sleep from six to eight campers. The boating facilities at this state park are excellent. There is a main dock with a pro shop, rentals, and fish cleaning stations. Campers with their own kayaks and SUPs will love the personal watercraft ramp where motorized boats are not allowed.

Easy Hikes with Big Views in Arches National Park

▷   Balanced Rock (0.3-mile loop)

▷   Double Arch (0.5-mile round trip)

▷   Sand Dune Arch (0.3-mile round trip)

▷   Delicate Arch Viewpoint (0.7-mile round trip)

Zion River Resort

▷   Virgin, Utah

▷   zionriverresort.com

▷   RV and Tent Sites, Cabins and Two-Bedroom Suites

Zion River Resort may be the nicest resort-style campground in all of Utah. Unlike some private RV resorts that can look like parking lots, this one is absolutely beautiful in every way. The Virgin River runs alongside the campground, and you can hear it from many of the sites, though views can be somewhat limited due to a protective berm. But the mountain views encircle the campground and the sight of red rock and blue skies will fill your heart with joy. The amenities here are also excellent. The heated pool and hot tub are perfect for a relaxing post-hike dip, and the communal camp kitchen with charcoal grills is a great place to stretch your legs and meet your neighbors. There is also a spa for guests who are fourteen years old and up. During the spring and summer months, the on-site takeout grill offers up hot and cold sandwiches, salads, and ice cream. The resort also offers a fourteen-person shuttle bus that will, for a fee, drop you off and pick you up directly in front of the entrance to Zion. This service could be clutch for those renting motorhomes and traveling without a car.

Cannonville/Bryce Valley KOA Holiday

▷   Cannonville, Utah

▷   koa.com

▷   Lodge, Camping Cabins and Deluxe Cabins, RV and Tent Sites

If you like gorgeous views, friendly service, and meticulous cleanliness, then this KOA might be for you. Stunning views of the red rock cliffs of Grand Staircase Escalante National Monument surround you at this KOA, and Bryce Canyon National Park is only 12 miles away, making this a near-perfect base camp for exploring the region. Some of the RV sites are a bit tight, but common areas like the communal outdoor kitchens and gathering areas with fire rings are beloved by campers who love to get social. Tent sites are excellent here, with level sand pads, electricity, and proximity to the aforementioned kitchens. The cabins and lodge offerings are cute, and comfortable linens are provided. The area around the campground is a natural wonderland for hiking, biking, and photography, and you will love returning to the park each night for relaxing campfires and ice cream socials under the stars.

-------- **City Escape: Antelope Island State Park** --------

Located just a couple of hours outside of Salt Lake City, this state park in northern Utah is perfect for a quick camping getaway. Enjoy the wildlife in the park and also the robust educational programs, including a Junior Ranger course. Here are some other area attractions to round out your stay:

- Hill Air Force Base and Museum
- Lagoon Amusement Park
- Cherry Hill Waterpark
- USU Botanical Center
- Eccles Dinosaur Park
- Golden Spike National Monument

ALSO GREAT

Under Canvas Moab

▷   Moab, Utah

▷   undercanvas.com

▷   Glamping Tents

Moab. The name alone conjures up epic adventures surrounded by pink and red sandstone cliffs. The landscape around Moab may be rugged, but your tent at Under Canvas will be nothing but luxurious. Imagine a queen-sized leather couch in your tent's lounge area and a wood burning stove with a stack of firewood nearby, and you will start to get the picture. You might get a bit dirty and rough around the edges after hiking and mountain biking all day—but your private bathroom with shower and organic soaps and shampoos will be waiting for you back at your tent.

Watchman Campground/Zion National Park

▷ Springdale, Utah

▷ nps.gov

▷ RV and Tent Sites

Beautiful canyon and mountain views abound as the Virgin River rolls by this astonishingly beautiful NPS campground. The location inside the park is also excellent. The visitor center and Zion Canyon shuttle stop are within walking distance. Generators are not allowed, but Loops A and B have electric sites. Loop B has gorgeous river view sites. Good luck trying to book a site there—they are in high demand.

Devil's Garden/Arches National Park

▷ Moab, Utah

▷ nps.gov

▷ RV and Tent Sites

Devil's Garden has no hookups, no activities, and no amenities, but the location in one of Utah's most iconic national parks more than makes up for it. The views of the slickrock outcroppings give this campground an otherworldly look, and there is direct access to bouldering and rock scrambling just steps away from the campground. This is a dry campground with no hookups at the sites, so take caution when camping in the heat of the summer. Most RV owners like the back-in sites better than the pull-off sites.

Moab Valley RV Resort

▷ Moab, Utah

▷ sunrvresorts.com

▷ Cabins, Cottages, RV and Tent Sites

Clean as a whistle and cute as a button, the Moab Valley RV Resort wins points for its proximity to Arches National Park and its friendly and helpful customer service. The red rock mountains of the Moab Valley surround the campground and provide views from every site. The pool and the hot tub are nice after a long day of hiking in the park, and downtown Moab has great food and shopping.

------- **Utah Unique State Park Accommodations** -------

Tepees

- Fremont Indian State Park and Museum
- Red Fleet Park
- Scofield State Park

Canvas Tents

- Palisades State Park

Yurts

- Dead Horse Point State Park
- East Canyon State Park
- Goblin Valley State Park
- Rockport State Park

Hammocks

- East Canyon State Park
- Red Fleet State Park

Wagons

- East Canyon Bay State Park

A Quick Guide to Zion National Park

When to Go

Zion National Park is open year-round. April through October are the busiest months. Spring and fall are the best times to visit if looking to avoid high temperatures. However, if you visit in the spring, the famous Narrows hike may not be open on account of high water levels.

Before You Go

Read: *The Complete Guide to National Parks of the West* and *Utah's Big Five National Parks: Adventuring with Kids*, both by Fodor's Travel

Where to Stay in the Park

▷ Watchmen Campground
▷ South Campground
▷ Lava Point Campground
▷ Cabins at the Zion Lodge

Where to Stay Outside the Park

▷ Zion River Resort
▷ St. George/Hurricane KOA

Where to Stock Up

▷ **Springdale:** This small town is just outside the south entrance and has groceries, camping supplies, and dining options.
▷ **Virgin:** A bit farther afield, this town has lots of outfitter options for biking, tubing, horseback riding, and other outdoor adventures.

How to Get Around

Zion is notoriously crowded during the summer months, and it is wise to make use of the park shuttle during your visit. The shuttle runs to all the major park attractions and has stops in Springdale.

First Stop: Visitor Center

Weather conditions are always changing in Zion, so stop at the visitor center to check on trail closures, water flow, and rock slide updates. You can also pick up a Junior Ranger packet for the kids there.

Hikes

- ▷ **Angels Landing:** One of the most notorious hikes in the park, this trail features a series of switchbacks before leading you high up to a narrow ridge of rocks. The narrow trail offers only a chain to help you stay anchored on the steep incline. This hike is not for the faint of heart.
- ▷ **The Narrows:** Another one of the most popular hikes, the Narrows takes you through Zion Canyon where the rim walls rise over 1,000 feet above the ground. Flash flooding is an ever-present danger on this hike, so consult rangers before heading out.
- ▷ **Riverside Walk:** This 1-mile paved trail runs along the edge of the river and offers a taste of the Narrows without the potential danger.
- ▷ **Canyon Overlook Trail:** This hike is another 1-mile round trip hike that gives visitors great views without a ton of strenuous labor.
- ▷ **Watchman Trail:** A relatively easy 3.3 miles round trip, this trail is located near the Zion Canyon Visitor Center and easily accessible from the Watchman Campground.

Biking

If you bring your bikes camping, enjoy the Pa'rus Trail bike path that starts at the visitor center and runs along the Virgin River.

· *Washington* ·

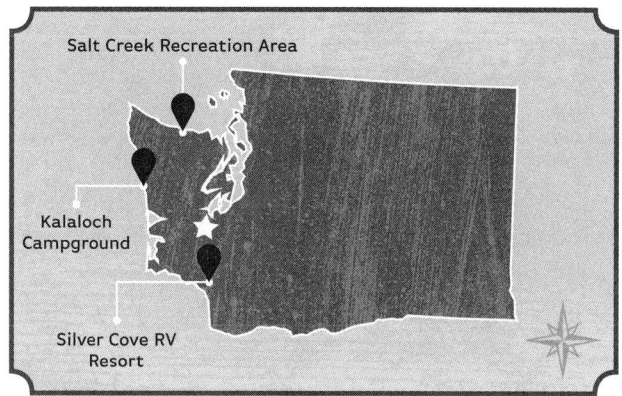

Olympic National Park is one of our very favorite travel destinations in the entire country, so that alone puts Washington at the top of our list for amazing camping states. There are NPS campgrounds in each of the remarkably beautiful and distinct regions of the park, including the coastal area, rain forest, and hot springs. You can also find a handful of decent private campground options outside the park in the gateway city of Port Angeles.

Washington offers so much more than just Olympic National Park, though, especially when it comes to dreamy camping opportunities. We never imagined that Mount St. Helens would be such a travel highlight for our whole family. Yes, the huge volcanic crater is amazing to see, but hiking in the Ape Caves—underground lava tubes—was simply unforgettable.

Another gift this state has to offer is the San Juan Islands, where places like Moran State Park on Orcas Island offer rustic campsites or even glamping platform tents with access to amazing hiking, biking, and fishing. Camper beware: A single night under the stars in Washington will forever alter your camping expectations.

BEST IN STATE

Silver Cove RV Resort

- ▷ Silverlake, Washington
- ▷ highwaywestvacations.com
- ▷ Cottages, Hunter Cabins, RV and Tent Sites

Silver Cove RV Resort is a delight from start to finish. It is our top pick for touring the Mount St. Helens area, which we think is one of the most underrated tourist destinations in the Pacific Northwest. Many of the cabins and RV sites are situated on the lovely fingers of Silver Lake. Kayakers and those who SUP will delight in launching directly from their sites or at the centrally located boat launch. Rentals are also available for a reasonable price. Ambitious paddlers can row out to Silver Lake, while those who want to relax can just goof around inside the campground. A stunning PNW-style lodge is available to rent for group activities, weddings, rallies, etc., and the common areas for grilling and chilling are also delightful. The cabins are cozy and comfortably appointed, and RV sites are nicely sized. Silver Cove gets everything right. The management is friendly and helpful, and the complimentary coffee in the camp store is served up hot and fresh all day long.

Salt Creek Recreation Area

- ▷ Port Angeles, Washington
- ▷ clallam.net
- ▷ RV and Tent Sites

When we post pictures of the campground at the Salt Creek Recreation Area on social media, our followers flip out and demand to know where it is located. It is just that beautiful. The campground is situated on a bluff above the Strait of Juan de Fuca, and the vast majority of the sites have views of the sparkling water. When we pulled into the campground our cell phones welcomed us to Canada, which is located directly across the strait. The location of this campground is stunning and dramatic in every way. The tide pools located just steps below the campsites kept our young kids occupied for hours, as did the basketball and volleyball courts. Outdoor activities abound for thrill seekers and nature lovers. Whether you love hiking, biking, kayaking, bird watching, or surfing, there is something for you on the property or nearby. Downtown Port Angeles is also close and filled with hip food, coffee, and shopping. If summertime on the Olympic Peninsula isn't near wild heaven, it's pretty darn close.

Kalaloch Campground

▷ Olympic National Park, Washington

▷ nps.gov

▷ Tent and RV Sites

For those adventurous souls who want to experience coastal Olympic National Park in all of its rugged glory and are willing to camp without hookups or shower facilities, there is no better place than Kalaloch Campground. There are a wide variety of site sizes and only a handful have ocean views, but all of them have easy access to the beach just below the bluff upon which the campground sits. The mile-long Kalaloch Creek Nature trail also makes for a lovely walk as you follow the water to its drainage point in the wild Pacific. Plan on spending hours at Kalaloch just exploring tide pools and looking for crabs and sea urchins. But make sure you keep your eyes peeled just past the waves because dolphins and whales make more than occasional appearances. Swimming is allowed but please take caution. Rip tides and gigantic floating logs pose real dangers. Smaller RVs will have more success finding suitable sites at Kalaloch. Those in tents should pay close attention to the possibility of rain and strong winds.

ALSO GREAT

The Fairholme Campground and Lake Crescent Lodge/ Olympic National Park

▷ Port Angeles, Washington

▷ olympicnationalparks.com

▷ Lodge, RV and Tent Sites

Lake Crescent is truly one of Olympic's most stunning gems. Its sharp blue waters are perfect for kayaking, and heartier souls (like our kids) will love diving in for a brisk swim. The campground and lodge are technically two separate, side-by-side facilities run by the same concessionaire. The campground could use some maintenance, but the views are breathtaking and the location is perfect for exploring Jeremy's favorite national park.

Olympic Peninsula/Port Angeles KOA

▷ Port Angeles, Washington

▷ koa.com

▷ Camping Cabins, Deluxe Cabins, Tent and RV Sites

Olympic is filled with rustic NPS campgrounds without hookups or amenities, but if you are willing to camp outside the park (near downtown Port Angeles) you can get full hookups, a pool, a hot tub, and other fun amenities at this charming KOA. There are still gorgeous mountain views, but the highway is nearby and you will have some serious driving to do to get deep into the park.

Cape Disappointment State Park

▷ Ilwaco, Washington

▷ parks.state.wa

▷ Tent and RV Sites, Yurts, Cabins

For epic coastal camping on the Long Beach Peninsula, look no further than Cape Disappointment State Park. The sites are spacious and plentiful, and fifty of them have full hookups. If possible, reserve a yurt or RV site right by the beach. There is some shade and protection from the rugged stretch of sand and sea just beyond the trees, but plan on windy conditions and don't leave the RV awning out when unattended.

Quick Guide to Olympic National Park

Olympic can be a tricky national park to navigate because it is spread out over nearly one million acres and encompasses multiple ecosystems from the coast to a rainforest to snow-capped mountains. You'll need a plan and the willingness to spend some time in the car, driving to all the amazing park highlights.

Where to Camp
Pick one of the amazing campgrounds featured in this chapter. Even though the campgrounds in the park are located in beautiful areas, we preferred to be near the gateway city of Port Angeles, a small city with great dining options.

▷ Olympic Peninsula/Port Angeles KOA
▷ The Fairholme Campground and Lake Crescent Lodge
▷ Kalaloch Campground
▷ Salt Creek Recreation Area

Visitor Centers
The main Olympic National Park Visitor Center, located in Port Angeles, is the perfect place to get acclimated and speak with the park rangers about your plans. The interpretative exhibits are engaging, but you shouldn't bother watching the video in our humble opinion. There are two short-but-sweet hikes at the visitor center as well: Living Forest Trail (0.4 miles) and Peabody Creek Trail (0.5 miles).

You should also visit the Hurricane Ridge Visitor Center and the Hoh Rain Forest Visitor Center when arriving in those areas of the park. Both places were helpful for us as we mapped out our adventures for the day.

Areas of the Park

▷ **Hurricane Ridge:** The Hurricane Ridge Trail is our favorite hike in the whole national park (and one of our favorite hikes ever). It's about 3 miles round trip and offers magnificent views along the entire trail.

▷ **Sol Duc Falls:** The Sol Duc Falls nature trail is an easy 1.6-mile out-and-back hike that runs through an old-growth forest and across one beautiful spring-fed creek after another, offering views of three waterfalls. You can also visit Marymere Falls and Madison Falls nearby. Our kids particularly loved the Sol Duc Hot Springs, which basically look like pools with varying temperatures that smell like sulfur. This wasn't a highlight for the adults, but the kids begged to go back throughout our trip.

▷ **Lake Crescent:** This lake is a great place for a day trip since it offers hikes, a picnic area, and recreation opportunities. The Spruce Railroad Trail runs for about 6 miles along the edge of the lake, but you can just hike for as long as you choose and then turn back. We enjoyed renting a canoe from the concessionaire, and there are also kayaks and paddle boats.

▷ **Ruby Beach:** If you are staying near Port Angeles, this will be a bit of a drive (1.5 hours), but do not miss visiting this part of the national park. Check the tides (rangers at the visitors center have the tidal charts) and make sure to visit during low tide, when visitors can hike out to the sea stacks and find colorful sea stars and sea anemones. Bring a change of clothes—you will get wet.

▷ **Hoh Rainforest:** Yes, there really is a rainforest in Olympic National Park, and it is one of the most beautiful places we have ever seen. There are two loop trails with trail heads right at the visitor center: Hall of Moses (0.8 miles) and Spruce Nature Trail (1.2 miles). These short trails are an awesome way to experience the wonders of the temperate rainforest. Note that this is a very remote part of the park, so plan ahead for meals and be prepared for no cell reception. The town of Forks is about an hour away and has limited food options.

Quick Guide to Mount St. Helens

Mount St. Helens is one of the most memorable sleeper hits from all our camping trips. We thought we were visiting a volcanic photo op. Instead, we found beautiful hikes, lava tube adventures, and amazing educational opportunities. Stay at the nearby Silver Cove RV Resort and take your time exploring.

The West Side

Start at Mount St. Helens Visitor Center at Silver Lake
Get your map and chat with a ranger about your plans for the day. You will find a chronological timeline of events leading up to the 1980 eruption, an educational movie, and a step-in model of the volcano.

Drive to the Forest Learning Center
This awesome place is on your way up Route 504 to the Johnston Ridge Observatory. The learning center is run by the Wyerhaeuser Logging Company and is chock-full of hands-on exhibits and jaw-dropping news footage of the time immediately before and after the volcanic eruption.

Hike the Hummocks Trail
This 2.5-mile loop trail is located in between the Forest Learning Center and the Johnston Ridge Observatory. The relatively flat trail offers beautiful views of Mount St. Helens as it meanders through fields of debris left from the 1980 eruption and mudslide.

Visit the Johnston Ridge Observatory
Even though this monument is run by the National Forest Service, your annual national parks pass is honored for admission. You do not want to miss the excellent sixteen-minute movie with a show-stopping ending.

The South Side

Explore the Ape Cave Lava Tube

Make sure you dress warm since the underground temperature is a chilly 42°F, and bring a flashlight or headlamp for everyone in the family. You can also rent lanterns at the entrance of the cave. There are two hiking options: The lower cave is an easy 1.5 miles round trip, and the upper cave is also 1.5 miles, but more challenging with rock scrambles and tight squeezes.

Hike the Trail of Two Forests or the June Lake Trail

The Trail of Two Forests is a short interpretive trail that takes you through an old growth forest entombed by a 1,900-year-old lava flow. If you are up for more of a challenge, the June Lake trail is a little over 3 miles and runs along a rushing stream before reaching the lake.

Swim at Lake Merwin, Yale Reservoir, or Swift Reservoir

Bring your swimsuits when you visit the south side of Mount St. Helens. There are a number of day use areas along Forest Road 83 that offer great places for an afternoon dip.

Wyoming

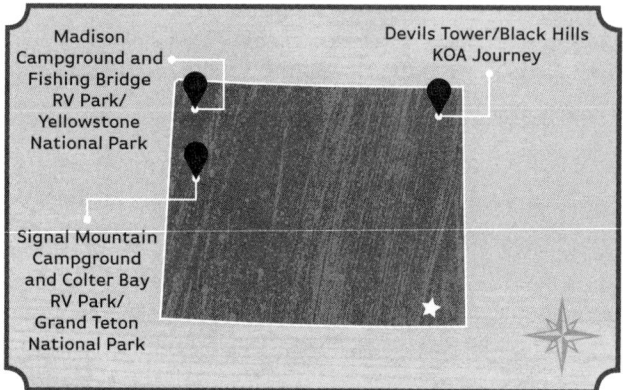

Madison Campground and Fishing Bridge RV Park/ Yellowstone National Park

Devils Tower/Black Hills KOA Journey

Signal Mountain Campground and Colter Bay RV Park/ Grand Teton National Park

Between Yellowstone, Grand Teton, and Devils Tower, Wyoming has more bucket list camping destinations than the typical state. We also find that Cody ends up being a favorite destination for many RVers who stop on the way to or from Yellowstone National Park. Southern Wyoming also offers a quick weekend getaway option for folks in the Denver area. This means that state park campgrounds fill up fast, so make sure you reserve the maximum four months in advance for May through September bookings.

Also be aware that people plan their bucket list camping trips to places like Yellowstone and Grand Teton more than a year in advance. If you have already missed that window, you'll have better luck with private camp-grounds than public ones. We've highlighted some of our favorites here, but also look at our Idaho campgrounds for recommendations near the west entrance of Yellowstone.

BEST IN STATE

Madison Campground and Fishing Bridge RV Park/ Yellowstone National Park

- ▷ Yellowstone National Park, Wyoming
- ▷ nps.gov
- ▷ RV and Tent Sites

If you are a tent camper or own a small RV and want the best that Yellowstone National Park has to offer, then Madison Campground may be a great choice for you. The campground is situated near the Madison River under a canopy of fragrant lodgepole pine trees. It is also located near some of the most popular spots in Yellowstone, including Old Faithful. Most spots are spacious and offer a bit of privacy, but many sites are not level and there are no hookups.

RV owners that desire full hook-up sites inside Yellowstone have one option, and that is Fishing Bridge RV Park near the Yellowstone River. Unfortunately, like so many concession-run campgrounds in the national park system, this campground has not exactly been well maintained over the years, and the sites are pretty small. At the time of this writing this campground is closed for major repairs, and we are hopeful that it will be dramatically improved. But even if it isn't, it's still worth recommending. The location inside the park is excellent and offers full hookups inside Yellowstone. You can sign me up again and again.

Signal Mountain Campground and Colter Bay RV Park/ Grand Teton National Park

- ▷ Moran, Wyoming
- ▷ nps.gov
- ▷ RV and Tent Sites

Signal Mountain Campground is situated in a gorgeous lodgepole pine forest with breathtaking views of Mount Moran. Much like Madison Campground in Yellowstone, this campground is excellent for tent campers and for those with smaller RVs. It has the added benefit of being close to Signal Mountain Lodge, which has a bar and several decent dining options plus other amenities like an ATM and gift shop. Sites are located just steps away from the scenic waters of Jackson Lake—get your cameras ready!

Colter Bay RV Park is a concessionaire-run campground that boasts a jaw-dropping location that is just five minutes away from the chilly-but-stunning Jackson Lake. This campground, much like Fishing Bridge in Yellowstone, has full hookups, but the campground itself is beautiful and the sites are nice. Fragrant pines give shade and privacy to most of the campsites here. There is pretty much nothing not to love here—except the no campfire rule. Colter Bay is the ultimate base camp for RV owners visiting Grand Teton, and it books up lightning fast—so if you want to go, get on it!

Devils Tower/Black Hills KOA Journey

- ▷ Devils Tower, Wyoming
- ▷ koa.com
- ▷ RV and Tent Sites, Camping Cabins and Deluxe Cabins

This KOA has an iconic location, and each night from June 1 to September 1 it offers a free outdoor screening of *Close Encounters of the Third Kind* right in the shadow of Devils Tower. Parts of the movie were filmed right at the campground. Pretty darn cool, right? Devils Tower National Monument is America's first national monument and should be a required stop on any cross-country road trip—if you can squeeze in an extra day or two. The monument and this KOA are not right off the highway, so you will need to commit some extra time to get here. But man oh man is it worth it. The KOA is part of the historic Campstool Ranch, which has been in one family for eight generations. Thankfully, it is not a one-trick pony. RV and tent sites are nice, and virtually all of them have views of the tower. The pool is also pleasant if you end up there on a hot summer day. Plan on spending a full day exploring the Devils Tower Visitor Center and the tower itself, and bring comfortable hiking shoes. Make sure to visit the Devils Tower Trading Post across the street, and grab some ice cream and *Close Encounters* souvenirs while you are there.

> --------- **Conquering Yellowstone National Park** ---------
>
> Clocking in at 2.2 million acres, Yellowstone National Park might be one of the more overwhelming parks to navigate. The Grand Loop runs for 142 miles, connecting northern attractions like Mammoth Hot Springs with popular spots in the south such as Old Faithful. You'll want to plan this trip in advance and think through a flexible itinerary. Here are some tips:
>
> ✧ Allow plenty of time to see the park. There are NPS sites that can be enjoyed in a single day, but Yellowstone is not one of them. Driving times will be slower on account of traffic and wildlife.
>
> ✧ Do your research before deciding where to camp. There are five entrances to the park and beautiful campgrounds near each one. Certain park highlights might be one to two hours from a particular base camp. Many visitors pick two locations (one on the east side and one on the west) and split up their stay.
>
> ✧ Pack a lunch and plenty of snacks every day. Navigating the roads and crowds in Yellowstone often means that you are nowhere near a restaurant when you are dying to eat. Ward off the "hangry" attacks by being prepared with your own food.
>
> ✧ Plan for a wide variety of weather conditions. Temperatures can vary greatly throughout the course of the day, so wear layers and pack rain gear. Nights can get below freezing, even in the summer. Bring plenty of warm clothing.
>
> ✧ Respect the wildlife and make sure your children understand park guidelines. It seems that many of the ridiculous videos of tourists acting inappropriately with wildlife come out of Yellowstone each year. Be a good steward of our national parks and leave no trace.

ALSO GREAT

Curt Gowdy State Park

▷   Cheyenne, Wyoming

▷   wyoparks.wyo.gov

▷   RV and Tent Sites

Curt Gowdy State Park is only about two and half hours away from the Denver metro area, so it is a popular weekend retreat for campers from the Mile-High City. Reservations are tough to get here, and it is easy to see why. This twelve•loop campground is stunning—and it is dirt cheap to camp here. Fishing and boating are excellent on Gowdy's three reservoirs, and folks come from miles around to hike and mountain bike here.

Cody KOA Holiday

▷   Cody, Wyoming

▷   koa.com

▷   Deluxe Cabins, Camping Cabins, Tepees, RV and Tent Sites

This top-notch KOA is located an hour away from the eastern gate of Yellowstone National Park, but Cody is a vacation-worthy destination in its own right. The Buffalo Bill Center of the West and the Cody Night Rodeo are well worth your time and attention, and so is this great campground—grab free pancakes in the morning before heading out to explore, then plan on spending some time relaxing in the hot tub when you get back each night.

-------------------   **The Yellowstone Top Five**   ----------------

1. *Old Faithful, Observation Point Trail, and the Upper Basin*: Just because it's crowded doesn't mean you shouldn't go. You have to see Old Faithful during your visit. Hike up the Observation Point Trail to watch the eruption with a bird's eye view.

2. *Old Faithful Inn:* This is just everything a national park lodge is supposed to be. Even if you don't stay here, visit the lobby to see the huge stone fireplace and enjoy live music in the evenings.

3. *Grand Canyon of the Yellowstone*: Hike the Brink of the Lower Falls Trail to look down over the edge of a waterfall. When you've had your fill of steaming vents and geysers, this is where you should go.

4. *Mammoth Hot Springs and Historic District:* This is like stepping onto another planet with boardwalks built over steaming, sulfuric hydrothermal features. The history of Yellowstone comes to life in this area of the park as well, housing the original visitors center and Fort Yellowstone.

5. *Yellowstone Lake:* This lake sits 7,000 feet above sea level and is full of native cutthroat trout and surrounded by towering pines. Drop your kayak in for a paddle, but be aware of safety warnings from the national park: Water temperatures are low even in the summer, and sudden strong winds can take even seasoned paddlers by surprise.

Cody and the Wild West

Cody tends to fly under the radar, being surrounded by so many natural wonders. But it ends up being a memorable and favorite destination for many families who camp there. Here are some of the highlights.

Buffalo Bill Center of the West

The center has five distinct museums under one roof, and there is a reason the entrance ticket is good for two days. You'll need that amount of time to explore the Buffalo Bill Museum, Plains Indian Museum, Whitney Western Art Museum, Draper Natural History Museum, and the New Cody Firearms Museum.

The Cody Nite Rodeo

Cody is the self-proclaimed Rodeo Capital of the World, and this one runs nightly from June through August.

Buffalo Bill Dam and Visitors Center

This dam was completed in 1910 and was the highest dam in the world at the time. You can walk all the way across the top of the dam and look down 325 feet to the Shoshone River.

Shoshone National Forest

This was our country's first national forest, and it has hiking trails, campgrounds, and picnic areas. There are also snowmobiling trails and cross-country skiing trails for hearty adventurers.

Buffalo Bill State Park

This park offers boating, fishing, paddle boarding, and plenty of other water recreation on the reservoir.

Appendix A:

CAMPGROUNDS BY STATE

Appendix B:

CAMPGROUNDS BY BADGE

 Family-Friendly Campgrounds

Glamping Campgrounds

Romantic Weekend Campgrounds

 ## Rustic Campgrounds

Waterfront Views Campgrounds

ABOUT THE AUTHORS

Jeremy Puglisi is the cocreator and managing editor of *The RV Atlas* podcast and website. He is also the coauthor of *See You at the Campground* and *Idiot's Guide: RV Vacations*. His work has been published in *Trailer Life Magazine, AARP The Magazine, ROVA,* and dozens of online publications. He loves nothing more than camping with Stephanie and his three sons, and he is always ready to hitch up and head out for the next adventure.

Stephanie Puglisi is the head of content for Roadtrippers and Togo RV. She is also the cohost of *The RV Atlas* podcast and coauthor of *See You at the Campground* and *Idiot's Guide: RV Vacations*. She most appreciates that campgrounds have allowed her to embrace her semi-outdoorsy personality—sleeping in the great outdoors while simultaneously enjoying a hot shower and soft bed at the end of every day.

You can follow Jeremy and Stephanie's camping adventures @thervatlas on Instagram and Facebook.